# The Letters and Notebooks of Mary Devlin Booth

Mary Elizabeth Devlin Booth
1840-1863

# THE LETTERS AND NOTEBOOKS OF MARY DEVLIN BOOTH

Edited by L. Terry Oggel

Contributions in Drama and Theatre Studies, Number 23

Greenwood Press
New York • Westport, Connecticut • London

Library of Congress Cataloging-in-Publication Data

Booth, Mary Devlin, 1840-1863.
  The letters and notebooks of Mary Devlin Booth.

  (Contributions in drama and theatre studies,
ISSN 0163-3821 ; no. 23)
  Includes index.
  1. Booth, Mary Devlin, 1840-1863—Correspondence.
2. Booth, Edwin, 1833-1893—Correspondence.  3. Actors—
United States—Correspondence.   I. Oggel, L. Terry.
II. Title.  III. Series.
PN2287.B637A4  1987      792'.028'0924  [B]       87-130
ISBN 0-313-25468-0 (lib. bdg. : alk. paper)

Copyright © 1987 by L. Terry Oggel

All rights reserved. No portion of this book may be
reproduced, by any process or technique, without the
express written consent of the publisher.

Library of Congress Catalog Card Number: 87-130
ISBN: 0-313-25468-0
ISSN: 0163-3821

First published in 1987

Greenwood Press, Inc.
88 Post Road West, Westport, Connecticut 06881

Printed in the United States of America

The paper used in this book complies with the
Permanent Paper Standard issued by the National
Information Standards Organization (Z39.48-1984).

10  9  8  7  6  5  4  3  2  1

**Copyright Acknowledgments**

The author and publisher are grateful for permission to reprint from the following sources.

Frontispiece of Mary Elizabeth Devlin Booth c. 1860. Courtesy of the Billy Rose Theatre Collection, New York Public Library

Illustrations of personal letters from Mary Devlin Booth to Edwin Booth (letter 54) and to Elizabeth Stoddard (letter 81).
Courtesy Hampden-Booth Theatre Library at The Players

Every reasonable effort has been made to trace the owners of copyright materials in this book, but in some instances this has proven impossible. The publishers will be glad to receive information leading to more complete acknowledgments in subsequent printings of the book, and in the meantime extend their apologies for any omissions.

for

Linda,

Amy and Kate

Ah! darling were you here, now, I
could talk so 'sensibly' I'm sure!
but that we are cruelly separated,
is greater reason, why we should
corrospond *carefully*, and
*thoughtfully*--for *letters* are
sacred things--

        Mary Devlin to Edwin Booth
          [12 February 1860]

# Contents

Mary Devlin Booth Chronology — ix

*Example of Letter (#54)* — following page x

General Introduction — xi

Calendar of Letters and Notebooks — xxxiii

Letters — 3

Notebooks — 107

Annotations — 117

*Example of Letter (#81)* — following page 138

Textual Notes — 139

Index — 161

# Mary Devlin Booth Chronology

| | |
|---|---|
| 1840 | born, May 19 (Sand Lake, New York) |
| 1848 | moves with family to Troy, New York |
| 1852 | appears on stage first time, 4 May (Troy, NY) |
| 1853 | performs in *School for Scandal* production with the Placides, Murdock, Wallack and Jefferson (autumn, Baltimore) |
| 1854 | performs under tutelage of A. W. Fenno as a danseuse using stage name of La Belle Elise, 17 April–4 July (Troy) |
| 1855 | performs first time in New York, 28 June, with E. Eddy<br>begins nearly continuous four-year association with Joseph Jefferson by joining Henry Jarrett's Baltimore Museum stock company, Jefferson managing, September<br>plays Michette to Heron's Camille, 31 October (Washington, DC) |
| 1856 | performs first time with Edwin Forrest, 24–29 March (Washington, DC)<br>performs with Dion Boucicault, 5 April (Washington, DC) and 12 April (Richmond)<br>becomes member of John Ford's Marshall Theatre stock company (Joseph Jefferson, stage manager), September (Richmond)<br>performs first time with EB, 24 November–12 December (Richmond) |
| 1857 | performs first time as headliner, 15–20 February (Richmond)<br>performs second and third times with Edwin Forrest, 4–6? May (Baltimore) and 15–20 May (Richmond) |

## Chronology

| | |
|---|---|
| 1858 | performs second and third times with EB, 23 February–6 March (Richmond) and 8–20 March (Baltimore) |
| | performs three times with Charlotte Cushman in her farewell tour, 26 April–8 May (Baltimore), 31 May–12 June (Boston), and 21 June–6 July (New York) |
| | performs in *School for Scandal* production with H. Placide, Gilbert, Blake, Davenport and Cushman, 3 July (New York) |
| | performs fourth time with EB, 25 October–13 November (Boston) |
| 1859 | is engaged to EB, July |
| | performs final time, and presumably fifth time with EB, 30? July (New York) |
| | begins year of seclusion and study, August |
| 1860 | marries EB, 7 July |
| 1861 | travels to England with EB on his first foreign tour, 20 August |
| | gives birth to Edwina in London, 9 December |
| 1862 | returns from Europe, 28 August |
| 1863 | dies, 21 February (Dorchester) |

1861

Sunday Afternoon

Dearest Edwin mine— I very much the weeks reviews. showered myself & now sit down for a little chat with you; feeling much more cheerful even in my loneness than I did this time a week ago— with the sorrow of parting from you before me. This time next Sunday I hope to see & welcome you home. Can you leave on that day?— Miss Corbyn was here to dinner with me yesterday. I allow her to she came back with me. I was astonished by Mrs Corbyn's account of Amasia Jones. Is it not disgraceful, that a fine girl like her, should be publicly living

Mary Devlin Booth's letter to Edwin Booth, 2 March 1862 (Letter 54), in which she reports the week's news about the London theatre world to Booth who was performing in Liverpool.

**Courtesy Hampden-Booth Theatre Library at The Players**

allow of any undue familiarity from
any person. Though, understand Love,
darling, none was offered me: only
Mr Braybear was that kind of man —
whom you would have me never meet
if possible. — & if it could not be
helped, solely only. Now, for the
comfort to be derived from this.
I will see Mrs Mathews & tell her
that I have heard since of the character
of her guests that Sunday — & I am
astonished that she should have invited me to meet such people: especially allowed one to be there without
my husband. And, that having been
betrayed once into such company
I will never trust again. Will say
too, have engagements you are about to
permit that be the best way to get
rid of them! — I enclose Auntyps's
letter. I forgot it yesterday also the
photographs. — Oh, darling, how

# GENERAL INTRODUCTION

Because Mary Devlin Booth died young, a volume of her letters and notebooks focuses perforce on a short span of years. The brevity of the period is compensated by its importance, however, for during those years she met and married Edwin Booth, influenced the development of his career, and left a record, albeit partial, of their brief time together.

During the earliest of those years--the time between their first meeting in late November 1856 and their engagement in July 1859--it seems clear that despite what has been written the relationship was slow to develop.[1] For example, there is no evidence that they met again or corresponded in 1857. Furthermore, though in early 1858 they performed together again--in February (Richmond) and in March (Baltimore)--evidence indicates that no understanding about their future together existed between them then. This is shown by Booth's formality in referring to Devlin in a letter (HRHRC; see p. xix for list of abbreviations) he wrote on 2 June 1858 (perhaps the earliest extant letter in which he mentions her). At the time MD, just turned eighteen, was performing in Boston with Charlotte Cushman on the latter's "farewell" tour, and EB, then twenty-four years old, wrote from Chicago to his painter friend Walter Brackett in Boston: ". . . I hope the Bostonians will treat my little friend Miss Devlin well; she's a good, little girl and very talented."

Till then, MD had apparently shown little interest in EB and indeed was almost engaged to the Boston lawyer R. S. Spofford. Thus, in the same letter EB remarks to Brackett:

---

[1] Most of what has been said originates in an essay of doubtful authority by Anne M. Fauntleroy ("The Romance of Mary Devlin Booth," *Ladies' Home Journal*, 21 [September 1904], 10) and the erring memory of Joseph Jefferson thirty-eight years after the fact (*The Players* [New York, 1894], pp. 38-39, repeated in Francis Wilson, *Joseph Jefferson* [New York, 1906], pp. 145-146).

>... it's all very well to say 'oh she'll come along by and by--' but my dear boy, she <u>has</u> been along--and passed on me too--just as I <u>had</u> a full hand--my game's blocked; I'll live and die an <u>old maid</u>. . . .

Apparently the acquaintanceship had developed slowly during the first eighteen months because of a reluctance on MD's part. But another letter by EB to Brackett later the same month (22 June 1858; HRHRC) shows that although a correspondence between MD and EB had by then developed, EB now shared MD's uncertainty:

> . . . she is indeed a dear, sweet girl, innocent as a babe, and I would give the world to see her high in her profession, and happy withal; but, Walter, marrying wouldn't achieve the latter--no, on the contrary, 'twould be to render her most wretched; I love her as a sister--nothing more.

Yet in a third letter to Brackett the same summer (23 July 1858; HRHRC) EB, though still formal in referring to her, reverses himself and shows more than merely a brotherly joy when he emphasizes that MD isn't to marry Spofford:

> Miss D. is up in the country--at Paradise Valley (the angel) Monroe County Pennsylvania--should you write to her--<u>don't</u> <u>congratulate</u> <u>her</u> <u>on</u> <u>her</u> <u>wedding</u>--'<u>taint</u> <u>so</u>.

Such reversals reveal EB's uncertainty about his view toward marriage in general and toward marrying MD in particular. Nevertheless, though there is apparently no evidence extant about their relationship during the months following the summer of 1858 (they did perform together--the fourth time--in October and November in Boston), it seems certain that they continued to correspond and that the acquaintanceship continued to develop, more or less by accretion. By late January, for example, in a letter to Brackett (30 January 1859; HRHRC), EB refers to her as "Molly," the name she herself used with her intimates. Several more letters from EB to Brackett through the winter and spring of 1859 (HRHRC) confirm this increasing familiarity. Still, the last of these letters, dated 11 June [1859], as well as MD's letter to EB dated 7[?] June 1859 (Letter 3 printed in this volume), shows that by mid-June they had not made a decision to marry.

That changed within a month, for sometime during July, while MD was performing at Niblo's in New York and EB was visiting his friend Adam Badeau in Jamaica, Long Island, MD and EB became engaged. In his letter to his friends Dr. and Mrs. Beale at the end of July (26 July [1859]; Folger) EB took pains not to fall "into the lover's strain" but rather to explain carefully the practical advantages of his decision:

> I felt the need of some gentler respite from the cares and excitement of my profession . . . . [A]t last I settled down into this calm conclusion --'Mary is the girl for me--there's no use in trying to give her up, and if she will leave the stage I'll make her Mrs B.' Now you must remember I have thought a long, very long time on this; 'tis no hasty step; no boy's love--. . . . Mary has all the qualities of heart--and of mind, though undeveloped--which I most need to make life cheerful to me. . . . [I]f she will . . . give up all thoughts of the profession as far as she is concerned, and by study improve her mind, she will make me a happy individual.

As EB says, to marry--especially to marry MD--was no easy decision. The reason for this is made clear in another letter to Brackett two months later (12 September [1859]; HU--TC):

> . . . from the first day I met her I felt the influence of her kindred spirit--purer--holier than mine, but still a kindred one; a fragile flower, breathing sweet odor on my withered heart. . . .

He continued by telling Brackett that although he had "resolved never to marry an actress," he had come "to the conclusion that the knowledge [MD] had gained in the trials & vicissitudes of an actor's life, would be an advantage. . . ."

This summary of the early years of MD's acquaintance with EB allows us to understand EB's thinking and to appreciate some of the elements which made his decision to marry MD not only difficult but unlikely. For as EB himself said to Brackett (12 September [1859]), instead of choosing a woman of wealth and beauty, which he could easily have done, he had selected a "humble actress with the angel's soul." The emphasis here should be on "humble" and "angel." EB's letter of 12 September [1859] provides the full explanation. MD's nature--her simplicity, her innocence ("purity")--were attractive to EB, who saw himself possessing just the opposite characteristics, as represented by his metaphor of a "withered heart." "It seems almost absurd in one so young as I to talk about a withered heart," he wrote Brackett, ". . . but could you read the history of my blighted youth, you'd wonder at my being still above the sod. . . ." From the first time he met her, more than two and a half years earlier, he said, he knew that she possessed "all the requisites to render my home a happy one--my heart a cheerful one, if aught on earth could make it so. . . ."

It was a role which, as many of her letters printed here show, she agreed to play, although for a year or more after the engagement she was less sure than he that she was well-suited for it. In the letters written after the engagement she reveals her uncertainty about living up to his expectations; while he was on his long southern tour during the winter and spring of 1860, she even speaks of her jealousy of the women in the cities on the tour who idolize him. With more or less blind faith, however, she trusts that eventually the "humble daisy" will win out over the "exotic roses." Not till the fall of 1860 does she seem confident in public and in private as EB's wife.

From EB's viewpoint, however, MD provided all the stability and virtue he could have hoped for to counterbalance his sense of his own recklessness. She did so, moreover, not only for the brief period of their marriage but for much of his later life. For instance, in his correspondence twenty years later with another painter friend, Jervis McEntee (Univ. of Tulsa), EB displayed a regard for her that amounted to reverence.

This influence on EB is one aspect of the major reason for MDB's enduring significance. The other is the unique private view she permits through the documents printed here of the character and personality of the young EB. That she was herself an actress of considerable experience and that her association with EB occurred during the formative period of his career only enhance her importance. Beyond a doubt, had she not met EB she would have remained an obscure young actress who, though she performed in several notable productions and acted with virtually every major performer of her day--Drew, Murdock, Boucicault, Robertson, Wallack, Heron, Davenport, Forrest, Cushman, Jefferson--would be unworthy of notice a century later. But in November 1856 she did meet and act with EB, and her life and his were permanently altered.

Attention has been paid to her, therefore, by scholars of late nineteenth century American theatre history. All modern biographies of EB recognize her importance. In his study of the development of EB's most famous role, Hamlet, Charles Shattuck even accords her, along with Badeau, primary status as EB's "educator." Shattuck concludes that part of EB's "artistic conscience" was lost to him when the "wise" MDB died.[2]

To a much lesser degree, another reason for continued interest in MDB is that she also had a brief but strong effect on Elizabeth Stoddard, the novelist. In his examination of Stoddard's literary achievement, James Matlack emphasizes the stabilizing influence MDB had on the "brash and independent" Stoddard. He concludes that the bond between Stoddard and MDB "was most vital to Elizabeth" and that the

---

[2]*The Hamlet of Edwin Booth* (Urbana, 1969), pp. 30-36.

consequences of MDB's death "shaped the rest of [Stoddard's] life. . . ."³

Her letters, as nowhere else, reveal the development of the woman who grew into this prominence, and when read in the light of her desire to fulfill EB's expectations (and, indeed, her own), they are of interest even when they are concerned with matters of such topical interest as the birth and progress of her daughter, Edwina, and EB's reaction to fatherhood; the deaths of friends; or Anglo-American relations during the Civil War as seen by Americans living in England. More important, of course, are the references to matters of abiding interest: EB's performances and the reaction to them by the press and the public; EB's tours and the development of his roles; his acquaintances and associates in and out of the theatre; her view of Badeau as she vies with him for "possession" of EB; her hopes for a visit to Italy (where, along with Germany, Charlotte Cushman had said the best acting was being done). In sum, these documents are a valuable portion of what remains of the record of the private side of the major tragedian and one of the best-known public figures of the age.

To preserve that record is the chief objective of this volume. Already one of the letters, extant some years ago, has disappeared. In 1969 Shattuck referred (p. 5n) to the presence of twenty-seven MDB letters at the Theatre Collection of the New York Public Library. By 1979, however, only twenty-six were available.⁴ Thus, only the passage that Shattuck printed remains.⁵

For the documents still extant, preserving the record also means correcting the texts now in print. Because they were created during times relatively unconcerned with textual accuracy, these texts are corrupt by modern standards. Using the term liberally, there have been two "editions" of MDB's letters, the first by Edwina Booth Grossmann in 1894 and the second by Otis Skinner in 1939.⁶ Grossmann included lengthy passages from what appear to be six MDB letters in the opening section of her epistolary biography

---

³*The Literary Career of Elizabeth Barstow Stoddard* (Unpubl. diss.: Yale Univ., 1968), pp. 294-295, 309.

⁴See my "A Guide to the Edwin Booth Literary Materials at the New York Public Library," *BRH*, 82 (Spring 1979), 90-104.

⁵"many, many evenings we will while away in peace rendered more delightful by Apollo's gift," Shattuck, p. 31.

⁶*Edwin Booth: Recollections by his daughter* . . . (New York, 1894; a portion of the section on MDB was also printed as part of Grossmann's "The Real Edwin Booth," *The Century Magazine*, 48 [October 1894], 803-815) and *The Last Tragedian* (New York, 1939), pp. 111-125.

of her father. These transcriptions, all without dates, contain incorrect readings and have large omitted sections unmarked by ellipses. One transcription (pp. 27-28), in fact, is a combination of passages from two letters written seven months apart. To make matters even worse, the second passage of this text is from the earlier of the letters (see Letters 4 [17 July 1859] and 30 [11 February 1860] printed in this volume). Skinner's presentation is a little better. Though he too prints inaccurate readings, he occasionally includes ellipses to indicate the numerous large omissions he makes, and he prints partial dates. However, one letter (pp. 111-112) of the eight he includes is not by MDB. The present volume is, therefore, the first edition of these documents in a critical text, one which aims to be as accurate as humanly possible.

By her own admission on more than one occasion, MDB did not relish letter-writing, despite her conviction that "<u>letters</u> are sacred things." More than for any other reason, she corresponded out of a sense of duty. Nevertheless, she carried on a lively correspondence with her family and friends. In addition, after she and EB were engaged she seems to have written him at least twice a week whenever they were separated for more than a week. She also refers (in Letter 21) to a notebook now apparently lost. Calculated conservatively, this means that between the summer of 1858 and February 1863 she wrote about 140 letters to EB and began at least three notebooks; and that from the time she began her independent stage career in 1855 to her death she wrote about 750 letters to others. All that remain from this total of nearly 900 letters and three notebooks are printed here (87 letters, less than one-tenth, and two brief, unfinished notebooks).

The chief reason for such a high rate of loss is clear. Since she pre-deceased EB by many years, all of her letters to him came into his possession; as for her other letters, following her death recipients returned them to EB as a courtesy. Of all these letters, EB rather systematically preserved several--ones which he wished posterity to read-- and he even annotated a few. He then destroyed the rest, in keeping with the convention of the age. Still other letters may have been destroyed by Edwina or by friends who wanted to protect the reputations of MDB or EB or who simply felt that private communications should not be viewed by public eyes. Regardless of who did the destroying or what the reason was, the result is that for the most part the twentieth century reads only what the nineteenth has consciously allowed it to read. Thus, we are guided, to a great degree by EB himself, in what EB and MDB's correspondence allows us to understand and reconstruct about them. Inasmuch as all his letters to her were also destroyed (for the most part also by EB, no doubt), it is fortunate that even this many of her documents have survived.

Introduction xvii

The Search for MDB Documents

To locate all extant MDB documents, I first contacted all known EB collections. This process uncovered the letters to EB and the two notebooks at two of the major repositories, The Players and the New York Public Library. Gradually I cast a wider net to include, first, collections of people associated with the Booths and then collections of people named prominently or frequently in the correspondence. This located letters to other, unexpected people, like Mattie Woodman, at less expected repositories, like the Manuscript Division at Harvard Univ. A list of the seven collections known to have material by MDB is given in the Acknowledgements section below. The complete list of recipients is as follows: EB, Emma F. Cary, Helen S. Cary, Charlotte Cushman, Emma C. Cushman, Mary L. Felton, Josephine Graham, Julia Nash, Elizabeth Stoddard, Richard Henry Stoddard and Matilda Woodman.

However, still more materials by MDB are no doubt extant and will gradually come to light. Later scholars pursuing these elusive documents can be aided by a list of the most promising among the additional repositories which were contacted--albeit in vain--in connection with this edition. This can be particularly helpful in eliminating leads which will prove false (unless, of course, those repositories acquire MDB documents in the meantime). For example, in a letter to Edwina Grossmann (27 November 1894; Players), Adam Badeau states that he has some MDB letters "written to me during her engagement and after her marriage." However, no known Badeau collection (Library of Congress, Princeton, Players, Rutgers) contains any MDB documents. (By 1901, however, the letters had apparently disappeared from Badeau's own holdings, for the catalog of the sale of Badeau's literary possessions in December of that year does not list any MDB letters.) False leads also occur with other collections or repositories which might be thought to have material by her on the grounds that they focus on individuals associated with the Booths: T. B. Aldrich collections at the American Academy of Arts and Letters, the Huntington, and the Iowa Historical Association; Stoddard collection at the Univ. of Delaware and Stoddard materials in the Stedman collection at Columbia Univ.; Joseph Jefferson collections at Princeton and the Univ. of California at Davis; Charlotte Cushman and Emma Crow Cushman collections at the Free Library of Philadelphia and Washington State Univ.; Julia Ward Howe and family collections at Radcliffe College, Colby College, Brown Univ., Univ. of Virginia, Berg Collection of the New York Public Library, Claremont College, Indiana Univ., Historical Society of Pennsylvania, Stowe-Day Memorial Library, and Rutherford B. Hayes Library; and finally Junius Brutus Booth II materials at the Manchester Historical Society. Indeed, except for the seven primary ones all collections referred to in this volume can be added to this list. Furthermore, all repositories in locations where MDB lived or performed and which reasonably might have material by her were contacted without success. These include Troy and Albany, New York; Richmond, Virginia; Boston; Washington, D.C.; Philadelphia; and New York City. Altogether, more than one hundred collections were queried for primary materials.

The Text

To present the materials gleaned from this search, a text was designed which would serve both the specialized scholar and the general reader. Both kinds depend upon the accuracy and scrupulousness with which the text has been prepared, but for the specialist the textual notes are a matter of scholarly necessity. Conversely, both kinds of readers no doubt will find at least some of the annotations helpful, but the general reader is likely to be the more interested. To meet the needs of both kinds of readers, I have used principles of textual scholarship codified initially by the Modern Language Association's Center for Editions of American Authors and currently maintained by that Center's successor, the Committee for Scholarly Editions. These principles have been adapted for documentary editing (the most common method of presenting materials not intended for publication) and have been promulgated through discourse within the Society for Textual Scholarship and the Association for Documentary Editing. Chiefly they call for reproducing all textually significant or potentially significant elements in the documents, and for providing full explanations of the procedures used to generate the printed text and of the means of resolving the cruxes which inevitably result from applying uniform standards to eccentric texts. The result is the first documentary edition I know of in nineteenth-century American theatre scholarship.

In this edition, the documents are presented in clear text: that is, no interruptive, distracting textual symbols have been intruded. (A full explanation of the editorial principles is provided in the Textual Notes.) The text is also free from superscript and subscript symbols to indicate the existence of textual notes and annotations. However, to alert the reader when a textual note exists a "T" appears to the right of the relevant line of the text; an "A" appears for an annotation. Line numbers are also provided to the right of the text. (An explanation of the guiding principles behind the annotation is given in the headnote to that section, immediately following the text.)

Some indicators and abbreviations have been employed. Square brackets are used sparingly, only seven times altogether. Intertextually, three sets occur. In the 12 November 1860 entry in MDB's Journal (Players), Edwina Booth Grossmann superimposed three words over her mother's writing, in effect emending the original text. Grossmann's writing is enclosed within square brackets in the present text. Elsewhere, square brackets are used three times extratextually to explain anomalous textual matters, as in "[remainder of letter missing]," and to give documentation data. They are used once intratextually, in "[addenda on inserted leaves]." MDB never used square brackets, so these indicators can not be confused with marks she made.

Arrows are used to indicate inserted material but since MDB usually used carets when she inserted writing interlinearly, these arrows are not symbols. Nor are line-throughs, which cancel writing the same way MDB ordinarily did. When the material cancelled is undecipherable, however, a free-standing question mark, lined-through, has been used. No confusion exists between this symbol and a question mark cancelled by MDB because she never cancelled a free-standing question mark.

Finally, for persons and repositories referred to often the following abbreviations have been used for convenience:

| | |
|---|---|
| EB | Edwin Booth |
| FL--BTM | Franklyn Lenthall--Boothbay Theatre Museum |
| HRHRC | Theatre Arts Library, Harry Ransom Humanities Research Center, The Univ. of Texas at Austin |
| HU--MD | Harvard Univ.--Manuscript Division |
| HU--TC | Harvard Univ.--Theatre Collection |
| LC--MD | Library of Congress--Manuscript Division |
| MD or MDB | Mary Devlin or Mary Devlin Booth |
| NYPL--MD | New York Public Library--Manuscript Division |
| NYPL--TC | New York Public Library--Billy Rose Theatre Collection |
| Players | The Walter Hampden-Edwin Booth Theatre Collection and Library at The Players |
| PSU | Pennsylvania State Univ.--Department of Special Collections |

Prominent Figures in the Correspondence

Several people (or groups of people) are referred to often in MDB's correspondence. The most prominent of these is, of course, EB, for whom no annotation is necessary. For the others, however, some identification is in order. A note or a cross reference in the annotation at each of the frequent mentions of these people would soon become tedious and needlessly distracting. Furthermore, for some of these figures, like Adam Badeau and the Stoddards, a comprehensive statement--more than what could be reasonably supplied in an annotation--is necessary. Hence, for the people who are referred to often or who are prominent, a full identification is given here. This suffices for general purposes and when additional information is necessary for a specific reference it will be given at the appropriate place in the Annotations section, immediately following the text. People are noted here in the approximate order of their appearance in the correspondence.

**Charlotte Cushman and Emma Crow Cushman:** Charlotte Cushman (1816-1876) is generally acknowledged as the first great tragedienne of the American stage. Unmarried, she adopted her sister's son Edwin Charles Merriman in 1851, when he was thirteen years old. In 1861, he married Emma Crow, daughter of Wayman Crow, Cushman's financial advisor in St. Louis. In this way, Cushman was both mother-in-law and aunt by marriage to Emma; from MD's references, Emma preferred to think of her as the latter. According to her memoir (LC--MD), Emma first met MD, who was one year her junior, in St. Louis in mid-January 1858--an impossibility since MD was not in St. Louis at that time and was regularly named in the cast at the Baltimore Museum in January of 1858. Probably they first met in the spring of 1861, as MDB implies in Letter 52, l. 8. Letters from Cushman to Emma and from Emma to EB following MDB's death (LC--MD and Players) reveal the closeness of MDB's relationship with Emma, a relationship focused on the birth of MDB's daughter and the expected arrival of "little Charlotte," Emma's baby (it miscarried in May 1862). Cushman even worried that MDB's death would be a severe blow to Emma's health. She also believed that the salutary effect MDB had on "her poor weak husband" was so important that her death would mean the virtual end of his career.

In her unique position as EB's wife and a favorite of Cushman, MDB sought to arrange performances starring the two in 1860. Her efforts bore fruit when the two performed together in December in Philadelphia. In April-May 1861, with MDB's aid, Cushman used EB's Hamlet "drapery" in New York and even got permission to have a costumer use it to make a pattern for herself (Cushman to MDB, Players; undated). Through MDB, Cushman strongly urged EB to go to Europe: "his intelligence would know what to eschew & what to receive, & the best Shaksperian actors *now* are in Germany & Italy" (NYPL--TC; undated). When the Booths did go abroad in 1861-1862, Cushman visited them in London and Paris.

**Joseph Jefferson:** Jefferson (1829-1905) was the most popular and most respected American comedian of the nineteenth century. MD might have first seen him perform when he appeared in Troy in February 1853 while she was presumably still living there. If Jefferson can be believed, MD's first professional association with him occurred in the autumn of 1853, when she was in the company at Henry Jarrett's Baltimore Museum under Jefferson's management; she joined him again in the autumn of 1855, returning to his company headquartered at the Baltimore Museum and, beginning in October, giving weekly performances at the National Theatre in Washington, D.C., also managed by Jefferson for Jarrett. In the fall of 1856 MD joined the company of John T. Ford's Marshall Theatre in Richmond when Jefferson had begun to manage there. During this engagement MD and EB met and first acted together (24 November-12 December). Years later Jefferson took credit for playing a significant part in uniting EB and MD (see Players Book for 1894 [Players], pp. 38-39; repeated with a change in the year, from 1854 to 1853, in Francis Wilson, *Joseph Jefferson* [New York, 1906], pp. 145-146). If his story about blessing them is true, however, the event did not occur in 1853, nor in 1854 as he implies, but perhaps in March of 1858. In time MD virtually became a member of the Jefferson family, even accompanying them in the summers of 1858 and 1859 to their summer retreat in the Poconos (see EB to Walter Brackett, 23 July 1858, HRHRC; see also Annotation for Letter 3, l. 18). All in all, Jefferson was surely the most important influence on MD personally and professionally prior to July 1859, when she became engaged to EB.

**The Devlin family:** MD was the fourth child in a large Irish Catholic family. Her parents, Charles and Nancy Ann, were born (in 1804 and 1812, respectively) and married in Ireland; they had their first child, Margaret, there in 1828. They apparently immigrated to Canada in c. 1830, where their second child, Charles, was born in 1834. By 1840, they had immigrated to the United States, to Sand Lake, a tiny village eleven miles southeast of Troy, New York. Three more children were born there: Catherine Celestine (1839), Mary Elizabeth (1840) and Letitia M. (1845). In the spring of 1848 the family moved to Troy; another child, William H., was born that year. The father was a tailor and evidently quite successful for in 1850 he moved his family up River Street to a location in the newest and most prosperous part of Troy's business district. Another son, John, was born that year. In 1851 the father opened a wholesale and retail dry goods and tailor shop of his own and began to run a large display advertisement in the largest Troy daily newspaper, the *Times*. MD made her first appearance on stage the following spring, on 4 May, two weeks shy of her twelfth birthday. The *Times* of 5 May carried her first review. In its entirety it read: "A Trojan danseuse, Miss Devlin, made her debut at the Museum last evening. She danced exceedingly well, and was honored with a hearty encore." By fall the business had prospered to the point that the oldest son, Charles, joined the father in the "Charles Devlin & Son" tailor shop. In October 1852 the family left Troy, ostensibly going to New York where the father was to work as costumer for the actor-manager A. W.

Fenno, though no New York city records bear this out. By 1857 the family was in Philadelphia and by June 1860 another daughter, Sarah, had been born. The oldest son, Charles, and his sisters Catherine and Mary were no longer living at home. Mary, of course, had by that time married EB; in 1858 Catherine had married Henry Magonigle (1830-1919). Magonigle, the "Harry" of these letters, developed a close personal and professional relationship with EB over the years, proving to be one of the few financial advisors EB could trust. Magonigle helped plan the building of Booth's Theatre and then managed it; later he was treasurer for EB and Lawrence Barrett; and finally he served as manager of The Players. By 1859, Magonigle and Catherine had an infant daughter, Sarah, referred to by MD and identified by EB (see Letter 34 and Annotation for it). For at least part of the year that MD spent in seclusion in Hoboken, New Jersey, following her engagement to EB, she lived with Catherine (referred to as "sister" and "Kate" in the letters) and Magonigle. Several references, one to her brother (Letter 15), two to "my folks" (Letters 9 and 15), one to "my parents" (Letter 15) and one to "all . . . here" (Letter 10), imply MD also lived with her family for part of that year.

**The Booth Family:** EB (1833-1893) was the inheritor of a name made famous in America by his father, Junius Brutus Booth (1796-1852), the British-born rival to Edmund Kean and generally thought to be the first powerful tragedian on the American stage. After the elder Booth's death, EB's mother, Mary Ann Holmes (1802-1885), and her unmarried daughter, Rosalie (1823-1889), stayed at the family residence, Tudor Hall (Bel Air, Maryland), until 1859 when, with EB's assistance, they took up residence in Philadelphia. Another daughter, Asia (1835-1888), married the comedian John Sleeper Clarke (1833-1899). Initially Asia had a strong dislike for MD, accusing her of pursuing EB for his money and his name and calling her a "deep designing artful actress." By the time of MDB's death, however, Asia had moderated her attitude considerably (see the Sherwood Collection of Asia Booth Clarke letters at the Peale Museum, Baltimore, especially: undated [summer 1859], Thursday [August 1859], 21 August and 28 October 1860, and 3 March 1863; see also Asia Booth Clarke, *The Elder and the Younger Booth* [Boston, 1882], p. 157). Asia became the family chronicler, writing *The Unlocked Book* (New York, 1938) on J. W. Booth in addition to her books on EB and her father.

The youngest of the elder Booth's children by Mary Ann Holmes (his second wife) was Joseph Adrian (1840-1902). The "Joe" of these letters was marginally associated with the theatre in his early years. In the spring of 1859, for example, he toured with EB and on at least two occasions he acted with him, though only "out of courtesy" because there weren't enough actors to play the piece, never "to make a business out of it" (John C. Brennan, "John Wilkes Booth's Enigmatic Brother Joseph," *Maryland Historical Magazine*, 78 [Spring 1983], 28). In 1861-1862, Joe acted as agent for

John Wilkes Booth in New York, and in 1868, when EB began the lengthy process of building his theatre in New York, Joe was named treasurer.

The most notorious member of the Booth family was certainly John Wilkes (1838-1865), who made his acting debut at the age of seventeen in Richmond and from that time forward was inevitably compared, usually unfavorably, to EB. From the start, Wilkes, who preferred melodramatic roles, had been appreciated in the south. By late 1862, however, he was also performing in the major northern cities and was rivaling the aging Forrest. Wilkes had been a witness to the marriage of EB and MD, and during January 1863, while he was performing in Boston, he visited MDB and EB often. Though EB had performed with Wilkes once (in 1858), it was not until 21 January 1863 that he first watched Wilkes act, when he and MDB attended Wilkes' performance at the Boston Museum. A month later, on his way to fill his engagement in Philadelphia, Wilkes stopped in New York and told EB that MDB, who had been severely ill, was recovering. Two weeks later, Wilkes and John Sleeper Clarke, also in Philadelphia at the time, returned to Boston for MDB's funeral.

**Adam Badeau:** General Badeau (1831-1895), soldier, author and diplomat, is best known as "court historian" for U. S. Grant, both as Grant's military secretary during the Civil War and after (1864-1869) and later as diplomat during and after Grant's presidency (1869-1884). In these capacities, Badeau wrote *Grant in Peace* (Philadelphia, 1868) and *Military History of U. S. Grant*, 3 vols. (New York, 1868-1881). He also served as amanuensis for Grant's *Personal Memoirs*, 2 vols. (New York, 1885-1886). From his diplomatic experiences (secretary, U.S. legation in London [1869-1870] and U.S. consul general at London [1870-1881]), he produced *Aristocracy in England* (New York, 1886) and *Our Relations with England* (n.p., [1870?]).

Badeau had been a writer from his early years, though of aesthetic criticism not of history. He had been privately educated in Tarrytown, New York, and by 1857 he was writing drama criticism for Noah's *Sunday Times* using the nom de plume "The Vagabond." In the spring of that year he first saw EB perform and though the actor was unpolished and in need of refinement and education, Badeau saw "the unmistakable fire, the electric spark, the god-like quality, which mankind have agreed to worship" ("American Art," one of Badeau's *Sunday Times* essays collected in *The Vagabond* [New York, 1859], p. 120). Badeau attended all of EB's New York performances during the spring of 1857, then promptly wrote EB an extraordinary letter (15 June 1857; Players) to introduce himself and praise EB's genius. He enclosed a copy of his *Sunday Times* essay on "Tragedy" and stressed that EB's performances were of such quality that Badeau needed to prepare himself to appreciate them fully: ". . . I have studied Shakespeare most diligently to recall your look and tones in certain parts, and in others, pardon me, to fancy what you might have said, and done, and looked, and did not." Badeau "ferretted out" old criticisms on Garrick, Kean and Siddons; he re-read Hazlitt's "A View of the English Stage" (offering to send EB a copy) and called into consideration his studies of Rachel, Grisi, Forrest, Wallack and Heron. He read "every scrap" that he could find in print about EB. He concluded that the rebirth of tragedy was imminent, in the person of EB: "There are certainly no heights you may not attain. . . ." It would take work, though, for EB lacked intellectual control; therefore, admonished Badeau, "During your vacation, I entreat you, for your own sake, to apply your wonderful energies . . ." to diligent study; "to the filling up, as it were, of your performances, to the acquisition of a complete control of your voice, to the absolute mastery of every character you play." Badeau concluded this marvelous letter with an invitation for EB to visit him at his earliest convenience. EB responded as fully as Badeau could have hoped and during the summer of 1857 Badeau did nothing less than tutor EB in the arts and in the history of modern acting. Years later, after EB's death, Badeau recalled: "I used to hunt up books and pictures about the stage, the finest criticisms, the works that illustrated his scenes, the biographies of great actors, and we studied them together. We visited the Astor Library and the Society Library to verify costumes, and every picture or picture-gallery in New York, public or private, that was accessible" ("Edwin Booth. On and Off the Stage. Personal Recollections," *McClure's Magazine*, I [August 1893], 259).

Beyond a doubt, Badeau was the most literate, sensitive mind EB had encountered. He was the best possible influence on EB at this time and, EB's father excepted, he had the most effect on EB prior to EB's marriage. EB came to depend upon Badeau. In early 1860, for example, when the play EB had commissioned by G. H. Hollister, *Henry II*, needed revision, EB presumed upon Badeau to "fix it." Nor was this close association without its benefits for Badeau. He was plainly enchanted at being so close to genius, to a family of geniuses. On one occasion EB took Badeau to his family home, Tudor Hall, built by the elder Booth, where they rummaged through theatrical wardrobes; read letters from Edmund Kean, the elder Mathews and Macready; and looked over old playbills ("A Night with the Booths," collected in *The Vagabond*, p. 348). By 1860, Badeau was emboldened to say that the theatre was the only truly representative art in America and that excellence in American theatre was best represented by EB ("Representative Art," *Atlantic Monthly*, V [June 1860], 687-693). Yet even as this essay was being written, the intensity of the three-year-old relationship between EB and Badeau was diminishing. MD had already signaled its fate by calling Badeau an "intolerable bore--a second Boswell" (Letter 17). By the spring of 1860 his sense of her inclining and his own declining influence on EB caused him to be more possessive than ever, and his praise of EB "degenerated into sycophantic hero-worship" (Shattuck, p. 28). EB's patience was wearing thin. As the new relationship waxed and the old one waned from the autumn of 1859

Introduction    xxv

through the spring of 1960, tensions among the three increased.

In September 1859, at EB's insistence, MD began a "year" (really about nine months) in relative seclusion in Hoboken, New Jersey, during which she was to further her education by reading, studying French, visiting art galleries and museums, and adding the guitar to her dancing, piano and acting accomplishments (the parallel between this year for MD and the summer of 1857 when Badeau tutored EB is unmistakable). As letters from Badeau to EB (Players) and several of MD's own letters printed here show, Badeau visited her often during the year, no doubt chiefly at EB's behest to watch over her while he was on tour and to aid her when necessary. Badeau's first visit occurred shortly before 23 September 1859, the date of the only letter extant from Badeau to MD (Players). In it he informs her that he is having a guitar sent to her, and he continues in a tone cordial though edged with anxiety: I "am so desirous of becoming associated with you in procuring his happiness. I trust indeed, that your music may have the power over him that David's did with Saul. . . . I am a little selfish, you perceive: I want to secure for myself in the heart of my friend, a place with all sweet and holy things and thoughts; with music that wonderful soother and charmer, with woman and wife the only charmer of more subtle and more lasting sway." Moreover, Badeau recognized that MD was more than mere charmer. "You needn't trouble yourself about her mind; she has enough. Character too," he wrote EB (6 February 1860) in a clear reference to EB's concern for her intellectual development. Later (18 April 1860) he added: "She is full of ambition for you. In fact she's the woman of the entire world for you. Whether she will have the requisite strength of character, time only can tell. But her love is strong. And she knows what she is about to undertake." To his credit, Badeau appears to have fought his jealousy of MD, though from her advent in the previous summer he had feared she would take his place in EB's eyes. In this same letter (18 April 1860) and in many others from this time forward, including his letters to Harry Wilson (1862-1865; Princeton), Badeau's jealousy is less disguised. Increasingly during the spring of 1860 his letters contain derogatory references to marriage and children, though not to MD herself, and he hints that he isn't willing to give EB up. EB bridled at some of this, but he was surprisingly tolerant and even had Badeau act as best man at his wedding. Yet by late spring 1860 the time of Badeau's dominant influence was over; in the rivalry, MD had emerged victorious. Gradually, EB weaned Badeau: in visits to Philadelphia and Boston early in 1860, EB shunned Badeau. Badeau's letters to Wilson suggest Badeau's pain of rejection.

Still, the relationship, though diminished, continued for many more years. In the spring and summer of 1863, for example, after MDB had died, Badeau was one of the few (the Stoddards were the others) to whom EB confided his grief in its depth. In the fall of 1863, recalling that his unique position between MD and EB during their engagement year put him in the best position possible to recognize the beneficial effect MD had on EB, in life and perhaps even more in death, he wrote Wilson: ". . . I tell you now [EB] is safer than when his wife lived, for her influence survives her" (12 September 1863). Even after EB's death, Badeau was loyal. Remembering the furor thirty-one years earlier about EB's culpability for MDB's death, Badeau wrote Edwina (6 February 1894; Players): "There never was a kinder or more loving husband, and I am sure your mother was more than satisfied with his devotion. I certainly had the amplest opportunity to know. . . ."

**The Cary family:** Sometime during the spring of 1860, EB met Richard Cary and his wife Helen Eugenia Shelton Cary, both of Boston. Before long MDB had also met them and soon the Booths became acquainted with the entire Cary family. Of all the Carys, Richard's unmarried sister Emma took the deepest and most enduring interest in the Booths. She corresponded with EB long after MDB's death.

The family was well represented among Cambridge intellectuals. One sister, Elizabeth, married the Harvard geologist Louis Agassiz (1807-1873). Another sister, Mary, married Cornelius Felton (1807-1862), professor of classics and from 1860 to 1862, president of Harvard. Shortly before the Booths left for England, Richard joined the Union army; his daughter Georgie was born while he was in the service. He died in the battle of Cedar Mountain (Virginia), 9 August 1862, coincidentally as the Booths were returning from Europe. Several of EB's letters (Players) reveal he felt extremely close to Richard Cary (see also Annotation for Letter 9, 1. 44), and letters to EB and MDB from Richard, Emma and Helen (Players and NYPL--TC) indicate that the Carys looked upon EB as a member of their own family.

**Julia Ward Howe:** Howe (1819-1910), writer and reformer, author of "The Battle Hymn of the Republic" (1861), was born into an old and wealthy New England family. She was a grand niece of General Francis Marion, the Swamp Fox of the Revolutionary War; her father was a wealthy New York banker whose father had fought under George Washington and whose grandfather was a direct descendant of Roger Williams. In 1843 she married Samuel G. Howe (1801-1876), the internationally known physician, educator, reformer and philanthropist. They established their home in Boston and soon Mrs. Howe became known as a woman of intellect and refinement whose home was a center of hospitality. By the time the Booths met her (1862) she was also widely recognized as a reformer in behalf of women's rights and the abolition of slavery and was associated with Theodore Parker and Margaret Fuller.

She seems to have been attracted to the Booths immediately (she had first seen EB perform in 1857, and in 1858 she had written a five-act play, *Hippolytus*, for EB and Charlotte Cushman). Apparently she had a maternal feeling for MDB, who was only a few years older than her oldest daughter, Julia (born in 1844; referred to in Letters 70 and

82, and by name in 42 and 83; the second daughter, Florence [1845], is also referred to in Letters 82 and 83). Many years later, in their biography of their mother, the two younger daughters, Laura (1850) and Maud (1854), recollected a party their mother gave for EB in December 1862, a party which MDB mentions in Letters 68 and 69. Their version (*Julia Ward Howe* [Boston, 1916], I, 205) illustrates MDB's charge that, though it was a "real ovation to Edwin," it was "tedious" for her and EB:

> We gave a party for him, and Beacon Street came in force to meet the brilliant young actor. Alas! the brilliant young actor, after the briefest and shyest of greetings to the company, retired into a corner with eight-year-old Maud, where he sat on the floor making dolls and rabbits out of his pocket handkerchief!

**Lucy Pry:** Lucy J. Pry of Boston was a friend of the Booths at least as early as the fall of 1861 and she remained so until MDB's death in February 1863. Her association with the Cushmans apparently preceded that, and by February 1863 she had also become familiar with the Stoddards. She was a constant visitor during MDB's final days. Her letter to Elizabeth Stoddard, 21 February [1863] (Players) is the best account extant of MDB's condition in the days immediately prior to her death. That letter makes clear that there were signs for hope and that the doctor in attendance, Dr. Miller, expected her to rally. The letter also gives details about what Pry had heard, from a friend of a friend, concerning the excessive drinking of EB who was performing in New York at the time of MDB's death.

**The Stoddards:** Richard Henry Stoddard (1825-1903), poet, literary editor and public official, and Elizabeth Drew Barstow Stoddard (1823-1902), novelist, both met MDB and EB in early September 1862, soon after the Booths returned from Europe. The couples were brought together by James Lorimer Graham and his wife, Josephine, New York friends of the Stoddards whom the Booths had met in England the previous winter (see letters from Graham to Stoddard, 27 July and August 1862; NYPL--MD). Letters by Elizabeth Stoddard and EB to Lorimer Graham (PSU) show how quickly the Booths made their way to meet the Stoddards upon their return from Europe and how remarkably intense the relationships among the four of them were: on 14 September Elizabeth wrote that they had spent three evenings together and on 9 October EB wrote, "Scarcely a day has passed without our seeing them. They are dear, good, splendid, noble, bully folks."

Most of the intensity was owing to the forceful, irascible Elizabeth. For one thing, she was strongly attracted to EB. A dramatic account of her first meeting him is recorded by Lillian Woodman (Mrs. Thomas B. Aldrich, *Crowding Memories* [New York, 1920], p. 13; see also Elizabeth's letter to E. C. Stedman, 30 July 1891, quoted in

Matlack, p. 593). But Elizabeth also felt strongly about MDB. When the Booths moved to Boston from New York in late November, for example, Elizabeth accompanied them, staying for two weeks to help MDB and her infant daughter get settled. In MDB Elizabeth had found "at last an enduring female confidante who could soften her temperament . . ." (Matlack, p. 287). MDB's death shattered Elizabeth; the consequences of it "shaped the rest of her life" (Matlack, p. 309). "She was devoted heart and soul to us--. . . ," wrote Elizabeth to Lorimer Graham, 6 March 1863 (PSU); "I . . . am cut adrift. . . . I had attached myself strongly to the lovely, affectionate, intelligent girl." Her poem on MDB's death appeared on the front page of the New York Post, 4 March 1863.

For both Booths, but for MDB especially, the friendship of Richard and Elizabeth Stoddard marked a great advance into the intellectual and cultural life of New York, for the Stoddards were at the center of a group of writers, critics, editors, sculptors and painters that included E. C. Stedman, Bayard Taylor, T. B. Aldrich, Fitz Hugh Ludlow, Jervis McEntee and Launt Thompson. The Booths were pleased to be included and quickly became familiar with the Stoddards' recent writing. MDB read Elizabeth's first novel, *The Morgesons* (New York, 1862), and when "Tuberoses," Elizabeth's short story featuring EB, appeared (*Harpers*, 26 [January 1863], 191-197), MDB received and immediately read an advance copy. Together MDB and EB read, and wept over, Richard's long narrative poem *The King's Bell* (New York, 1863). "Edwin's hobby now is--what d'ye think?" asked MDB in a letter to Elizabeth in late January 1863 (#84). "Stoddard's poems!"

The strength of this extraordinary four-way relationship was shown in other ways. For example, Elizabeth's brother, Wilson Barstow, a captain in the Union army, was stationed for a time at Fortress Monroe, an important supply base located at the mouth of Hampton Roads, Virginia. When Richard visited him in late December 1862, EB made special arrangements to accompany him, to meet Barstow and see some of the war zone. Later, EB stayed with the Stoddards during his engagement at the Winter Garden in New York in February, and plans called for MDB to join him at the Stoddards' as soon as she was able. Finally, when EB was summoned to Dorchester because of MDB's serious illness, Richard accompanied him, and after MDB's death EB poured out his grief to the Stoddards more than to anyone else. In December 1863, the Stoddards' third son was born, named Edwin after EB. The intimacy of EB's relationship with the Stoddards, particularly with Elizabeth, decreased sharply about a year after MDB's death for rather obscure reasons having to do with EB's behavior during MDB's final illness (see letter from Elizabeth Stoddard to E. C. Stedman, 30 July 1891, quoted in Matlack, p. 593).

**Dr. Erasmus Miller:** While in Boston for EB's engagement there (24 November-20 December 1862), MDB's ever weak condition worsened significantly and she visited the "celebrated"

Introduction xxix

(her term) Dr. Miller of Dorchester, just outside Boston. His treatment included much quiet and rest, more than she could have in a hotel room in the city, so she and EB rented a cottage "out" in Dorchester to be nearer Miller. Whatever his credentials, Dr. Miller had the confidence of MDB, so much so that she rejected the advice of Elizabeth Stoddard to seek treatment in New York. She planned to rest for six weeks in Dorchester and, when she had regained her strength, travel with EB to New York for his Winter Garden engagement. But by early February it was clear that she was not better, so EB was required to go alone. In this peculiar set of circumstances, Erasmus Miller, altogether unpredictably, came to have a disproportionately large role to play during the final weeks of MDB's life (and indirectly during the rest of EB's life, as well).

For a supposed specialist in diseases of the sort MDB had, Miller was remarkably ineffective both in treating MDB and in accurately assessing the seriousness of her condition. Perhaps her case was hopeless so that no treatment would have been effective, yet there is no satisfactory way to account for why Miller was continually hopeful and encouraging, not only to MDB but also to EB, even during the final few days. Because Miller was so optimistic, however, EB had no reason not to leave MDB in Dorchester when he went to New York, nor was there reason for him to return to Dorchester during what turned out to be her final days. But this explanation was not apparent to others, such as Elizabeth Stoddard and Lillian Woodman (later Mrs. Thomas Aldrich). To them, EB was irresponsible in not being at MDB's bedside, and for years afterward they blamed him for this and charged the dereliction to his heavy drinking while he was alone in New York and not under MDB's direct and beneficial influence.

Yet, as Dr. Miller contributed to the misfortunes of the Booths, evidence discovered after his death helps repair some of the damage he caused. Two letters from him to EB, 18 and 19 February 1863 (NYPL--TC), exonerate EB at least from the implication of callousness and irresponsibility. In the first of these letters Miller wrote:

> I am very happy to be able to inform you that Mrs B, has been gradually gaining since yesterday morn-- . . . I hope you will not give yourself any undue anxiety in regard to the actual condition of Mrs B. for I assure you that should any change in her symptoms for the worse occur, (which I do not expect) you shall be notified at once-- I am stating the case to you as it is, & I feel to day, that there is little doubt but what every day will find her better--

On 19 February, less than forty-eight hours before MDB died, Miller confirmed what he had said the previous day:

xxx  Introduction

> I am happy to say that Mrs B. has passed a comfortable night-- . . . Don't give yourself undue anxiety, for I have given my word that if any thing does not progress satisfactorily, you shall be instantly notified--

From EB's point of view, these letters from MDB's doctor were sufficient reason not to be in Dorchester on 21 February 1863.

### ACKNOWLEDGEMENTS

In preparing this edition I have accumulated many debts. I am grateful to Northern Illinois Univ. for a research leave and to the Graduate School of Northern Illinois Univ. for a travel grant which enabled me to do research for the edition and to read my transcriptions against the originals. For their encouragement and cooperation, I am also indebted to Edwin and Mary Devlin Booth's heirs, Mrs. Richard Cutting (Edwina Booth Waterbury Cutting, daughter of Mildred Grossmann) and Mrs. Lois Rathbun (Lois Fellows White Rathbun, granddaughter of Edwin [Clarence] Booth Grossmann). Most unfortunately, Mrs. Cutting died before this volume was completed. In her behalf, her foster son, Joseph Kinner, lent his support as fully as Mrs. Cutting had.

On a practical level, this volume could not have been completed without the conscientious labors of several people at Northern Illinois Univ. Much of the work for the context of the text of these documents was done with material borrowed through the interlibrary loan department of Founders Memorial Library. To the heads of this division, first Mrs. Mertie Podschwit, then her successor Mrs. Tobie Miller, and to their staff, I am grateful for their persistence and resourcefulness. Research assistants assigned by the Department of English also contributed much to the effort, especially Ann Litow, Tan Zhiming, Ma Bing-gong, Xie Lihong, Penelope LeFew and Nathalie Monsaint. A special thanks to Mary Risseeuw, of the Faculty Development Office and the Department of Art, for help with production, and to Peggy Sullivan, Dean of the College of Professional Studies. Most of all, I am grateful for the diligence and thoroughness of Yao Fusheng, Department of English, who did the bulk of the text editing on the university's mainframe computer; of Gai Littler, Department of English, who helped establish the Lenthall texts and who created the index; and of Cheryl Fuller, of the Word Processing Center, College of Liberal Arts and Sciences, who did all the micro-computer word processing.

So many persons have been helpful in ways too numerous and varied to enumerate that this list is necessarily incomplete, but gratitude must be expressed to Alan Golden and

Introduction xxxi

Katherine M. Smith, Poe Museum, Richmond; Sarah Shields, Valentine Museum, Richmond; Richard W. Flint, Peale Museum, Baltimore; Ellen Keyes Gamache and Cara Janowsky, Troy (New York) Public Library; James Hobin, Albany (New York) Public Library; Robert J. Zietz, Mobile (Alabama) Public Library; Professor Thomas Liszka, Pennsylvania State Univ. at Altoona; Martha Mahard, HU--TC; Howard L. and Dorothy E. Fox, Tudor Hall, Bel Air, Maryland; John C. Brennan, Laurel, Maryland; Donald Anderle, Associate Director of Special Collections, and Susan Davis, Curator of Manuscripts, New York Public Library; Stephen T. Seames, Maine Historical Society; Jean F. Preston, Princeton Univ. Library; Dr. Constance Head, Cullowhee, North Carolina; Jeffrey Sowder, Merl Kelce Library, Univ. of Tampa; Paul M. Bailey, HRHRC; David Farmer, formerly of the HRHRC and now of the DeGolyer Library, Southern Methodist Univ.; Laetitia Yeandle, Folger Shakespeare Library; Professor Joseph Leach, Univ. of Texas at El Paso; Mr. and Mrs. Ynhui Park, Boston; and Robert H. Gruber, Navy and Old Army Branch, Military Archives Division, National Archives.

Acknowledgement is made to the following individuals and institutions who own the MDB documents printed in this volume: Allison-Shelley Collection, The Pennsylvania State Univ. Libraries; Anthony Collection, New York Public Library --Manuscript Division; Charlotte Cushman Papers, Manuscript Division, Library of Congress; Edwina Grossmann Collection, Billy Rose Theatre Collection, New York Public Library; Franklyn Lenthall--Boothbay Theatre Museum; Hampden-Booth Theatre Library, The Players; and the T. B. Aldrich Collection, Houghton Library, Harvard Univ. At these institutions, certain individuals and their staffs provided special assistance: James H. Hudson, Chief of the Manuscript Division, Library of Congress; Charles W. Mann, Chief of the Rare Books and Special Collections Division, Pennsylvania State Univ. Library; and Ray Wemmlinger, assistant curator at The Players. Most of all, I am indebted to Louis Rachow of The Players and to Dorothy Swerdlove of the New York Public Library's Billy Rose Theatre Collection. Franklyn Lenthall was especially considerate in arranging a convenient means for me to examine the letters he owns.

In addition, for permission to quote materials relating to MDB I am indebted to the HRHRC, the Peale Museum, Princeton Univ., Players, PSU, NYPL--TC, LC--MD, HU--TC, the Folger Shakespeare Library, the Univ. of Rochester, FL--BTM, HU--MD, NYPL--MD, Mrs. Lois Rathbun, and Mr. Joseph Kinner.

Finally, I want to acknowledge my obligation to three colleagues. Professors Daniel Watermeier (Univ. of Toledo) and Stephen Archer (Univ. of Missouri at Columbia) have willingly shared information which they have gathered in the process of writing biographies of Edwin Booth and Junius Brutus Booth, respectively, and they have been sources of encouragement and counsel. Professor Thomas Marshall, Emeritus, was chairman of the English department at Kent

State Univ. when I entered there as a Masters student. His career also spans both literature and theatre in nineteenth century America. More than just interested in American theatre history, he was one of the moving spirits behind the founding of the American Society for Theatre Research twenty-seven years ago. He has been a valued advisor and friend to me over the years. He readily agreed to read the entire typescript of this volume and his comments were clear and cogent. The volume has benefitted from them. Any deficiencies that remain are my responsibility alone.

L. T. O.
1 September 1986

# Calendar of Letters and Notebooks

| Letter | Recipient | Date | Location |
|---|---|---|---|
| 1 | Charlotte Cushman | 4 Nov 58 | Players |
| 2 | Charlotte Cushman | 4 Nov 58 | LC—MD |
| 3 | EB | 7? Jun 59 | Players |
| 4 | EB | 17 Jul 59 | NYPL—TC |
| 5 | EB | Jul—Aug? 59 | Players |
| 6 | EB | 16 Aug 59 | Players |
| 7 | EB | 19—20 Aug 59 | NYPL—TC |
| 8 | EB | 23 Aug 59 | Players |
| 9 | EB | 24? Aug 59 | NYPL—TC |
| 10 | EB | 12 Sep 59 | Players |
| 11 | EB | 13—14 Sep 59 | NYPL—TC |
| 12 | EB | 15? Sep 59 | NYPL—TC |
| 13 | EB | 19 Sep 59 | NYPL—TC |
| 14 | EB | 21 Sep 59 | NYPL—TC |
| 15 | EB | 29 Sep 59 | Players |
| 16 | EB | 7 Oct 59 | Players |
| 17 | EB | 11 Oct 59 | NYPL—TC |
| 18 | EB | 11 Oct 59 | NYPL—TC |
| 19 | EB | 13 Oct 59 | NYPL—TC |
| 20 | EB | 14—15 Oct 59 | NYPL—TC |
| 21 | EB | 28 Nov 59 | NYPL—TC |
| 22 | EB | Dec 59 | NYPL—TC |
| 23 | EB | 16 Dec 59 | Players |
| 24 | EB | Dec 59 | NYPL—TC |
| 25 | EB | 28 Dec 59 | Players |
| 26 | EB | 4 Jan 60 | Players |
| 27 | EB | 24 Jan 60 | NYPL—TC |
| 28 | EB | 7 Feb 60 | NYPL—TC |
| 29 | EB | 9 Feb 60 | NYPL—TC |
| 30 | EB | 11 Feb 60 | NYPL—TC |
| 31 | EB | 12 Feb 60 | NYPL—TC |
| 32 | EB | 20 Feb 60 | NYPL—TC |
| 33 | EB | 23 Feb 60 | NYPL—TC |
| 34 | EB | 24—25 Feb 60 | Players |
| 35 | Julia Nash | 26 Feb 60 | Players |
| 36 | EB | 1 Mar 60 | Players |
| 37 | EB | 19 Mar 60 | NYPL—TC |
| 38 | EB | 10 May 60 | NYPL—TC |

xxxiv  Calendar

| | | | |
|---|---|---|---|
| 39 | EB | 19 May 60 | NYPL–TC |
| 40 | Mary L. Felton | 29 Sep 60 | Players |
| 41 | Julia Nash | Winter 60–61 | NYPL–TC |
| 42 | Julia Ward Howe | 30 Jun 61 | *NEM*, 1893 |
| 43 | Emma F. Cary | 3 Jul 61 | Players |
| 44 | Emma F. Cary | 30 Aug 61 | Players |
| 45 | Emma F. Cary | 1–2 Oct 61 | Players |
| 46 | Emma C. Cushman | 4 Oct 61 | FL–BTM |
| 47 | Josephine Graham | 1 Nov 61 | PSU |
| 48 | Emma F. Cary | Oct 61 | Players |
| 49 | EB | 22 Nov 61 | NYPL–TC |
| 50 | Emma C. Cushman | 13? Jan 62 | FL–BTM |
| 51 | Mary L. Felton | 14 Feb 62 | NYPL–TC |
| 52 | Emma C. Cushman | 26 Feb 62 | FL–BTM |
| 53 | EB | 28 Feb 62 | Players |
| 54 | EB | 2 Mar 62 | Players |
| 55 | Mary L. Felton | 22 Mar 62 | Players |
| 56 | Emma F. Cary | 26 Mar 62 | Players |
| 57 | Emma C. Cushman | 12 Apr 62 | FL–BTM |
| 58 | Emma C. Cushman | 11 May 62 | FL–BTM |
| 59 | Mary L. Felton | 13 May 62 | Players |
| 60 | Mary L. Felton | early Sep 62 | NYPL–TC |
| 61 | Mary L. Felton | 10 Sep 62 | NYPL–TC |
| 62 | Mary L. Felton | 22 Sep 62 | Players |
| 63 | Elizabeth Stoddard | Oct 62 | NYPL–MD |
| 64 | Mary L. Felton | 31 Oct 62 | Players |
| 65 | Emma C. Cushman | 10? Nov 62 | FL–BTM |
| 66 | Helen S. Cary | 25 Nov 62 | NYPL–TC |
| 67 | Elizabeth Stoddard | 7 Dec 62 | Players |
| 68 | Elizabeth Stoddard | 13 Dec 62 | NYPL–MD |
| 69 | Emma C. Cushman | 13–16 Dec 62 | FL–BTM |
| 70 | Elizabeth Stoddard | 16 Dec 62 | NYPL–MD |
| 71 | Richard H. Stoddard | 20 Dec 62 | NYPL–MD |
| 72 | Elizabeth Stoddard | 21 Dec 62 | Players |
| 73 | Mary L. Felton | 22 Dec 62 | Players |
| 74 | Elizabeth Stoddard | 24 Dec 62 | Players |
| 75 | Elizabeth Stoddard | 30 Dec 62 | Players |
| 76 | Mary L. Felton | 1 Jan 63 | Players |
| 77 | Elizabeth Stoddard | 7 Jan 63 | Players |
| 78 | Mary L. Felton | 7 Jan 63 | Players |
| 79 | Richard H. Stoddard | early Jan 63 | Players |
| 80 | Richard H. Stoddard | 15 Jan 63 | Players |
| 81 | Elizabeth Stoddard | 19 Jan 63 | Players |
| 82 | Elizabeth Stoddard | 20 Jan 63 | Players |
| 83 | Emma C. Cushman | 22 Jan 63 | FL–BTM |
| 84 | Elizabeth Stoddard | 29 Jan 63 | Players |
| 85 | Matilda Woodman | 29 Jan 63 | HU–MD |
| 86 | EB | 9 Feb 63 | Players |
| 87 | EB | 12 Feb 63 | NYPL–TC |

Notebook

| | | |
|---|---|---|
| Record Book | 4 Oct 60 | NYPL–TC |
| Journal | 4–12 Nov 60 | Players |

# The Letters and Notebooks of Mary Devlin Booth

# LETTERS

1: to Charlotte Cushman (Players), 4 November 1858

                              Boston Nov 4th/58        T

Darling Miss Cushman,
    Need I tell you how grateful I am for your <u>thought</u>
of <u>me</u>, and how pleased I was at your present,--suffice it
to <u>say</u> that through the politeness of Capt Leitch I         A
received it safely and longed for your presence to <u>kiss</u>,
and <u>bless you</u>. I am at the Boston Theater, but most
uncomfortable; Mrs Davenport rendering it unpleasant,          A
however I shall try and bear it with gentleness and
<u>patience</u>, and hope for better
    Your instructions, <u>dear</u> <u>to</u> <u>me</u>, as ever, are not
forgotten or neglected <u>by me</u>, but studied carefully and    10
cherished most dearly ~~by me~~. Mr Pray I see often; his       A
son was married ~~last~~ ↑this↓ week they are all well and      T
received your love with rapture. I will not presume to
ask you to write me <u>often</u> ↑the knoledge of↓ your
extensive correspondence forbidding me, but let me
sometimes hear from, you that I may feel I am remembered
by <u>one</u> whom I <u>love</u> <u>so</u> <u>dearly</u>. God bless you no one gives   T
me candy now!
                              Your "<u>Juliet</u>"         A


2: to Charlotte Cushman (LC—MD), 4 November 1858

                              Boston   Nov 4th/58      T

Darling Miss Cushman,
    Need I tell you, how grateful I am for your kind
thought of me, and how pleased I was at your present of

the "Pearls";--suffice it to say that I received them safely, and only longed for your presence to <u>kiss</u>, and <u>bless you</u>!

I am most uncomfortable at the <u>Theater</u>, Mrs Davenport, rendering my position unpleasant,--however I shall try and bear it with gentle patience, and hope for better. <u>Your</u> instructions, are not forgotten or neglected by me, but studied carefully, and cherished <u>most dearly</u>. Mr Pray I see often; his son, was last week married; they are all well, and received <u>your love</u>, with rapture.

I will not presume to ask you to write me <u>often</u>, the knoledge of your extensive correspondence forbidding me, but let me some times hear from you, that I may feel, I am remembered by <u>one</u> I love so dearly. Nobody gives me candy <u>now</u>! God bless you

Yours sincerely

Mary.


**3: to Edwin Booth (Players), 7? June 1859**

Buffalo-June 1859.

Dear Edwin

I take advantage of the first leisure moment afforded me from travel and sickness to write you. The day before leaving N. Y. I was quite ill, and but for Mr Jefferson's entreaties, would have given up all thoughts of a pleasure tour. I am quite recovered now however. Niagara, had the same effect upon me as upon others I presume overwhelmed with its grandeur &c, &c. This city I confess myself agreeably disappointmened in,--it has been forever associated to me with canal boats but I find on the contrary a very great deal of style in both city and people.

Last night I saw for the first time, (and I hope the last) 'Histrionic acting', such ranting, and tearing, it has never been my misfortune to behold. How ↑<u>you</u>↓ can act, surrounded by such people, is more than I can answer.

Mrs Jefferson and myself play for Joe's benefit, on Saturday, then leave for Paradise Valley, stay one week, and return to the city. After I have made my arrangements for next season (I hope they will be the last) I shall go to <u>Phil</u>, and hope to see you then if not before. I have no news to tell you, but that Joe thinks of going to England--has had very fine offers; I hope he

will accept them.
       Are you well yet, and are you a good boy?--and do
you ever think of me?--It seems to me that lately, by
some unaccountable agency, I have been estranged from you    T
no doubt the feeling comes from you--ah well when I see
you, it will be all right.--Do you hear from Walter he       AT
has not yet answered here in regard to Borg.                 30
       I miss them, Walter and Louise, very much; they are
both such good souls.  Excuse the careless manner in
which this is written, but I am labouring under two
disadvantages, bad pen, and paper.
       God bless you, that is my nightly prayer,--If you     T
write to N. Y. the same as before, I will receive it
safely.  Good bye, let me hear soon from you
                                  Mary.


4: to Edwin Booth (NYPL—TC), 17 July 1859

                                           New York
                                           Sunday Morn.

My darling Edwin,
       As you requested I saw Mr Baker last evening,--he     A
cannot get from Mr. Eddy the precise date of the benefit,    A
until tomorrow Monday, when you shall be immediately
apprised.  I impressed upon him the importance of his
doing so.--I am so happy to day, dear Edwin, and I begin
to realize, fully, the indescribable joy, and intense
happiness, you in your loved and goodness, have bestowed
upon me,--ah, I shall so study to deserve it--by giving
my whole thoughts, and heart and soul into your loved
keeping, my confidence in you, assures me that they will    T
be well guarded and never abused.  God bless you, my        11
future ambition, will be to see you, great, and good, and
if, devotion of mind, and intellect, but what is still
more influencing and absorbing,--affection--↑can
accomplish it↓ you shall be everything, that the world
has predicted.  This morning I wrote to my Sister asking
her to come ↑on↓ immediately as my future welfare was
concerned, and I am sure she will do so.--To De Bar I       A
have also written, a copy of which I shall send you and I
will keep in possession a copy of the answer to Mr.         A
Spofford, that you may see it--Last evening, you left       21
town I presume, as you were not at the Theater.             A
Davenport had a very fine house despite the weather, and    A
gained by it I beleive.
       The day here is most oppressive, but I have so many
happy thoughts about you, that my mind--is quieted, and I
feel more capable of enduring the sultriness--
       You must endeavour to enjoy yourself, in the country

and think of me--Come up as soon as possible--for I shall
count the moments until I see you.
God bless you--Adieu--

Molly.

Write me soon.


5: to Edwin Booth (Players), July-August? 1859

Teusday Morn
6 'o clock.
P. M.

Darling Edwin
I write you thus early, for I am not happy this
morning--and will not be until I have written you dear
the cause. In the letter I wrote you, yesterday, I
mentioned ↑having had↓ an invitation to the Theater, and
that I should not accept it;--but my friends were so
disappointed at my refusal, that I consented to accompany
them--and in doing so, I had written you an untruth.
My punishment though was sufficient for the wrong I
~~may have~~ committed--for the play, beautiful--and
interesting as it seemed to others, gave me no pleasure,
if I had written this before I went, so positive am
I, of your entire approval that 'twould have been
otherwise--but to be obliged to sit there, feeling that
the mail was fast bearing to you ↑a↓ promise already,
broken made every word seem a bitter reproach. I see
your smile of forgiveness already, and beleive me when I
say, that never, never, will I again give myself cause
for unhappiness, by breaking my word to you darling.
You will not receive this until tomorrow morning,
and only when I am sure you have read and answered it,
will I be content.
God bless you darling--you are never so dear to me
as when I go into the world, where my thoughts are
distracted by those around me, then it is I long for my
own--room quiet and peaceful, where every thought is of
Edwin.
This is early morning--and the spirit of this
letter, should be as bouyant and free from sorrow, as the
bright sun, and lovely morning, never fails to call forth
in the pure heart.--but they are not welcome to me to
day, for I have told you a falsehood; and I am not worthy
to enjoy them. In a few hours I expect to hear from you,
and if my lesson does not detain me past mail time, I
shall write you again to day. Heaven bless you

dearest--my heart aches so, to have your reply to
this--Adieu
                              Your unhappy little
                                    daughter
                                              Mary.




6: to Edwin Booth (Players), 16 August 1859


                              Teusday Morn
Edwin dearest--
     You received this morning I hope, my letter written
on <u>Sunday evening</u>,--and I shall await with impatience the
answer.  Yesterday, I saw <u>Prof Harold</u>, made arraingements
with him for my French lessons, and this morning I began
my task cheerfully.--
     He has just finished giving me my lessons and I do
assure you that he has given me a greater insight into
the Language than has ever been my lot to know,--he says
I will speak very soon and easily--then I shall be so
<u>happy</u>, when I can sit upon your knee, and instruct you,
and say all kinds of pretty sayings in <u>French</u>.  I have
not yet procured a Guitar teacher, but have had one
recommended and will call on him immediately.
     Yesterday I visited the "Dussoldorff Geallery" of
Paintings, and found so much to admire one painting
especially "<u>Othello</u>"--you may have seen it--that which
struck me most particularly was the <u>dress</u>, the details I
impressed upon my memory, that I might suggest them to
you darling, when you are preparing to act the part.
     I must not forget to tell you, that dear little
<u>Molly</u>, while walking with me this morning fell down in a
<u>fit</u>  For a moment I imagined she was going mad, and was
naturally, very much terrified,--but love for the little
creature, predominated over fear, and I took ~~it~~ ↑her↓ in
my arms there being no person by, and plunged it in cold
water, that was fortunately not far off.  I came home in
a most lamentable condition, mud from head to foot, but
<u>she</u> got better and I was content.  For a long time she
<u>was</u> unconscious, and although I called, "Molly, Molly"
she never opened her eyes; poor little thing, she is well
now, and snoozing comfortably at my feet; she is a great
companion for me, and I would not lose her for the world.
     Edwin I feel your absence most keenly, and time~~s~~
seems endless to me--shall I not see you soon?--say yes!
Have you given your Richard dress to be made, when it is
finished tell me how it becomes you.
     I have been thinking seriously, since leaving you,
that 'twill be too much for you to play <u>Richard</u>, every
night, & sure you will get exhausted, and worn completely
down,--take every care of yourself however and as much

repose during the day as is possible. God bless you
darling--love me dearly, think of me, every moment, and
come as soon. Has Joe, got home yet?--Give my love to
all, and to yourself, dearest, a shower of kisses, and
loving thoughts. I must set to work now, upon my <u>Verbs</u>,
the rocks a-dread, of the French Language, and the
everlasting torment to all Students.--but with determined
perseverance and constant study, and <u>your</u> precious love,
encircling, and elevating me, I shall acquire reach the
most desirable goal. Write me every day, tell me all
about your dear self, and all your thoughts and wishes,
that I may be allowed the felicity of assisting in their
fulfilment. Once again May God in Heaven bless and
protect you and bestow upon you the happiness, I am sure
you desire to enjoy, and which you so richly deserve.
And if your little "daughter, baby and Wife", can always
look in your face, as she does <u>now</u>, and deserve from you
the endearing words, "God bless you Mary", an eternal
peace will be enjoyed by her. although the "Grand House"
pictured by us, may never rear its head, we will have the
groundwork, and foundation of Love, and congeniality of
Soul, and the affluent will envy us. Adieu
        Devotedly Yours
              Mary.


## 7: to Edwin Booth (NYPL—TC), 19-20 August 1859

                Friday Afternoon

This is one of those, cold, rainy, disagreeable days,
when the good fairy of the household, seems to have
deserted her post, leaving all dark, and cheerless--when
books are closed in disgust, because they bring no
sunshine. Such days I like, especially,--when I can sit
and clasp another's hand, and talk of the past,--but
reflecting with oneself is so wearysome, and since I may
not clasp the hand I love, can at least talk to you with
my pen--although a ↑day↓ must pass before you hear what,
I say.--
    Everything looks brighter, now that I have commenced
writing ah, truly, truly, Edwin, there would be no light
for me were you, lost to me. If you could only see into
my heart, how full of hope and love it is,--it comes to
the surface in, tears--and very often, your bosom, will
be their recipient--
    Don't fancy that I am weeping now, no--not a single
tear--but last nght after writing you--for one long hour
I never ceased, until at last, I hushed my ↑sobs↓ fearing
that you might hear them--and knew how pained you would
be that you were not here, to kiss them away.--My sister

calls me I must leave you, for a time. God bless you, darling--
                    Mary.

                              10 o'clock A.M.
I will write a few lines, before saying my prayers, darling--and then finish in the morning.--The letter for Mr Sothern came the tone, pleased me very much--I am sure he will be delighted,--you will not regret the recommendation, for he is an honourable gentleman--she a well bred lady.--
    Mollie is not 'dead'--but is quite well and as naughty as ever--your instructions should be followed, but only as a last ~~resrost~~ resort, as she frequently kisses me--and from that fatal moment--she never more could be officer of mine.
    I'll bid you a loving, 'good night'--take shelter under my mosquito net--and dream of you. God bless you.

                    Saturday Morning
    Another gloomy, rainy day--this morning I have practised already two hours my Guitar--I have learnt, "Some one to love" it sounds charmingly.--Tomorrow is 'Sunday'--I will write you, a long letter; in one week more I shall see you, shall I not?--God bless and, guard you,--I am well and happy--and hope you are the same darling.--My best love to Mother, Rose and Joe--I am so glad he is well again. Adieu
                         Ever Mary.--


8: to Edwin Booth (Players), 23 August 1859

                         Teusday Morn

Edwin darling--
    An hour ago your dear letter, written Sunday came--preceeded by the <u>Doctor</u> and succeeded by '<u>Robonb</u>'--and 'Gruel'.--Instead of finding myself better this morning--I'm much worse, but could not bear that you should be a day without a letter so hastened to make a trial of my pen--my sister kindly offered to write for me, but <u>that</u>, I knew would frighten ~~to~~, and make you think I'm a great deal worse than I really am.--
    Last evening I wrote a long to you darling, you will get it at 'Dumpling' time ↑to day↓--I take my, french in the afternoon now--and fortunately--for this morning I could hardly ↑have↓ conjugate the verb 'Amen'.--I wonder, darling, if you love me better, when you are ill than at other times--I'm sure I do <u>you</u>--I'm afraid you will have a good deal of trouble with your baby--for people say I'm

very delicate--I never wished for health until now--God
grant me it!--Enclosed you will find a letter this
morning received from R. S. Spofford Esq.--heroic young
man--he takes it like a philosopher does he not--tell me
what you think of it--and burn or keep the letter as you
please.  I wonder where he heard of my engagement?  he
will devote himself now to the "labours of the State" no
doubt.--The letter darling for Southern has not been
there, my mâlidie--having prevented--I'm tired of writing
that word 'ill'.  You will forgive the brevity of this
dearest I am sure--this afternoon I will if possible
write you again.--Have you received all my letters--are
you happy?--God bless you all I can think of is, that a
few days will bring you to my longing arms--Yours evr
                                                          Mary.
(That is a Kiss)
   'Baby'


9: to Edwin Booth (NYPL—TC), 24? August 1859

                                                 Wedensday Morn.

Darling--Your 'daughter' is better to day--and if the sun
only shone, she would be bright and happy once
again;--but it is raining and consequently everything
looks black and gloomy--save the sheet upon which, I
write, and love brightens that.
    From, some cause or other, no letter has come to me
since the one written Sunday.--you cannot be to blame I'm
sure--they may come to day.--I have been able to attend
to my lessons, every day as usual--and yesterday had a
written, 'convérsation francaise"--prepared for him, 'ma
premier effôrt'--and he praised it highly--and told me I
soon would be a 'french ladie'.--Heaven bless you Edwin
darling--I shall pay every attention to my studies--that
your, goodness to me, may not be thrown away--You need
never tell me, Edwin what your motive is for having me
seclude myself this one year--I know you, better than you
know yourself,--and that it is for me, for me alone, that
your bounty gives so much--I know you too well, to think
that you would fear what the miserable world would
say--you love me, and dearly too, my heart tells me, your
every action proves it--and all the improvement you
desire in me, is ↑because↓ that you know 'twould make me
happier.--See, dearest am I not content?--never think me
dull and lonely--often I would give the world for a
'kiss'--and a "God bless you Mary" from your own
lips--rather than by letter--but when that cannot be I,
content myself--by keeping my 'kisses' warm in my heart,
until I do, clasp your neck--and sit down quietly and

think over the future, and all the good things, I am
going to do, to soothe and comfort you, in your tired
moments.--I picture to myself, a great-armed-chair you
sitting in it--with your 'great meer chaum'--and <u>me</u> your
'little wife' upon your knew--reading, or singing,
something pleasing to you;--then, the foot-lights will
fade, the cares of your profession be forgotten--and the
'great artist'--become a <u>man</u>! Ah Edwin, I shall so
strive to make you happy--<u>I</u> love you too fondly, to do
aught else--and if I succeed, "mine the joy--" mine the
bliss." In the <u>night</u>--when no one sees, or can read our
souls, save <u>He</u> who joined them--you will tell to me, your
heart's sad story of the <u>past</u>; I will kiss your pale
cheek--dearer to me, for the trouble that has robbed it
of its hue--and persuade you into forgetfulness.--Edwin,
I am often inclined to believe in, 'Spiritualism' not ?
in the same way fanatics do, but--I'll tell you how I
mean.--I feel,--frequently when alone thinking of
you--that your father's spirit--, speaks to me, and gives
me to see the true nature of his son;--why if I continue
in this strain, I will make you melancholy, and, you must
not be so.--This morning I shall hear from you no
doubt--if not--"I'll sit me down and weep.--" All my
folks send love--and give mine to your Mother, Rose and
Joe--Adieu. God bless you
                                              Mary.


10: to Edwin Booth (Players), 12 September 1859

                                      Monday Evening--

My darling Edwin
     I left <u>Phil</u> in--the 11. o'clock train,--a ride of
four hours brought me safely home, and with the exception
of a slight headache I am very well. Never since I have
loved you, have I felt so keanly the pangs of separating
from you, as the parting of last night.--this morning, I
thought more calmly of it--but still my heart seemed torn
into a thousand peices;--<u>three</u> more must take place, and
they I hope will be the <u>last</u>. This <u>will</u> not reach you,
until tomorrow afternoon,--had I arrived early enough, I
would have written from N.Y--but the mail had gone, when
the cars reached there. My visit, was a most happy one,
the only regret was saying 'Good Bye'. God bless you,
darling Edwin, you have made me so happy. Tomorrow
morning, I will begin my studies, with renewed attention,
and shall make up, the time lost. Every hour of the two
weeks to come, I shall count--and when I again clasp you,
in my arms--will be able, to sit at your feet and sing
and play on my Guitar for you. "Not mine (dear Edwin)

the sweetness, and the skill"
"But mine the love, that will not tire". I pray
that your voice, and health may continue good--take
excellent care of yourself, love 'your daughter'--and
think of her. I am so fatigued, that I must take some
rest--tomorrow I will write at length--excuse this stupid
epistle, I have not got sufficiently settled to collect
my thoughts. This is simply to inform my darling papa,
that his daughter, is safe, and happy--God bless and
guard you, from every danger. To Joe, your dear Mother
and Sister my best love--what do they think of your
choice dear--that I can make you happy?--
    All are well here, and send you, love. Molly
behaved herself very well, on the cars. Adieu dearest,
write me immediately, but that I am sure of--
                                        Your own
                                          Mary.


11: to Edwin Booth (NYPL—TC), 13-14 September 1859

                                    Teusday Night--
Before going to rest, Dearest, I must write to you, for
the morning is so occupied, that time sufficient is not
allowed to address you, only briefly--The entire day, I
have studied unceasingly, and it was with real pleasure
that I came to my room to have this chat with you--Your
picture is placed immediately before my eyes, and, I gaze
alternately from the sheet I am writing on to it--seeking
in its deep spirituelle expression, the many workings of
your nature--and with heart, and soul, fervently implore,
that no fault, or lack of duty, on my part, may ever
cause those eyes to change, that look so mildly from the
ivory, as I write, to indifference and reproach.
    When I came home from Phil, a letter awaited me from
Louise--filled with the most graphic descriptions of the
country, they have been visiting--interspersed with long
dissertations upon, her great theme--'Love'.--most
assuredly I sympathized, with every word she wrote--and
my heart longed to see her, to tell how blest it is,--I
wrote her to day, but though many words were employed
they failed to express, the joy of ~~of~~ my overflowing
heart. Now that I am away from the busy world, of which
I was once a member--the different faces, associated with
me during that period--all pass before me, and no desire
of mine, bids them linger, for a single moment--two only,
I care to have remain--those are, Walter and Louise--they
are good and true.--Forget, darling that she ever 'swore'
(only used for stronger emphasis), and you will see a
great deal to admire in her;--let the east-winds of,

Boston, that Doc Holmes says, gives a pungency to the
speech, and robs it of feminine delicacy--be her excuse.
You are about leaving the, Theater, at this hour and,--my
heart whispers me "perhaps, Edwin will go home and write
his 'baby"--In the morning I will add a few lines--Good
night--"I'll go pray"--Angels guard you--
Mary--

Wedensday Morning
I have had, dear Edwin, a glorious night's rest--dreamed
oh, so sweetly of you, it does not occur often, although
I wish for it, so much. This morning, my music teacher
comes, and I must practice yet, an hour--to be prepared
You will have this, for breakfast tomorrow, relish it,
for my heart is in every word. God bless you darling,
Adieu, Your own
Mary.

12: to Edwin Booth (NYPL—TC), 15? September 1859

Thursday Evening.

Darling--
    My french teacher left me a moment since, and my
first inquiry was--'is there a letter'?--none--my heart
sank, and I was just coming to my room, to think over the
cause of ~~my~~ the delay--when lo! the post-man comes--and
the disappointment has only made your letter dearer. The
day, has been cold, and cheerless, reminding us, that
Summer's reign is over;--I for one, am content, to
dispense with her gladdening influence, for when she
holds her court again, she brings to me, untold joys for
the future--the 'future'--ah, Edwin dear, what may it not
contain of joy--perhaps, of <u>woe</u>, for our two anxious
young hearts, that wait impatiently to know it; but
whatever it may be, shall we not share it?--I will be
ever at your side, as, soother--child--and wife--your
sympathizer in sadness and ill health--your <u>child</u> to play
with and carress, when light of heart--your <u>wife</u>, always.
My reward too--how great 'twill be!--your bosom for my
nightly pillow--your heart my home--and the hand dearest
to me on earth, to clasp and cling to. I shall never
grow weary either of loving and serving you;--in the day,
when absent from me think of the heart all yours waiting
the approach of your footstep, and with sincere joy clasp
your neck;--and at night, when thousands of eyes, look
upon you in admiration--my heart will beat faster
still--for the felicity will be mine, to take to my
breast and calm the, weary Artiste--'Artiste' no
longer--but <u>man</u>, one who will whisper in my listening

ear--'God bless you Mary'! my youthful fancy, hopes for this an will enjoy it too, I'm sure--for the wish is pure and placed in my heart, by Him, who joined our souls.

    Edwin darling--we must ever dwell 'above the, thunder',--treading beneath our feet, the black clouds of dissension.--You are too great, ere to descend to discord--I have too high an appreciation of the 'divine spark'--God has gifted you with and which you entrust to my care--ever, to cause you to seek another sphere, from your natural one--where Music, and Poetry--together with your little wife--who will endeavour by her devotion, to make it a charmed one.

    Then if you smile, and say with heart as well as lips God bless you--the 'fine lady' whom, I have sometimes though with beauty and talents, might come, and cause you a sigh of regret, when turning--your eyes would fall, upon the foolish child, who knows but may not aid your genious--the fine lady then, would haunt me no more; and she will never come I know, for surely you would hate her, for trying to rob, your baby, of her life. I have written you this evening, darling--my lessons being over--and your letter just received, my soul yearned to talk with you--this will be welcome I know--therefore I send it--God bless thee
    Adieu.
                      Mary.

---

13: to Edwin Booth (NYPL—TC), 19 September 1859

                                    Monday Morn.

Edwin darling--
    This morning I did not receive as I expected, letters from you--the cause I have just now learned from my sister--the trouble with the workmen on the N. J----R. R. has prevented the cars from running, and not doubt, it has affected also the delivery of mails in Phil, and if you have not learned ere this the cause--I'm being 'blessed'--for, 'not writing' 'neglect'--&c. This morning took as usual my music lesson--my teacher tells me I have improved wonderfully and I think he speaks truly--but my very weak fingers cannot keep pace with my ambition--that makes me impatient often--but, never mind, Edwin by the time we hear the roar of 'Niagara' I shall be strong, love will inspire me then, and with the little cottage--little wife--and little Guitar, shall you not be happy.--You might, think, from the style, that word, 'happy' is written in--that surely I must be

unacquainted with its meaning--not so, I'm weak, and ill
to day--let that be my excuse for this scrawl.--I have
endeavoured to forget it, while writing you dearest, but
my feeble hand reminds me, of the disagreeable fact.
This day is so beautiful, all trace of the recent storm
has passed, and this will be now an 'Indian Summer'. I
liken the time to you darling--your love, for me,--is it
not, the Indian Summer of your heart? enjoy and be as
happy in its sunshine, and warmth, as she is, whose life
it gladdens. All the clouds of your life must pass away,
and let the sunbeam, which your love, has created in me,
fall on its threshold and brighten what is within. This
afternoon darling--your letters will come I think--then I
will write again to night--God bless you--my best love to
all
    I must close in haste as it is mailtime, and what
would my darling papa do, without his breakfast tomorrow
morning--Adieu
                                                  Your own
                                                    Mary.--
P.S.
    Ah--how badly this is written--forgive your baby.--



14: to Edwin Booth (NYPL--TC), 21 September 1859

                                      Wedensday Afternoon

My darling Edwin,
    The door has but closed upon you, and I have
hastened to my room to write, what, Mr Badeau's presence
forbade me speaking. As I anticipated he talked to me
seriously and without reserve, but with so much kindness,
that I opened my whole heart to him at once.
    He has made me feel darling, more truly the
responsibility of the precious life and heart, entrusted
to my care,--and gave me advice which shall never be
forgotten or neglected by me; and in the happy, blissful,
time to come, when that 'life' shall be mine forever, his
love for you, will I hope be only more closely cemented,
by the knoledge that there is another heart, beating in
unison with yours, to whom, his every look, and action
for you, will be doubly dear. He like myself, would see
you, great and glorious, and with his friendship, my
devoted love, added to your own noble soul, 'twill be
happiness unspeakable
    Edwin dear, forget your past life, which has taught
you, a sad, but withal a useful lesson, and in my bosom,
every throb of which, beats for you, find that joy, and
repose, that your nature requires--
    I know your every feeling and the abundence of

goodness, hidden beneath your seemingly cold exterior
    Everything will I study, to charm, and interest you,
and although a brilliant education, has never fallen to
my lot, I am sufficiently well informed, to appreciate
the good, and beautiful--the rest will come, I doubt not.
Forget if possible, as I shall that the Stage, ever
claimed me as its votary,--and any love I may have had
for the <u>Art</u> I transfer to <u>you</u>--where I shall see my
favorite authors made greater by your genious and
talents.
    What could I wish for more?--than to be at home to
receive my husband weary from his professional duties,
with kisses, and open arms--that, will constitute to me,
a life of ecstacy and joy!
    You will be here on Saturday, will you not darling?
untill that interminable time Adieu, and
        "May all good angels
trusted in and loved
        Attend thy rest"
    God bless you dear heart
                        Forever Thine
                                Mary.




15: to Edwin Booth (Players), 29 September 1859


                                    Thursday Morn.

Edwin darling--
    The sun still refuses to gladden us--and but that I
am reminded by one of your precious letters, that in the
event of such an expression of sentiment I am to be
'hated'--I could almost exclaim 'diable'! on the weather
but as I do not wish to cultivate your scorn, in the
Spring-time of your love--I'll suppress the ~~the~~ word, and
use its modification, 'plague upon' it!--
    Yesterday, your letter, written in three several
parts, came, at the, wished ↑for↓ hour--it had a great
deal that was interesting to me--only Edwin dear, pray
don't ever expect me to 'time' a letter properly--for I
never know the date, by any chance, and if writing in the
afternoon I am almost sure of calling it A.M;--the same
thoughtlessness causes me to forget naming my parents to
you, in my letter often--letter writing I'm most unhappy
at, and I don't dare to read after having written, or I
should not post one letter in the week.  I take most
kindly all the scoldings I get from friends, on this
point--but this good intent fails to cure me of the bad
habit of <u>haste</u>, ~~that~~ which, like my impulsiveness of
mind, ~~is~~ ↑was↓ born with me.--Harry will enquire at what
time the trains leave for 'Buffalo',--that reminds me,

that I have great cause for anger ~~at~~ ↑with↓ you
Edwin--how is it, that you come here, <u>to my house</u>, in the
night, visit, my brother's pillow, and forget to come up
stairs to me?--I will explain--he had, two nights ago, a
most singular dream about you, saw you playing in the,
Theater, and was himself, playing 'second to you'--he
acquitted himself so well that he intends negociating
with you, when you come on, to support you in your, tour.
  Yesterday, I was sewing on your 'smoking coat'--my
thoughts went faster than my needle and could the 'seams'
be read--what promises to the future at every 'stich'
would sew.--This will be my <u>first</u> attempt, at any thing
so important and if I succee<u>d</u>--"Bertha, the spinner--the
"Queen of Helvetia" could not have been prouder, than I
shall be.--I am getting better, slowly--the climate I do
not think affects me--as your letter suggests--my health
has failed me, within the last two years, more I fear,
than I'm aware of--the slightest change, makes me
<u>ill</u>--Are you well darling? I hope so.--
  Write me in your next, the day you will be here--ah,
the joy in anticipation!--My love to all--You are very
kind to send tickets to my folks--they will appreciate
your courtesy I'm sure,

                  Mary--


16: to Edwin Booth (Players), 7 October 1859

              Friday--Oct 7th
                1859.

Edwin darling--
  I wrote you a long letter last night, in answer to
the one received in the afternoon, I presume you will
get this as soon; I have just finished my musiic
lesson--and played for the first time on the Guitar, ? 'A
lowly youth' &.--It sounds charming!--Yesterday I had a
visit from Mr Jefferson, he told Mr Clark had been in N.
Y--and slept at his house.
  This afternoon, I will receive I hope a letter from
you, if you wrote in the day, dear instead of at night--I
would have your letter a day sooner. yet withal, I
prefer to have your 'night thoughts'--so continue to
write whenever you think best, and have the most time, I
know I shall never be forgotten or neglected.
  Has your business, improved any--I would not play,
if I were you--the second week, unless it 'payed'. How
cheerless and dull it, must be there, those <u>lake cities</u>,
in the fall season are ever so;--then if the company who
support you, are not good, and the audiences slim, you
cannot surely feel very happy--never mind Edwin

darling--after this season, you shall never have an
unhappy moment, if I can prevent it.--Joe of course is
perfectly content--it being a new field of action for him
     Give him my love--and tell him to be a good boy.
     Adieu Edwin--I am writing before dinner--and after a
long lesson--so pardon brevity, and I will write you, at
greater length this evening--I can think best then.
     God bless you darling
                                           Mary.


17: to Edwin Booth (NYPL—TC), 11 October 1859

                                 Teusday Morn.

Edwin darling,
     This morning I arose early and fet well and
cheerful--I wrote you a few lines last evening before
retiring--and gave them to Hary to direct.
     Yes darling, I am well, and cheerful again--you must
not think that I ever feel lonely or get weary in your
absence, save when I am suffering bodily and you know
well enough how that affects the mind. This morning
another sunbeam fell upon my already happy heart--a long,
loving letter from you, with more kindness in it, than my
peevishness deserves. I regret so much, the anxiety you
have had on my account. I was only afflicted with
cold--which with careful nursing is well again.--I sink
almost under every pain, I have now, for with your love
life is so dear to me--and the thought of not enjoying
it, sometimes saddens me. I answered Mr L.'s note to
day, and it pleases me that he feels so friendly.
     You mention in your letter, that you would like it
could I visit Boston--I agree with you perfectly that
'twould be imprudent--and I do not care to mix again with
the world, until I am your wife.
     You must continue to write me ↑of↓ all the pleasant
times you have and I enjoy reading them almost as much as
if were there. Mr Bader's visit will doubtless place
some restraint upon you--what a pity he is not like other
men--then his friendship would ever be welcome to
you,--you must tutor him, or he will continue through
life an intolerable bore--a second Boswell--I fancy that
is what he most desires to be.
     The mail closes soon, so I must 'close'--I will
write at greater length tomorrow. My love to all--God
bless you darling--be assured that I am happy--as happy
as I ever can be in your absence.
                           Adieu
                              Yours
                                       Mary.

18: to Edwin Booth (NYPL—TC), 11 October 1859

                              Teusday Evening.--
My darling Edwin
     This afternoon I went for an hour or two, to N. Y.
and as usual returned out, of humour and greatly annoyed
that I had gone,--perhaps you will say, 'why did you go
then Mary'?  I'll tell you why!  ladies have a
custom--stupid and formal, in the extreme--which your
sex, is fortunately free from--that is, 'calling', or
rather 'paying calls'--and besides, Mr and Mrs Jefferson,
fancy that I have entirely forgotten them lately, and as
I esteem them both highly--I feel it a duty to 'call' at
least once a week upon them.  To day I met John Ford at
this table--he has gotten quite 'fleshy' in the service
of the 'rif-rafs' and 'plug-uglies'--my pen almost
refuses to deface this sheet by the tracing of such
names.  I said I returned dissatisfied--did I not? ah
yes--but your letter was waiting me--so full of love and
kindness, and now I am quite happy again.
     I wrote you a long letter this morning but it
affords me so much pleasure to sit and pen my thoughts to
you, that I cannot refrain from talking with a little
while this evening.
     This morning in my 'walk'--I was thinking of the
strange being God had given me, to influence and cherish!
for you have ever seemed to me like, what Shelley 'says
of himself--'a phantom among men'--"companionless as the
last fading storm"--and yet my spirit ever seems lighter,
and more joyous when with you--this I can only account
for by beleiving that a mission has been given me to
fulfil, and that I shall be rewarded by seeing you rise
to be great and happy.
     Ah, the Angels surely, will rejoice in Heaven, when
that is completed!  Edwin darling--I have nev told you,
yet, have I--of all the odd thoughts, I have had, and do
have, about you?--well--↑on↓ some of the nights to 'come'
when I am influenced by your loved presence, and after
the singing of some pretty song, perhaps--I will tell you
all."  then you will laught at me I'm sure--when my tears
fall, and I say--"Edwin I'm so happy"--and I will be
happy too--joyous the whole day long--until wearied by my
continual prattle--you will exclaim, "why did I take this
rampaging girl into my house".
     I am forced to close this, the servant being
impatient, to go.--
     Adieu  God bless you--Do you hear from me everyday?
love to Joe.
                    Your own
                              Mary.

19: to Edwin Booth (NYPL—TC), 13 October 1859

                                        Thursday Morn.
Edwin darling,
     This will be the last letter directed 'Buffalo'--two
weeks have nearly passed--why, it does not seem possible!
two more rounds of the moon, and my arms will be
'a-round' your neck. Have you received all my letters,
for I have written an innumerable quantity--I should not
be surprised if the post-master, attributed such a
<u>furious</u> correspondence to a conspiracy against the State.
I will write you at Boston, that you may have a letter on
your arrival; tell Joe (you remember him)?, the
call-boy--to bring you your letters on Sunday morning--he
is with E. L. I beleive. My muse has deserted me this
morning--I feel very stupid--and cannot think of anything
that would interest you at all--except that I am very
happy--and persue my studies with the same gusto.
Yesterday Edwin, I was struck by quite an original
idea--to make during the next six months <u>all</u> <u>my</u> <u>own</u>
<u>wedding</u> <u>cake</u>! and then send it only to our particular
friends;--the custom I do not like, as a general
thing--but making it myself--would be a novel thing, and
something I should be very proud of.--I will make the
trial at all events, and if I spoil my work, I can eat
it.  Yesterday I got the song 'Bid we discourse' it is
very beautiful--but difficult  I shall have learned it by
the time you come to me; and everything that's pretty and
sweet, which I think will charm your ear. That I will
ever be indefatigable in my efforts to please you--you
already know--and 'twill be to me, so much more a
<u>pleasure</u>, since I feel convinced that in my society you
expect to be soothed and made at peace. Give Joe, my
best wishes for his success 'before the footlights'--
advise him Edwin to avoid the passions of the world,
~~that~~ ↑which↓ inevitably bring sorrow upon men. he loves
↑you↓ so, he will listen I am sure. Two french verbs
must be written this morning, or I will see black looks
from Mr Harrold--this must then be drawn to a close.
     You are engaged with studying 'Shake' and have not I
presume, opened your french books--when we are together,
I shall not allow them to be neglected. When writing you
last evening, the servant was waiting so impatiently for
the letter--that I was annoyed--and have thought since
that I made in it, a wrong quotation; it has worried me
ever since--and as I do not wish you to accuse me of
negligence, I will correct it here,--"Companionless as
the last cloud of the expiring storm--whose thunder is
its knell"--did I write it so?  I cannot remember.  This
I said you ever seemed to me!--let me hope to be the
<u>sunshine</u>, to follow so close, as to cause ↑all↓ traces of
the recent darkness to pass away.
     Adieu darling--why it seems to me, that I am parting
with you--I will be with you again--in Boston, as soon as

you arrive.  God bless you my prayers shall be offered
for your safe journey thither.--Continue to write me
every day--Adieu encore,
                                    Your own
                                         Mary.


20: to Edwin Booth (NYPL—TC), 14-15 October 1859

                              Friday Evening.
Edwin darling,
     Your letter written 'after 'Richard' came this
evening,--I am so delighted that the time has come for me
to write you again--yesterday--I cannot tell why--it
seemed as if I were parting from you--and after my letter
was posted--the last, to Buffalo, a feeling of sadness
came over me, and it continued the remainder of the day,
and I longed for tonight to come, that I might talk with
you.  Ah, Edwin, how desolate would the world be to me
now--deprived of you!--that would be such a sad, sad day,
when I could no longer look in your face and bless
you;--but this is a calamity I think not of--for every
word, your letters contain, prove to me that life is now
dear to you.  Once--do not blame me--I thought
indeed--that for the love you knew I bore you--you had
consented, to give the 'child' the 'toy'--she coveted
thinking that it must be broken--and her hand would hold
the shattered peices as carefully as another; but now
darling, all that, has proven untrue,--and I am sure you
are willing to forget the Past,--which has tinged your
youth with sadness--in the happy Future, I am, and ever
will prepare for you.  When I first met you,--you
remember, I was quite young--from the first moment, a
longing, for the sweet privilege to be mine, to give you
contentment--and to see your genious, so brilliant, but
so wayward a source of happiness to yourself;--the
feeling so pure so disinterested grew into a deep and
lasting love, and all the dreams, so stupid in a girl of
sixteen, are being more than realized to me, in my
womanhood.  God bless you darling,  I will ever try and
merit, the joy, God has given me in you.
     Good night--I will finish this tomorrow.
                    Mary.
                              Saturday Morning.
I see that my watch stopped this morning darling, at the
very hour you were to leave Buffalo, but since no other
misterious sign has been made--it is to be presumed, you
are safe and well, and the 'watch stopping' sufficiently
accounted for, by my carelessness in not winding it up.
last night.

		The great excitement for the past few days, has
been Miss Bartlett's marriage--a grand affair--
completely turning the heads of the 'crinoline' beholders.
The whole affair, is summed up in one word--
'rediculous';--made so however I think, ~~from~~ by the,
"blue B's"--and 'red B's' more than the parties
themselves.--I send you the paper with the full
account--you though have most likely seen it--give it,
however to Louise, women take an especial interest in
such things.  Yesterday on Broadway--the principle topic,
was 'diamonds,' and 'point lace'.--The bride's trousseau,
being picked to peices, to find the exact cost of each
article~~s~~--descending even to the costly 'garters'.  The
marriage ceramony of course interested me mostly--and I
came to the conclusion, that Archbishop Hughes, should
not join our hands,--the 'part' being entirely too long
to study.  A Badeau was ~~fa~~ most likely one of the favored
'B's, 'red,' or 'blue' and will give you, a full accout.
		Dear Edwin, write me of your 'opening night'--your
success--who of the audience were distinguished--and
everything about it.  Kiss Louise for me, and Walter too
if you like.--Act better than you have <u>ever</u> done, and
tell Louise to keep a seat for me, by <u>her</u> in the boxes,
for I shall be there in 'spirit'.  God bless you I will
write everyday the same as usual--be good and happy--and
think of me.  My love to Joe.
		Adieu
					Your own
							Mary.

### 21: to Edwin Booth (NYPL—TC), 28 November 1859

						Monday Afternoon.

		I was not disappointed this morning, darling--two
letters instead of <u>one</u>, gladdened me, so loving too, and
full of tenderness for me!  I am so sorry you found your
dear Mother ill--I hope you did not reproach yourself,
for not having seen her sooner, but for me you would have
done so,--she is well now I trust.
		Your news regarding the mad step, John has taken--I
confess did not surprise me--if you remember, I told you
I thought he would seize the opportunity.  'Tis a great
pity he has not more sense--but time will teach
him--although I fear the discipline is hardly severe
enough to sicken him immediately ~~of~~ ↑with↓ a "soldier's
life"  I hope nothing serious will occur there, for that
would frighten your mother so--and you being absent too.
I was astonished that you had been reading the play of
Taylor's, I wrote you of yesterday--how strange that we

both should have 'hit' upon it--another proof of the
great sympathy between us.  Mr Jefferson has a great idea
in view, for your opening in the Autumn in N. Y--I will
tell you all about it when you come.
   The unhappiness of 'Thanksgiving' must be cleared
away too--what a wretched day it was--I have recorded it
in my journal, and next year on the same day we will
compare, the <u>present</u>, with the <u>past</u>.  My health continues
to improve, and on Wednesday I will meet you, with a
'well mouth'--and a 'merry face'.  and oh Edwin, I have
so much to say to you--you shall know every feeling
lurking in my heart--that in your absence should sadness
ever cross you, you will close your eyes, and think only
of 'your daughter', who with every breath she draws,
invokes from Heaven a blessing on your 'devoted head'.
God bless you darling--it seems as though the time will
never come, when I can repay and tythe of the happiness,
you have given me.  My kindest love to, Mother, Rose and
Joe, I will not write again--but each hour pray God to
bring you safely to my longing a̶r̶s̶ arms!  Adieu
                                     Your own
                                         Mary.


22: to Edwin Booth (NYPL—TC), December 1859

                                   Wedensday Morn

Darling--my eyes were hardly open this morning when the
good post-boy, brought me a letter--and such a sweet one
too!  I kissed it and said--"Edwin must have been happy
when he wrote this"!  Your success is certainly very
flattering--I hope for its continuence.  The book you are
to send me, I shall look for anxiously--how kind and
thoughtful you are to me always--and considerate of my
tastes; the "brown and cherry" cannot suit your
complexion more admirably, than the 'Miller's daughter'
does mine.  I have read it frequently but from your
hands, I will value it still more highly.  The
classics--I never hope to cultivate a taste for--those I
will leave for you--m̶y̶ little 'rustic' poems--like the
one named above, I enjoy most; innocence and love make up
the sentiment--and they find deep sympathy in my
heart.  How precious all your gifts will be to me
hereafter--no matter what cares may cloud or wrinkle our
brows as years pass over us--they cannot fail to awaken
memories of our youthful love.--God bless you
darling!--How indignant Mr Badeau will be at the receipt
of the fruit-card you sent him--I laughed heartily at the
drollness, of the idea; he has not been to see me yet,
nor do I expect him, while this cold weathe lasts;--it is

very cold indeed, this is a barbarous climate
    Last night I sat by the window thinking of ~~u~~you and disturbed only by the mournful sighing of wind, I wondered in "this stillness of the world without, and of the soul within" what our lives in the future would be, and looked to see, if upon the clouds I could trace any semblance of it.  this led me into an odd train of thought, in which I recalled ~~an~~ susceptability of yours, you once told me of--you remember--'twas that a passing wind sometimes suggested to you the past--and carring you years back--set you dreaming!--it is not wonderful that you should have such emotions--sensitive natures are prone to them; then why, I ask myself, should my eyes have filled with tears, and trembled lest you should experience them again--ah, dear Edwin, 'twas a fear that they would lead you from my side, and leave me once more <u>alone</u>:
    I am very wrong doubtless to have allowed so simple a fact to have impressed me, and am still more to blame, to repeat it here, for have you not "died into life"--as Keats says--and I should wean you from all rememberance of the tomb--and so I promise to do!--it is only in your absence that I sometimes ponder thus ernestly upon the strange being, who has singled me from all 'my kind' to soothe and make his home a happy one!  I do not dare to pause alone, upon the responsbilities of the <u>Artist's</u>, and "<u>Man</u> of <u>Genius's</u> wife"--that is a task I am unequal for--but you have given me your tenderest love, and that will strengthen me to make your 'home circle' at least a charmed one and that will serve to brighten perhaps the 'higher sphere'.  I agree with you that it is better, you should be this winter away from me--'twas wisely arrainged--and only think, darling, of the meeting--why, 'twill more than repay us for ~~absence~~ ↑separation↓--only I beg that after this winter, 'twill never be repeated.
    Tell Joe I condole with him in his 'nervousness'--but he must pay the forfeit of the 'sock and buskin'.  Dear Edwin--God bless and guide you study all the new parts you have on hand, for you know what a detriment I am to <u>blank</u> <u>verse</u>, and I want you to be 'au fait' when you come to play before the great 'Moguls'--Then won't I be proud!  Adieu
                                        Mary.

### 23: to Edwin Booth (Players), 16 December 1859

Friday--Dec 16th/59.

Darling
    Another day has passed and I have twenty four hours less to wait ere seeing you--yes, every blessed night I lay my head on my pillow--I say "tomorrow's sun brings me nearer Edwin" that I shall be, thus philosophical the whole five months, I will not promise. I dare say that I will write many a 'peevish' and impatient letter ere the time is up. In <u>this</u>, I should give you a "feast of reason", for I have enjoyed the livelong day, a quiete peaceful love! even my french teacher, did not disturb the tenour of my thoughts--perhaps he divined them; we read from "Le Memorial"--one chapter upon youthful love and marriage--my interest and delight, he saw no doubt in ↑my↓ face, for the pure and natural sentiment found a deep echo in my heart--nor did I attempt to hide it from him, any more than I would have done before my 'darling papa'--for he loves the <u>young</u>--and he gratified me by comenting long, and <u>earnestly</u>, upon the responsible position a woman takes when she assumes the holy title <u>Wife</u>! and what he said strengthened my resolves. Dear <u>Edwin</u>, if you were here at this moment, I would give all the world--if only for a moment, that I might fall at your feet, and pour forth the utterings of a grateful heart, for having separated me from the cold world, and surrounded by your love, which makes all, 'golden tinged'. A thousand times in the day I close my eyes, and try to form the atmosphere, which I pray, we may breathe in this world together! I see our home, and as I wander up and down, now, into this room, now, into that--the walls seems to whisper to me--"all your girlish dreams are now fulfilled--Love, the great corner-stone was laid in earnest, Time, has made the ediface complete--you see your husband <u>great</u> and <u>happy</u>!" then I stop to cry as now I do, for very joy! This is wandering far into the future, though for well I know, 'home-luxury' will not be ours for some years at least--but notwithstanding we can bear with us the foundation. No letter from you today, darling. I miss them so much, accustomed so long to receive one every day. Yesterday afternoon, Mr Badeau called and stayed with me three or four hours, during which time you were never <u>once</u> named of course.
    He told me of the alteration he has made in the 'denuement' of the 'Fool's Revenge' I think it might be effective. Why have you never proposed to him the writing of a play, I fancy he has the ambition to do so--I am not so sure about the talent though. He is a good fellow--how that term would schock him--and a true friend of yours--I had almost begun to think he had forgotten you by not calling to see me. I took ~~accoun~~ ↑advantage↓ of the opportunity to let him see I was not

26    Letters

the 'child' he thought me, told him my knowledge of some
of your strange susceptabelities, which rather startled
him I think; he has promised to come soon again.
    God bless you my darling one!  I hope your throat is
better--your health now, is my only cause of
anxiety--when I am its guardian it shall be carefully
tended!  My love to Joe,
                            Yours
                                    Mary.




24: to Edwin Booth (NYPL—TC), December 1859


                                        Friday Evening.

Darling Edwin
    You have been, but a few hours from me, and yet I
have a thousand things to tell you--first, let me beg
your forgiveness, for the weakness I displayed, when
taking leave of you last night--'twas my duty to have
cheered and lightened, not, saddened your heart,: and I
would have done so, had we have been left <u>alone</u> together.
After you went away, I retired immediately, and releived
my overflowing heart with tears--sleep, soon closed,
however, my aching eyelids, and my sorrow was drowned in
forgetfulness.  When I awoke this morning--I poured forth
a prayer, for you--and asked of Heaven consolation, and
strength!
    You will be glad to hear that I am better, my cough
has not troubled me to day and I have been quite cheerful
too, and took my music lesson with ease and pleasure this
morning; and you, darling, did you arrive home safely and
find the 'loved ones' well--I hope so--your mother must
not scold Mary, for keeping her son, so long from her
presence.  I have endeavored to think all day, that you
have really left me, for the 'long journey', and my
duties seem graver, and more serious than heretofore.
You will see me on Wednesday will you not?--and I shall
not lose a single moment of the few short hours left me,
to disclose to you, the truthful, steady, course my love
will persue in your long absence, and will try and take
my arms from your neck, with a happy, smiling face, and
say Adieu, as if we were to meet the next day.  I will
pray for a letter tomorrow, but will not fancy myself
forgotten if one does not come, but patiently wait
another 'sun'.  God bless you darling--the beautiful
flowers you sent me, breathe their delicious perfume as I
write and seem to whisper--"live with us--we will shade
your path, through life, if you but tend us in purity of

heart!" Good night be happy until we meet again
     My love to your Mother, Sister and Joe. Adieu
                                  Your own
                                         Mary.


25: to Edwin Booth (Players), 28 December 1859

                                   Wednesday Evening.
                                       Dec 28th/59.

     Darling--I am very, very, happy tonight! three
letters from you today--two through the post here, and
one from Harry, with the "Miller's Daughter"--but of
that, anon. I doubt whether I shall have time this
evening to answer all the pretty things those dear
epistles contained--or tell you half, what I have to say,
if not I must add more in the morning.
     This is the last night you play in Montgomery, and I
rejoice, for evidently you are most uncomfortable there;
how is it possible for you to act, situated as you have
been in those small towns. it shall be different next
year, I promise you; no cheerless room, no
half-extinguished fire--but all bright and pleasant;
Providence, has given to the hand of Woman, a certain
delicacy of touch, which wonderfully transforms things
into beauty, and grace; how admirably God has adapted
us for each other--our very weakness gives you
strength--is it not so?--I grieve for John's
trouble--foolish boy, what can he be thinking of--talk to
him Edwin seriously, ere he destroys his youth. Mr
Badeau paid me a visit yesterday he had just received a
letter from you and from Mr Howe also, which he read to
me; he speaks most kindly of Mr Booth, he will tell you
all about it, so I will not anticipate him. He complains
bitterly that you do not write him often enough;--do not
neglect him I pray you. You complain that I did not
repeat to you, our conversation (Mr B's and mine) you
must forgive me, I would take great pleasure in doing so,
and will, whenever anything occurs that would interest
you. You would not care to hear, what was worn at the
last grand ball, or how distanguè the attendance was at
the Opera, and positively he talks of but little
else--save yourself, of course and did he confine himself
to your merits, and interests, that would be
all-sufficient for me--but "his only fault is loving
thee" and I sometimes feel as though he were a love-sick
school girl, I am consoling--for I am sure he is much
more inclined that way than I am--although I never do
talk 'sensibly' to you; do not think by this that I am
weary of him, on the contrary I value his friendship for

'my Edwin' very highly--perhaps set a greater price upon
it than he does, himself--and his visits afford me a deal
of pleasure, for he loves and can talk of you, to me.  He
says he will bid you Adieu, on your wedding day, that he
does not expect your attention after that--I consoled as
well as I could the 'neglected child'.  He does not like
one act he has read of H.'s new play--be very careful
Edwin in accepting blank-verse peices.  you know the day
for the <u>stately</u> and the grand, is passed vary your
repertoire, by things more suitable to the present age;
people live in the Future now, not in the Past.  If a
play was written on the manners of a century yet to come,
the public would more than likely rush to see it.  I will
devote the remainder of this sheet, to thanks, and kisses
for the pretty book you sent me--'The Miller's
Daughter'--and then begin a fresh one, with sweet
words--thought of all the time but not expressed.  Your
Christmas-gift came safely, and with my own hands I tore
the several covers from around it; and I was <u>alone</u> too,
so I kissed it a thousand times, and said, "what a dear,
good Santa Claus to think of me when so far away!"  then
when I read your affectionate dedication, a film passed
over my eyes and for many minutes, I could not look
clearly at the 'pretty pictures'--ah, why are you so
kind to me, that you make me cry?  all night I dreamed of
'Alice'--and this morning saw before me the pure
'unclouded life' your prayers, and love would have me
enjoy!  Call me your 'humble daisy' always darling, I
wish for no higher title, for am I not worn where the
proudest 'rose' will envy me? and I know too, that you
will be happier, breathing the air of 'ivee tipped modest
thing" than the close atmosphere of the rich exotic:--see
how conceited we, of the 'wild heather' are--therefore I
am happy when you indulge me, in stories and pictures of
a pure and innocent life, for it proves to me, you are
satisfied that I should take example and encouragement
↑from↓ this humble heroine and introduce ~~to~~ in the home
you will give me, the simpleness, which makes theirs so
beautiful.  You cannot imagine dearest, what holy and
earnest thoughts this little book has given me.  I wish
there was an Alice in the world from whom I could
learn!--and in 'after years' you then might say,
          "And now those vivid hours are gone,
       Like my own life to me thou art,
          While Past, and Present, wound in one
       Do make a garland for the heart!"
God bless you darling--and may you enjoy in my love
all the happiness your noble nature deserves!  You must
not fail to tell me all your sorrows, let my bosom be the
sanctuary of your griefs--do not fear to write me
gloomily for although I would rather know that you were
happy--yet I would wish if necessary to be your consoler.
I do not hope immediately to see those dread 'moods of
melancholy' pass entirely from you, more especially as
you are not under my imediate influence--but in time
they will I'm sure.  The Spectator--which I read every

day--contains a wonderful deal of information regarding,
the unhealthy spirit, which has got possesion of a
certain young gentleman with whom, <u>you</u> and I are
acquainted  I have always contended that waywardness and                    T
melancholy, was inherent with genious and though for a                     101
time, the restless one, might be soothed and quieted, yet
volcano-like 'twould burst forth again--happily, you have                   T
competed this, and I sure that with the 'careful                            T
watching' and 'gentle guidence' you have told me of, I
will see you enjoy that repose which is so necessary to
~~you~~ your talents, and life.  I hardly know what I have
been writing--they are all talking around me, fearful                       T
that I shall say something very stupid, I will close, and
bid you a loving good night!  The Faust you are to send                    110
me--'Edwin's book' shall be well taken care of, else how
are we to form the talked of library.  All send love--you
will be weary reading all the letters which await you at
N.O--I hope your success will be complete there, never                      A
go--again if you can help it to the small towns you have
just left.--I should expect to be scolded and 'snubbed'
the whole time if your business was very bad, Adieu God                     T
bless you and keep you mine.  I am improving in my <u>music</u>.
                    Love to Joe,
                           Mary.


26: to Edwin Booth (Players), 4 January 1860

                                 Wedensday Morn.
                                   Jan 4th/60.

Darling--
    No letters, gladdened me yesterday--I hope for one
today--then I shall expect no more until next
week--presuming that you did not write on your route to
N. O.  God grant you arrived there safely--and that you                     A
are better in health than you were,--your 'corporeal
welfare' is all I fear for--tell me that you are well!
    Last night, I went with Harry to skate--'twas
moonlight, and we enjoyed it immensely.--I am better and
stronger <u>now</u> than I have ever been; I enjoy my quiet life
too, so <u>much</u>.  You thought 'twould become wearisome to me                10
did you not? ah, no darling I am happier this day, than                     T
I ever was in my life before--and grow more happy each
new day, because it brings me nearer you.  Have you
thought of the joy of our <u>first</u> meeting yet--I have, a
thousand times--do think of it, every time I lay my head
upon my pillow at night! ah, dear Edwin I would not                         T
exchange the bliss of that <u>hour</u>, for all the riches earth
could offer me! yet--how I <u>shall</u> tremble to meet
you--tremble, lest I should not have accomplished <u>well</u>,

the pleasing tasks you have set me.  Will you love me
just as dearly, if I should chance to fail--will you not,
reproach me with neglect of your dearest wishes?  no, I
will answer for you--no, you will not, but will kiss me,
and bid me try again.--O Oh, if I beleived you would
regard me low--how I should hate my books, and music--for
then I could say to them, and justly too, I think--"'tis
you, Edwin loves, not me, go I will never touch you
again;" but 'twill not be so.  I am progressing more
rapidly than I had cause to hope for--and, who
knows--some of these days, you may be as 'proud' of my
intellect, as of my heart--would you not be happy
then--happier even than you are now; and it shall be
so--when I am under your immediate influence--and I have
your eyes, and your 'ears' to assist me.--
    When night comes--after the 'play', when you are
weary and 'brain-sick'--how more than happy 'twill make
me, to take your loved head upon my heart, and read you
some pretty, simple, soothing story--to quiet and rest
you, from the tiresome 'blank-verse' at the Theater.
Yes, dearest, your life shall be a poem if I can make it
so--for I have held converse with your higher self and
know well, the food it needs to nourish it--and keep it
alive--am I not right?  but you must assist me at the
'feast' and contribute to it.  Our first quarrel will be
I suppose about your loved 'meer chaum'--for positively I
will not inhale its 'odiferous perfumes' oftener, than
'twice a day'--and I shall be unyealding in my good
resolve--for despite all your excellent arguments to the
contrary 'tis that 'same pipe' which affects your
'speaking organs'.--
    'Tis now late in the morning, and no letter
yet--Harry perhaps will bring me one--so I will conclude.
Give my love to Joe--advise him for his good in life--and
make him a 'good boy'--
    Write me all the 'news' you have, I am so far from
all worldly gossip--above all, write me of yourself--your
wishes, your hopes, your inmost thoughts.  they will find
a sacred shrine in my heart be assured.  Study your own
heart, learn its ways; this self-examination is necessary
to us all!  God bless you my own Edwin
                                                Mary.


27: to Edwin Booth (NYPL—TC), 24 January 1860


                                          Teusday Evening--
                                              Jan 24th/60.

Darling--Another letter yesterday, 'crosser' than any I
have yet receved--this makes the third now--so that I am

sure for three days at least you did not love me a 'bit'.
I remember that I did send you one or two 'curt'
letters--but be assured darling, 'twas not willingly I
made them so--my time, was limited--you will forgive me
will you not.
    I know you have been annoyed with your new peice--
and felt perhaps the need of sympathy--so for your
'unloving' letters lately I pardon--and kiss you! Last
night I went to the 'W. Garden' to see the new play
'Lesbia'.--<u>intensely</u> French--and <u>horriblly</u> 'dramatic':
the 'scene <u>is laid in Venice</u>'. Wallack plays the Cheif
of the 'Council of Ten' as weak old 'Richelieu'--much
less impressive in <u>body</u> than in <u>mind</u>--and his fearful
mannerisms did not assist the character any. Miss
Hernon--Lesbia--is a spy from the 'Ten'--and is in love
with an enemy of the State--Mr Jordan--who is in love
with someone else--the daughter of the <u>Chief</u>;--as in all
such plays--there is a great deal of mystery 'black
cloaks' ↑being↓ worn by everyone--and a continual
description of their several families, for the six
hundred years past--calling eachother by long
'unpronouncable' Italian names: the scenery was very
fine--but the sentiment wretchedly commonplace; Miss
Heron acted in her usual 'grotesque' manner; the play is
accounted a failure I beleive--and though it may sound
unkind in me to say it--I am glad that it is
so.--'<u>Camilles</u>' <u>Medeas</u>--and <u>Lesbias</u>--are fit only for the
French stage: the atmosphere of the <u>courtezan</u>, is
unhealthy--and can produce no good! society is
sufficiently corrupted without being taught immorality
from the Stage--where it is seen in its most dangerous
and seductive form too! Women without principle or
virtue--represented in 'gold' and 'jewels'--and pearls,
and diamonds falling from their lips--enlisting the
sympathy of an ignorant audience.--To see an~~d~~ Art as <u>holy</u>
as the Drama--so desecrated--and perverted--is it not
outrageous. how glad I am dear one, that the branch you
were fitted for has not been disgraced for though
unappreciated <u>now</u>--the day will come, when "gorgeous
Tragedy" will have its sway! you, are held as its only
true representive ~~now~~ in this day--and you can, if you
<u>will</u>, change the perverted taste, of the public, by your
truth--and sublimity and you <u>must study</u> for this! Dear
Edwin I will never allow you to droop for a single
moment--for I know the power that dwells within your
eye--and my ambition is to see you surrounded by
greatness--is it not a laudable one? Ah, you do not know
how close a <u>critic</u>, I will be of your 'Genious'--a child,
who requires more nursing than the helpless babe, at the
Mother's breast!--Three hours have passed, dearest, and
my letter was laid aside for my French teacher--he has
gone--and I will resume. He brought to me today, a
<u>friend</u>, a veritable <u>friend</u>--not one of flesh and blood,
but <u>Genious</u> and <u>Truth</u>--the most lofty--and the most
<u>simple</u>--the works of <u>Mr. Jules Thierry</u> the great french
historian; ah darling, I cannot tell you how proudly

my heart beat--when I saw--and felt that I could
understand those glorious pages;--not merely because
their greatness impressed me--but my fondest wish was
accomplished--my great reward for the <u>toil</u>, I had
suffered had come! ah--I thought, "how happy this will
make Edwin"! my teacher does not look upon me
entirely as a <u>child</u>--and confine me to the narrow circle
of my 'Memorial'--he allows me to judge--<u>society</u>
also.--In the

[remainder of letter missing]


28: to Edwin Booth (NYPL—TC), 7 February 1860

                              Teusday Morn.
                               Feb--7th/60.

Darling--
       I wrote or rather <u>scribbled</u> you a long letter last
evening--telling you of Mr Badeau's visit &c. I did not
sleep well during the night--and feel very unwell this
morning;--during the past two weeks, I have been up late
for several nights--and it does not agree with me, very
well: I'm so accustomed now, since the summer--to retire
early, that I find myself with pale cheeks--and
headache--when I deviate from my usual habits: This
morning already, I have studied two or three hours--and
learned a sweet song--"What thought so heavenly as that,
I shall meet thee"--'tis operatic but most simple, and
charming: I take up my Guitar and sing it at least a
'dozen' times in the day--it reminds me so, of the joy in
store for me'--when I shall meet <u>thee</u>'. I have not
gotten through yet, with all the 'reading' you so kindly
furnished me with, although not a single day passes--that
I do not read a page from one or the other of our books.
I was beginning to be '<u>Victor Hugo</u>--'mad'--but Mr
Horch--said my mind was too youthful, and too ardent, to
read this author, without being intoxicated, and
consequently unfit, to judge of his works properly;--so I
promised him, I would be content, with having read 'Le
Roi s'amuse'--and would not read another until I become
<u>older</u>; his views for my education are precisely the same
as yours darling--I must be, he says, learned, and
intellectual--but retain with it all, the simplicity of a
child!--so you see that I am in the 'hands' of one, like
yourself--and you need not fear that I am being taught
anything, contrary to what you would desire. Dear
Edwin--a lady friend of mine was <u>evil</u> enough to say to
me--when she had asked me if I was 'happy'--and I
answered her--'as the was long'--ah, said she--"this is

your 'summer of the heart--'take my advice, and remain
lovers"; why, 'tis only the 'April' of our love--is it
not darling? for now we have clouds--as well as
sunshine--at least I do,--clouds which rain only tears of
joy, however;--but after marriage, the rain-bow will
never leave for a single day--our horizon I hope! You
threaten me with prolonging your stay, if I am not good,
and attentive to my duties;--ah! I promise
everything--will do everything so that you but return
soon: but perhaps you are not anxious to see me--the
imaganary me, which you tell me, is constantly with
you--perhaps she does quite as well--as the reality! is
it so? then I shall not be selfish--and break the
illusion by calling you away from it. God bless
you--darling, every day, you become dearer to me! Mr
Clarke was in town one day last week--he told Mr
Jefferson--he would like to have seen 'Mary' but he had
no time to come. "I told the parson, and the parson
tolled the bell"--'comprenez-vous, cela?' This I will
direct Mobile as I know not where you play--next
week--and they will forward it, doubtless. Are you well,
and what conquests have you made; last winter you used to
write me all about your sweet-hearts and now you never
say a word of them. 'Tis quite time to have a 'little
bit' of jealousy, but I cannot 'make beleive'--unless you
give me some cause. God bless you--that is the last
thought I shall ever have, I'm sure! when you write to
your Mother, you always give my love--I trust--I always
intend, though I often forget to send it. I have not
heard from, Louise, she wrote more frequently when you
were in Boston--but "out of sight--out of mind," I
presume. God bless you again, and again--tell me all
about yourself--and don't fancy that your gloom,
annoys me--I can always, discover illness and melancholy
from coldness; the latter, chills my sympathy, the
former, accuses it! Adieu, write me long letters or I
shall scold you severely--!

                                        Yours
                                           Mary.


29: to Edwin Booth (NYPL—TC), 9 February 1860

                                      Thursday Morn.
                                        Feb 9th/60.

Darling Edwin
    This morning I awoke and found the sun shining so
brightly--the air so sweet and balmy, that I loved myself
and all the world besides! You were my first thought--as
you ever are--I asked Heaven to bless you, and to

strengthen me to make you great and good; sometimes I
think I am very presumptuous,--erring, and weak as I
am--to expect my prayers to be answered--and yet I have
been favored beyond my hopes;--very little I have craved
for myself but all for you--darling--and I am rewarded I
see your fame increase--your health being restored,--your
<u>beauty</u> preserved--the great soul God gave you, filling
with purity and truth--Today, we enjoy the most delicious
atmosphere imaginable; I felt 'twould be wrong not to go
abroad and enjoy its perfume--and with a happy, contented
spirit, and my soul filled with a strange longing for
you--I left my books, and sauntered out, to walk, and
think of you and happiness! "such days as these--I said
to myself--will come again, when I am happier even than I
am now--and when Edwin will be with me to enjoy them
too--how happy he will be, after a tedious rehearsal--to
escape with me into the country--where nature will prompt
our loving hearts to goodness"! all this is in store for
us, is it not? ah! let us darling, grasp it while within
our reach--or earth's 'rude cares' will snatch it from
us. No wonder I am proud, and think my self 'God's
chosen one'--for 'tis not a little thing, to know one's
self beloved--and with the assurance of <u>truth</u> like
your's! the friends for whom, formerly, <u>I felt</u> an
interest are wearisome and tedious to me <u>now</u>--I live
alone for you and your happiness; for well I know, how
much you needed a <u>true friend</u>--one who would study to
please your nature--and calm your fevered soul! all
this, no one but a <u>wife</u> can perform; few think to follow
the <u>artist</u>, after the 'curtain falls'--they bear to their
homes the memory, of his 'matchless form'--his 'voice so
musical'--his passionate strains!--they pause not to
think, ~~of--~~ nor is it well they should, save a <u>few</u>--of
the exhausted frame--weary restless brain--the <u>lonely
heart</u>--which succeeds! many there are no doubt, more
worthy than I to fullfill the blissful office of your
friend and <u>nurse</u>; but Heaven told you of the yearning of
<u>my</u> heart and you have chosen <u>me</u>--shall I be worthy to
perform the holy task? <u>Time</u> will tell! I earnestly
pray, that I may be spared until it be fulfilled. I am
<u>serious</u>, this morning, you observe--but only for excess
of joy--I have not, nor can I write you <u>one tithe</u>, of the
content which encircles me today,--I have only one
craving on earth, and 'tis for your presence--but you are
"palpable to feeling", if not 'to sight',--time will soon
pass away now--and you will be mine <u>forever</u>. After my
French lesson, I will add another sheet.--When I am
<u>illnatured</u>, I long for my teacher--he invariably succeeds
in quieting me--but to day, I am sufficiently joyous--I
require no stimulant. God bless you--I must study now
for an hour--I have been very indolent this beautiful
morning though. I would like you to be here,--put on my
riding habit--take a hack--and both of us, ride miles
away, to some pleasant place.
    Adieu, till afternoon. God bless you
                    Mary.

30: to Edwin Booth (NYPL—TC), 11 February 1860

                                    Saturday Morn.
                                    Feb--12th/60.   T

    I awoke in a charming humour, this morning--and was
repaid for my amiability, and hour or two after, by a         T
long letter from my 'bien-aimee': partly loving and:
partly 'saucy': 'saucy' for he called me jealous! now,        T
'my champion you'--attack him upon this score, for
me--for you know darling that I am not--and I am too
happy now--and love him too well--to waste words--in my
own defence. I will apologize, however for the sad tone
of my letters for two or three days to you; the clouds
which sometimes cross me--are very few--and then they         10
never wear the threatening aspect, of a storm at
night--but such as we see hiding the hill-tops of a
summer morning--and which the bright sun, soon
scatters;--you are my sun, and when you seem hidden, then
I am sad--for no other light can cheer me but 'distrust'
you for a moment?--why, darling, suspicion is a stranger
to me--would I be worthy of you were it not? I have
purged from my bosom--every illiberal thought I found
lurking there and I am freer--else I could not love you
as I do--nor could I rest happy in the schackles of           20
'jealously':--now, do you not beleive, that I have been
all the time your 'little daughter'?--yes, dearest I have
been--my heart has never responded to one 'ugly' or
impatient--word my pen has dictated you. I am happy the
live-long day--so confident that "Edwin loves me
dearly"--ah! I'm sure you must think me very 'bad' now--I
wish I had never written you those hateful letters!
there!                                                        T
    The improvement you have made in the 'Cardinal'           A
charmed me; you must not forget to tell me of your            30
studies, they interest me alike with the movements of
your heart--my heart--for 'tis mine, you tell me.
    The 'conversational', colloquial-school you desire
to adopt--is the only true one Edwin, for the present
day! but as you very resonably add--too much is
'dangerous': for example--Miss Heron--(don't shudder, I       A
will make no comparison) in the beginning of her
career--was praised for her 'naturalness'--and deservedly
so--and while she 'used it' in moderation was
successful--but now could you see her! she gives you so       T
much of 'Mrs John Smith'--endeavors--or rather labors to      41
walk so very commonplace--that 'tis simply
ridiculous--and even her greatest admirers--can find no
merit in her now. Acting, is an imitation of Nature, is
it not?--then 'tis Art--and the 'Art' must be seen
too--for nature upon the stage would be most ridiculous.
Mr Badeau's 'luke-warm' praise of Faust was only
affectation--for he praised it loudly to me:--he fancies,
that 'nonchalance' will win your regard--where anxiety
and attention on his part has failed. I like and shall        50

ever respect him for his unselfish love for you--and he
is very talented too--but darling--he is very weak in
many, respects--the goddess 'Fashion' we must blame for
that though. Let us retain dearest--our 'primitive
nature' always--then we will enjoy life--and know nothing
of the torment, of the blasè! 'Tis too late for the
mail--so I will leave this unsealed--and add my 'Sunday
morning' thoughts. God bless you my own! I take my
french lesson--today--Adieu

                                                                         Mary.


### 31: to Edwin Booth (NYPL—TC), 12 February 1860

                                               Sunday Morn.

I promised you my 'Sunday morning thoughts'--and you
shall have them, darling as "fresh and dewy, as the bush
affords"! and this morning too. I verily beleive they
would outdo--'Titian', in bright coloring but I lack the
artist-skill, to give them proper form: but truth will
give them 'tone'--and to noble eyes, 'tis more acceptable
than beauty's self. The snow lays cold and hard upon the
ground--and bears a strange contrast, to the warmth
within my cozy 'cage'--where all seems pleasant, like a
June-day! no grief, or strife, in my heart, I enjoy a
sweet forgetfulness of the past--and am cheered by
blissful visions of the new world, your love has opened
to my grateful eyes! ah! darling were you here, now, I
could talk so 'sensibly' I'm sure! but that we are
cruelly separated, is greater reason, why we should
corrospond carefully, and thoughtfully--for letters are
sacred things--and yours--why, they seem to me fragments
of your soul, let loose--therefore I look in them, for
pulsation! I often reproach myself--that I do not talk
differently than I do, when writing you--but very
frequently I am deprived of this great joy--by lack of
time--but be assured, not a single day passes, that I
fail to place, a bead of pearl upon the golden thread,
you have given me! 'tis very long, 'twas measured with
our lives,--and is tender as 'tis beautiful! we hold
between us, its delicate fibres, which time alone, will
strengthen! and, ah! darling, for every unkind word--or
thoughtless act--a bead will fall--and we may look in
vain for its counterpart, among the jewels of the earth!
they are from Heaven! We are now standing--as two
individual souls, each responsible for the other! ah,
this is something to be thought of well, is it not?
Yours, I think I comprehend thoroughly--the voice of
Reason, often questions me--if I do not regard you too
'spiritually'? no--I prefer to work from such a model

then, the greater sculpter <u>I</u>, if the <u>flesh</u> and <u>blood</u>, I
carve is made to equal it!--if I talk this way, you will
be apt, to exclaim--"what, my little daughter would be
Master--eh?" but you know well enough that could never
be--I only desire to <u>make you free</u>! <u>we</u>, <u>ourselves</u>, are
our greatest tyrants, undoubtedly. Darling, every day my
love for you increases--but for your dear sake, <u>wisdom</u>,
must accompany it! if my love is <u>selfish</u>, you will never
be <u>great</u>--a part of you belongs to the world! I <u>must</u>
remember this, and assists in its 'blossoming'--if I
would taste of the ripe fruit--that will prove a rich
reward! why, I am stepping out of my 'lay-clothes' and
talking to you like a 'sage'! you will not frown upon me
I am sure--for your nobleness, has given me a prouder
office, in love, to 'sympathize with thought'--than in
the <u>higher</u> one 'to think': the former is a woman's
sphere--unfortunate she, who is compelled to seek the
other. This reminds me, of what I have often thought,
that your sister, whose talents I have heard so
praised--should have been married--you will pardon what I
am about to say--to some noble man--in <u>intellect</u>, you
understand me,--a wearisome thing it must be, to 'tug' to
raise--what should be the superior creature--to your own
height!--this remark, seems not well placed--'twas not
meant unkindly, however let it pass. Four pages of
'grave discourse' and not <u>one line</u> of 'baby talk'--
wonderful! "a happy relief" you will say--and for your
wickedness--you shall not escape--I shall put on my
'lay-clothes' again--lay aside my 'serious garb'--begin
another sheet by rattling 'my coral' in your ears.

[remainder of letter missing]


32: to Edwin Booth (NYPL—TC), 20 February 1860

            Monday Evening.

 What shall I say to my darling, ere I go to bed? my
teacher was with me <u>three hours</u>--and he extracted from me
all the brains, necessary--and I am very much
fatigued--but my <u>heart</u> is not--it will talk with you, for
a little while, with the pen--there in my 'little bed', I
will find repose, with your head resting upon it! I
began this afternoon another book, which promises to be
as good a friend as the 'Memorial' is--and by the <u>same</u>
<u>author</u>; the language is simple, but <u>true</u>: truth, is never
arrayed in gaudy colors you know! besides what can be
more interesting than to follow the writings of those
whose teachings find a response in our own
hearts.--'Hurry up philosophy'--our own vanity

aggrandizes us sufficiently--what we require most is to
be humbled! Darling, we find as much perfume in the
forest wild-flowers--~~and~~ ↑as↓ in the richest of the,
conservatory--and they spring up watered only by the
power of God, these little works, I praise--belong I
consider to the 'hedges' of life--and I hardly think they
would find a place upon the rich and learned savant's
table--but they breathe of ~~of~~ life well spent--duty
fulfilled--and love pure and holy!  I am certain 'twill
never displease you that I love these humble
companions--they encourage often my trembling heart--and
tell me too, there is no nobility save in the mind, and
soul!  for you must know that sometimes, I am a very
naughty, disobedient 'daughter', and think sadly, of
things which you have forbidden me to think of--and which
are wrong even to enter my busy, prattling thoughts,--for
have you not thought me a worthy inmate of the richest
palace the earth holds--your bosom's love--and I reign
there darling--as happy as a Queen!  You are my prince
and peasant--lofty to all the world--as I would have you
but gentle and yealding to me!--you see I boast my
powerer, ah! may I always be good enough to hold
it!--Tonight, within my soul--there is a plaintive voice
whispering me--ah! so many good and lovely things shall I
tell them to you?  no--for what from my own life, might
charm you--would look ugly and senseless upon paper--so I
will keep them all locked in a corner of my heart--until
I have your shoulder to lay my head upon--then you will
not dare to scold me--for I would kiss you, if you so
presumed.--One, sound I always hear, echoing
sweetly--"Edwin loves you dearly--depend upon his
truth"--and I hearken to it--above all others too--and
often, often its kindly tones, makes me cry.--ah, what a
happy little daughter, you have made me!  but are you as
joyous as I am?  You know what I have told you--"Your
eyes must grow brighter every day"--and though I would
not for the world have your cheeck lose its delicacy and
paleness--yet your heart must be as rosy as the dawn!
God bless my darling one!  Good night.  I will venture to
direct this Memphis--my 'Geography' informs me--'tis
nearest--N. O--I hope to hear tomorrow for a certainty
this morning I had no letter--and you see how 'amiable' I
am withal~~l~~--kiss me and pray for me--I need your every
thought!  selfishness personified, am I not?
    Mr love to Joe--God bless you
                  Your Mary.

33: to Edwin Booth (NYPL—TC), 23 February 1860

                                                              A
              Thursday Morn.
              Feb 23rd.

    I arose this morning, lighthearted, and full of
love, darling! the sun was just 'peeping' through the         T
clouds, which 'gave token' of a pleasant day.--I
breakfasted--then went to the piano, and practiced two
hours--and my arms were so fatigued that I said to Kate,      A
'Edwin can have no letter from my pen, tody--I'm
afraid'--and I sat down to 'Cameille'--but my restorative     A
came in a few moments after--"No 1860"--gave me renewed       A
vigor--and the weariness of 'octaves' and 'chords' was in
an instant dispelled!--The description of your                10
'suffering' with Mdme Le V-- amused me exceedingly--          A
darling--'tis very evident that you have no predilection
for the 'honourable escort' of 'unlofidated feemales'!
I trust you met with no annoyance until you reached
Memphis--and God grant you arrived there safely!--Your        A
request, made for your little friend--Miss Nash--I will       A
most readily comply with--and not only to please you
darling--but also myself. I will dictate it--as from 'a
child'--to 'a child'--I would disguise my nature, did I
use 'grand composition',--and children, you know, always      20
consider me one of them, wherever I go;--they come to me
to dress their dolls, and tell them fairy stories! and I
am as happy in conforming to their pretty innocent ways,
as I would be in delighting a 'thoughtful' mind: so your
little sweetheart--shall have the letter, you have
promised her--and by sweet words, wear perhaps some of
her love, for you--how will you like that--sir Edwin?--       T
then you will grow jealous of me! a friend told me the        T
other day, that the ladies, will never try to take you
from me--after they once know me! so I think 'twill be an     30
admirable plain--just by way of self-defense--to be           T
exceedingly amiable to all, whom I suspect don't you
think so, darling?--I am truly indebted to the attentive
'prompter' who shifts the scene of 'splendor' and
'fascination' before your eyes--and takes you to my
longing presence, 'tis my 'wickedness' that will not let      T
you 'stray' from me--and enjoy the 'rich-exotics'!            T
even though you wear your 'daisy' in your button-hole--you
will be out-performed by the roses--so, still keep it out
of sight--press it closely to your heart--'tis much           40
happier there, I know--for the little bee, who sucks its
honey, has 'buzzed' me this! God bless you darling
papa--this day is, oh! so beautiful--just such a
one--that I would love to 'mount' a horse, and with you
ride into the country--and enjoy the 'free and liberal
air'--we will do this some of these days, will we not
darling? Oh! how beautiful, lay our lives before us now!
they seem almost too short, to enjoy all the happiness my     T
soul conceives: some day--darling--if the day I hope for,
ever comes--I will tell you, of a strange desire, I have      50

ever had: I will not name it now--'tis not the time--and
besides 'twill leave me hereafter, I'm sure, unless 'tis
gratified then, by Fate!--This afternoon, I take my
French lesson, and I have a deal to study yet--so I will
not add more <u>now</u>  Mr Bader will call, perhaps tomorrow,
he is in mourning, and consequently--excluded by Fashion
from the sympathy of friends!  ah, deliver me from this
foolish Goddess!  Tomorrow I will write you a longer
letter, dearest--and enclose the note for <u>Miss Julia</u>.
God bless and guard you--I hope you are well--tell me
your wishes that I may fulfill them--Adieu, Your own
                                               Mary.



34: to Edwin Booth (Players), 24-25 February 1860

                          Friday <u>Afternoon</u>
                                <u>Feb 24th</u>/

Darling--
     The day is charming--it reminds me of the pleasant
Spring-time:  this morning I took <u>two</u> music
lessons--learned a new piece for <u>the piano</u>--which I know
will charm you: "The Sheppard's little bell"--you love
'pastoral poems'--do you not--(of course, <u>I'm</u> a 'pastoral
poem') then you will love <u>music</u> of the same style!--
perhaps, after we are married <u>some time</u>--you will weary
of 'Mollie's sitting at your feet and singing to you--and
will be very glad, to send me over in one corner of the
room--to the <u>piano</u> then to the 'tinkling' of the
'Sheppard's Bell,' you can fall asleep: this
accompaniment, will give my darling, pleasant
dreams!--these are the thoughts, encourage, and gladden
me--when my head becomes weary, with 'crotchets' and
'quavers'--and my little finger, almost breaks in
stretching, 'half a mile' across the keys;--my recompence
is all to come, in smiles from you, and could I desire a
greater? no, indeed!--Little 'Mollie' is out on the
balcony, running and playing, with the uncouth
'Newfoundlander', of Harry's--I almost envy her; were it
not that I expect Mr Bader, here this afternoon--I would
say--"Darling papa, for this once, forgive me, for a
short and stupid letter--and give me leave, to go out in
the glad sunshine, of this lovely day; I will put on my
'bonnet and cloak'--and take a long walk--with the
sweetest companions in the world, happy thoughts of your
love, and goodness"!  but, though sure of your permission
I will not go, lest--Mr B-- come--and he would be very
much disappointed--for he told me he should visit me
frequently <u>now</u> (he is excluded, you know, by his
breavement--from his more fashionable friends!)  I had no

letter from you, darling--today--although I did not
expect one--as sufficient time, has not elapsed yet, to
hear from <u>Memphis</u>: tomorrow I will write you again--the
last I shall send to <u>Memphis</u>--(dear me, the time is
going!) and will enclose for Miss Julia, the letter, I
have promised her; I would send it now--but, I must send
to town, today for 'petite' note-paper; since she is a
'little' girl--she must have a 'little' <u>letter</u>.
Yesterday I wrote <u>Louise</u>--in her last--she desired me, to
tell her, something of my 'internal nature'--she must
think me an 'anatomist' and '<u>all</u>' about my 'approaching
marriage' and '<u>all</u>' about '<u>Edwin</u>';--'I bethought' me, of
'a loud talking women'--and so in writing avoided as well
as possible'--<u>our</u> <u>affairs</u>: she forever boasts of her
intimate ↑knowledge↓ of 'Edwin Booth's' nature'--and
anything, that I would write would be most likely
repeated: and besides I desire to preserve you--if
possible, from a p̶ repetition of the annoyance, you
endured from her, before--when <u>we</u> visit Boston.--You
know, darling--that I am going to be a <u>perfect</u> <u>women</u>,
when others are by--'tis only in <u>your</u> <u>arms</u>, I shall be a
'yealding child'--and you shall witness how, well I shall
'clothe' myself in 'dignity' to protect you--from the
familiarity of strong-minded women!--The baby is
<u>screaming</u> at the 'top of her 'compass' and I cannot <u>hear</u>
myself <u>write</u>--, so I will draw this to a close--God bless
you my darling
    I will write you tomorrow at lenht: Are you well
and happy--Heaven grant it--
    Give Joe my love--Adieu
                    Your own
                    Mary.

    Thus far I have been writing in a most 'insipid'
vein--will you have courage to 'pick out' another
entire sheet--not without an exclamation or two of
disgust, I'm sure. The day is so dull and gloomy, that I
hardly know, what--save your presence--could give me
pleasurable thoughts, or feelings--'tis just such an
afternoon ('twas morning, when I began this) that I would
most desire to be at your side, reading one of my <u>pet</u>
<u>poems</u>--the 'Miller's Daughter' for instance--while you
smoked contentedly your meerchaum--and when your
breathing told me you were--no, not asleep--but
'unconscious' simply <u>unconscious</u>--I would drop the book
upon my lap--and pressing a kiss upon your eyes--only to
close them faster--would lay my head upon your knee, and
enjoy--unconsciousness' too--but you are not here, but
<u>far</u> <u>away</u>, and so I must indulge in no useless 'wishes',
for as you say--or rather 'Hamlet'--it is all the same
however, "the readiness is all"! this month has passed
rapidly away--if the next is no more tedious, I shall be
satisfied! Little Mollie, is streched out at my feet,
she looks more graceful to me, than ever: dear little
creature--she loves me so dearly I cannot move--but she
follows me--I never expected she would have lived through

the winter:--last night going up stairs to bed--she was
in my arms--and I said "Mollie--soon Edwin is coming
home--to take me with him--and you shall go too--and in
the summer, we will go where there are green fields, and
I can run and play with you on the green grass"; and she
looked so proud--as if she understood every word I had
said to her; I do believe, she will speak to me some day!
then won't she scold you, papa, if you ever make me cry!
You may say indeed to me--what the hero of the little
poem you sent me--says of his Alice--"Dear eyes--they
have not shed as many tears,--since first I knew them":
for they have not, darling--all my being is filled with
joy now--joy, of the many blissful hours, I have spent
with you--joy, in the present--with thoughts of the
ecstasy 'to come'! surely if there was any danger or
misery in store--I would apprehend it now: but there is
not in my soul a single fear, but that life shall be free
as a 'bright May-day'! I feel my arms clasping your
neck, now--and see in your eyes, an eternity of love and
truth, which will never fade, so I but guard and cherish
it! Oh! those thoughtless ladies knew not of the bliss
they would rob us of, when they questioned you 'why you
married'?--did they darling? leave to me the 'answering'
them. the 'problem' now is wonderful to their eyes. a
year or two, will 'solve' it for them--will it not?--if I
am good, that is:--and when they see 'Edwin' more
beautiful, and happier grow--ah! they will not wonder
then, he gave his heart into a single, woman's keeping!
they may give, and you receive this honest homage from
their boxes--but bestow upon me, your quiet moments when
the 'sock and buskin' are forgotten--then let me, take to
my bosom and soothe the brain their plaudits made so
weary! Darling, I could not love you better than I
do--(or have I commenced to love you yet?) I could not
yearn, more ernestly for your happiness on earth--if
angels, themselves had borne me in their arms from
Heaven, schooled, and tutored in 'your cause'! carefully
guide me Dear Edwin, that the lessons I have received,
may never be neglected by me
    God bless you
                            Mary.


35: to Julia Nash (Players), 26 February 1860

                           Sunday Morn.
                           Feb 26th/60.

My dear Miss Julia--
    I received a letter from Mr Booth, a day or two ago,
in which he requests me--to write to you, his 'little

Southern sweetheart'--and the pleasure I shall feel in
complying, decided me at once to do so: for although I
have never experienced the delight, of <u>seeing</u> you--yet I
seem to know you well; your <u>heart</u>, by the fondness, you
have, for 'our dear Edwin'--and I retain, alas, the
remembrance of an <u>innocent face</u>--worn by him, for a long
time, in a 'tiny' <u>locket</u>, attached to his watch-guard!
so we will immagine, that we know each other <u>well</u>,--for
'<u>Uncle Ned</u>' has told you of <u>me</u> too, has he not? told
you--'that Mary will love you dearly'--yes, that I
will--with all my heart I'm sure--and 'that you may love
him just as well, when I am by his side as <u>now</u> you
<u>do</u>'--and I promise you little Julia, that <u>you</u> shall!--I
am not a <u>tall</u>, <u>grand</u>, and <u>beautiful</u> lady, that will chill
and intimidate, your--young childish heart; 'tis not many
years, since <u>I</u> ceased playing with my 'dolls'--and I have
not forgotten yet--to sympathize with the <u>loves</u> and
griefs of a child: I know many, many, 'pretty stories'
too--which, I often, sit at Edwin's side, and tell
him--and he listens as <u>patiently</u> as though they were,
<u>marvelous tales</u>--and I will teach them to you, some
day.--and now we know each other, and will become the
best of friends, I hope--and you must never be <u>jealous</u> of
'Aunt Mary' but try and love her as you do 'Edwin': now,
listen, to <u>all</u>, I promise to do, for 'our
sweetheart'--but you must not betray me to
him--remember:--I love Edwin, <u>dearly</u> oh! you cannot think
how dearly!--why should I not? is he not good and
noble?--and he shall have the whole devotion of my life,
simple though, that be: and his home the <u>happiest</u>--if
'sunshine' and affection can, ~~can~~ make it so: he has
always, suffered much, from gloom and sadness, you
know--well, he promises to know them, no more! then will
you not be glad, and happy--to see the eyes we love, grow
brighter every year--his <u>genius</u> and his <u>beauty</u>, still
preserved, and in his <u>Art</u>, attain to <u>greatness</u>: you will
be a young lady grown then--but will still retain, I
hope, the same fondness for, 'Uncle Ned' as in your
childhood; he needs, dear little one, the soothing
influence of gentle hearts!--When he revisits the
South--he has promised, to take <u>me</u> with him: I hope to
see you then--and <u>two</u> hearts will cherish you instead of
<u>one</u>. Many weeks, must elapse, ere I see Edwin--and the
days, seem so long and so tedious, waiting his return--do
not you pity me. but to know him well, and happy, more
than repays me for his absence. I will enclose this to
Edwin, and he will forward it to you--and you will <u>answer</u>
this will you not? call me 'aunt Mary'--and think of me
often and, kindly. Remember me to your dear parents--and
ask them to receive me to their <u>hearts</u>, as an
affectionate friend. Adieu, dear little Julia, accept,
the love and kisses, of your <u>new</u>,
                    '<u>Aunt Mary</u>'

36: to Edwin Booth (Players), 1 March 1860

> Thursday Morn.
> March 1st/60.

Yesterday, as I told you in a previous letter--I was to make a 'lay-figure' of myself--which I did for a long space of <u>three</u> <u>hours</u>--went with the Jeffersons to the 'Royal Circus,' now playing at <u>Niblo</u>'s: its 'Royality' is a <u>humbug</u>--but notwithstanding, they are very clever: the great feature is the 'leap' made by the brothers <u>Harlow</u>; 'tis really wonderful, and terrific. Miss Ella Zoyara--(P)--the public are in doubt, whether she is 'une femme'--so they ask now--"well, what do you think, <u>it</u> is?" she is a very fine horse<u>man</u>--and creates the greater amount of curiosity. <u>I</u> returned this morning in the midst of rain and fog--found only <u>one</u> letter from you--dated 24th the second only since <u>you</u> have been in <u>Memphis</u>: I cannot understand it--the only reasonable conjecture is, that the young lady of the generous proposal--which 'proposal' you enclosed ↑to↓ me--has become desperate, and intercepted in her 'madness' your little daughter's letters! for I cannot think you neglected her, from Monday till Thursday night! to return again, to my 'original' suspicion of the 'Raphaelite' <u>Madame</u> perhaps she found as she hoped--'all well' and you have consented to become the 'pilot': darling--is it possible the~~y~~re are <u>women</u> no, not <u>women</u>, simply 'waves of crinoline'--who, can consent to render themselves in the eyes of a sensible man--so perfectly rediculous: do you know--I think there is a certain duty you can perform toward humanity--coming as you do in contact with such 'species'--in giving them a retort deserving of their own <u>shamelessness</u>: though this is by no means the <u>caméne</u>, I would have you fulfill--but since they fall oftener in <u>your</u> way, than in most men's--assist to your utmost, in their extermination. This is the beginning of Spring but the 1st looks most unpromising; we have not had a dozen clear days, in the same number of weeks: the <u>time</u> has not seemed so long to me, though as I anticipated; I have grown quite patient lately; 'tis, perhaps--that I feel the 'future' is 'drawing nigh'--and instead of the teazing--tormenting--restless, impatient 'child'--I am going to be a 'wife'--with duties and requirements, totally different, from those, which now posess me! They will be more <u>serious</u> too, and I must tutor my <u>brain</u> as well as <u>heart</u>, to meet them ~~boldly~~--bravely--is better.--I never intend, to make my forehead, wrinkled though, with two much 'serious thought' my hope and desire is, to smooth them away, only from 'my papa's' <u>brow</u> and <u>heart</u>! by gentleness, and have affection brush away the 'cobwebs' of the wretched <u>past</u>--and like a good <u>housewife</u>, establish 'cleanliness,' 'partout'. Edwin--I would pray earnestly for <u>death</u>, if I failed to meet your great soul's requisites! and must I

confess to you--that sometimes, I feel my heart grow
faint, and tremble, thinking upon the 'holy work'
allotted to me, in life: the only thought which at such
times, strengthens and consoles me, is--Edwin, knows well
my life, the love and devotion, I bear him, will cause
him to forget the faults of my nature now--and he will be
content to have me as his 'child-wife' until a just
experience, which two or three years will give
me--eradicates my imperfections, and association with him
makes me, a <u>womanly wife</u>": for you are young too--and
have so many <u>things yet</u> to learn--is it not so? and you
can teach me to 'think' darling, until my mind obeys you
as does my heart. "I do wish Mary wuld say, something
new"--I hear you say--"the same thing, over and over
again" well, 'tis all for you, so you must listen to
it--I desire that you should know it by heart; however, I
will not weary you longer, today--you are a good 'pupil'
and may be 'dismissed' My intention was to have written
only one of these sheets, <u>full</u>, for I can't well, write
<u>every day</u>--and be 'interesting' unless, I have something
to respond to--now, as I have only had <u>two</u> letters, in
<u>six days</u>--you must not blame <u>me</u>, if my correspondence is
'dull' and 'stupid'. Mr Jefferson, promises to write to
John--for though he may not be in management himself he
can always procure, him, an engagement. I cannot 'write
myself down' <u>well</u> today, for the weather makes me feel
most miserable: when with you, I shall never care how
much it rains; on such days, you will have the fewer
'<u>calls</u>' to take you from my side and you can sit and read
to me all day--won't that be jolly! God bless you write
me 'once in a while'--ask Joe for me, to still continue,
'dodging', he will receive from me a note of thanks,
for 'protecting' you, in your absence: these 'females'
who are willing to forsake 'home and friends'.
Adieu--God guard you--and bring you safely to me
                       Mary.


37: to Edwin Booth (NYPL—TC), 19 March 1860

                    Monday Morn.
                    March 19th/60.

Darling,
    Harry sent me this morning per express, a <u>luttle
box</u>--which came to him 'per express'; 200 <u>golden kisses</u>
from my darling papa!--I did not expect <u>half</u> so many, nor
their coming so soon: so it was a <u>great</u> <u>surprise</u> for
me;--you are very, very good and kind to me; many
thanks!--I only wish night were come--that I might feel
satisfied of your arrival in <u>Charleston</u>; all day,

yesterday--and last night, I could think of nothing, but
your long and tedious journey; a dozen times in the night
I awoke with a prayer on my lips for your safety! God
grant that it was heard! Yesterday I wrote you, but
could 'conjure' no sweet thoughts or harmonious I heard
only the '<u>chu</u>-<u>chu</u>-<u>chu</u>-ing', of the horrid cars, and felt
your throbbing aching head, against my bosom! I had a
bunch of beautiful violets sent me towards evening--and I
amused myself for a time, tieing and untieing, the
fragrant gift;--I pressed them into a tiny wreath for my
kind papa, 'pressed' them with <u>kisses</u>--and my imagination
was filled with a 'thousand' lovely images while I was
arrainging them: "last Spring violets, when your sisters
bloomed, I had no 'sweetheart' to send them to, and were
neglected by me; but now, ah! I am blessed indeed! I
have a true friend--a beautiful, loving papa--and ere you
blossom again, will call him <u>husband</u>": and I felt so
glad, and so happy--that I forgot entirely, how fragile
and ~~delel~~ delicate, were the slender stems, and I broke
many of them off 'too short', and spoiled them. Where
are you Edwin, now and are you well and happy? who can
tell me--no one at this moment! I must 'hope and pray'!
Has Mr Badeu sent you, yet--Hawthorne's last work on
Italy; he intends doing so, and one to me also; he seems
crazy now, to have you go on the 'Continent' for a few
months; then return to England and play: he won't
'<u>marry</u>', he says if you do this. When he told me of this
'marriage de convenance'--I told him I could not
understand it, "for <u>I</u> loved so dearly"--but
added,--hoping to find some affection in his
nature--'Your motive, of course, is not entirely a
<u>selfish</u> one, for you hope to confer happiness upon the
lady'--'no,' he said--she has been educated in purely
French style, and knows nothing of the heart'--ah! Edwin,
how I pitied them from the bottom of my heart! "to go
through life unloving, and unloved"--why, I would not
exchange the pure, unselfish devotion that <u>I</u> feel--for a
princess's diadem! would you, darling? no, I'm sure you
would not--for a '<u>prince's diadem</u>'! I have two music
lessons to take this morning so I will kiss my dear, dear
papa and promise him a longer letter <u>next time</u>. Have you
heard, yet the 'Petruchian Waltz'--please don't listen to
it--I shall, assuredly be jealous of any 'ten
fingers'--which offer to play it--before you come to me.
God bless you Edwin--pray be careful of your health--and
avoid discontent, wont ↓you,↑ but if you are sad, don't
conceal it from me--for I have not 'cried' for a long,
long time, and promise, I will not, soon again--so tell
me all your <u>fears</u>, and I will calm, and pacify them.
Adieu--God guard you safely.--give Joe my love.
             Your own
                 Mary.

38: to Edwin Booth (NYPL—TC), 10 May 1860

Thursday Morn.
May 10th/60

No letter yesterday--pourquoi? I did not feel lonely though as usual, for I knew you must have arrived home, and was satisfied that you were so near me!--Yesterday, I posted you a 'kiss,' but did 'twas one of the day previous--I spent half the day, with my 'modiste', and did not find time ↑to↓ send another; she is a 'Madame Françoise'--and I always take occasion to 'parle' with here: she, of course, as all French do, admires the 'Demoiselles Anglaises'--and I have no doubt that my acquaintance with her 'native tongue', will induce her to doubly 'frenchify' my 'dresses'. they are so pretty--I wonder if you--will like them; you have ever praised so highly my 'bon goût' that I must not lose my reputation in this instance--or I presume I will 'never more be officer of yours'. The other day, I dined and remained an hour or two after--with Mr Jefferson; I met there--not for the first time--but the first time socially, George Jordan; instead of a fastidious coxcomb, as I had always heard him, described to be--I found him, the most intolerably vulgar men, it has ever been my ill fortune, to come in contact with; it 'sickened' me of the house--I hardly tho't, I shall ever sit at their table again; for I have always esteemed Mr J. so much for his choice of guests; I am satisfied now, that things have changed, since 'my times'; and I shall be 'wary' in the future! How very glad I am--that I always held at a proper distance 'peoples du Theatre'--when I was 'of them'! how few--how very few--leave their 'tinsled gew-gaws' for the night--and in their proper places--no, they drag them to their homes, where they lose their charm and show their 'nothingness': I refer, of course, to the generality, now: and am I not right?--The society of 'Artists' in all countries but our own, is said to be more charming than of all other classes--for art, with all, save us, is 'religion' we shall see this when we go abroad; 'twill encourage and assist you, darling--in the mission you are to perform, towards, your 'sinking art' here; and if ↑you↓ will only choose to follow, the course ↑which↓ my judgement, prompts me is the direct and proper one--you will arrive ere long at the 'end', you are so nobly fitted for.' I would never have you inculcate a spirit of haughty pride--and a conpemptuous regard for all those who toil beneath you--as our friend Mr B-- would have you--and which is neither good nor proper--but the dignity and gentleness, of a worthy Chief, towards his subjects!--and you will be happier to live thus, as 'twere, within yourself--for 'tis glorious to rule, when we have the power ↑to rule↓, but sublime, when swayed benignantly!--I wonder if you ever reflect, upon ↑the↓

influence your talents, can bring to bear upon, the good
and the evil, of the sphere you move in!  I ask no
greater proofs, of this--than the notes, and tokens, you
used to enclose me now, and then--seemingly absurd, and
fit cause for laughter--but pause to think what victims,
they might become--were you not good--my good papa!  and
as your love, sacred and pure, will impart to your soul,
tranquillity of and holliness of purpose, so must you
instil their 'loftiness' into others!  What a pity you do
not read French fluently!  but this regret, shall be of
short duration--you must acquire it immediately; at
least, as soon, as I am permitted to sit by your side,
and instruct you!--There is one, single 'discourse' of
'Cousin's' that will more than repay you, for your
study!--'tis that you are not able, to read and profit by
its instructions, ere 'donning' your Hamlet dress
again--that I have said, and repeat again--what a
misfortune that you do not read the language!--but never
mind--you shall do so, soon--I will be the most arbitrary
and tiranical of 'professors' until you can read Cousin!
Mr Badeau, tried to discourage me--by telling me, "you
will not succeed--he will not listen to the
'abstract'--you will turn and find him, pondering upon
something else!"--I told him 'your gallantry' would not
permit such heedlessness--but dear papa, I do not place
much faith in your 'gallantry'--'tis your 'happiness' I
look to, for attention and regard!  you will have
forgotten then, I hope, the ugly face of the Past and
take interest, alike with me in the Present, shall it not
be so?--let us think, that we have deffered the 'reality
of life'--until our marriage--there seems to me--to be so
much of 'human promise' in it!--What a strange
disconnected way, I have of writing; I break my subject
generally into a dozen different parts; it must strain
your 'wits' to thier utmost, to find a 'link', and very
often, indeed there is none; this is a fault--experience
I hope will rid me of it; I can feel sensibly and
truly--but am at a loss, to defend my principles;
'spontaneity' is admired by all the world--but one, good
reflection, will scatter and 'upset' all its hasty
unfounded judgements.  I am too young and too happy to
'reflect' much yet--but quick to confess, you will be
ready to forgive!  Very little occupies me now--~~except~~
↑besides↓ the thoughts and eager hopes, for your
'coming'.  I begin to breath, 'short and quick'~~ly~~--as the
time draws near; I enjoy every thing I see and hear--for
all the world seem~~s~~ good to me now!  every day, I tell
'little Mollie', who is coming home!--she 'wags her tail'
and looks very glad--but 'tis a selfish 'wag'--for she
immediately leaps upon my lap--and falls asleep--hearing
nothing more I say; so I have come to the conclusion,
that she pretends, but really knows nothing after all--of
who 'Edwin' is--and cares only to get a warm place, upon
my lap--to luxuriate in.  We have had a storm--and it has
most likely reached you--, if so, your 'opening' must
have been injured by it, tell me all the news, and write

me often; morning is almost gone, and no letter yet!  God
bless you

                                      Mary.


39: to Edwin Booth (NYPL—TC), 19 May 1860

                                    Saturday Morn
                                    May 19th/60

My birthday darling!  <u>20</u>, and so happy--so very
happy!--This morning ere I arose the sky was storming,
and unpromising--but while braiding my hair, the sun
shone forth in all its splendor--and now 'tis "the
lovliest day of all the glad New Year" were <u>you</u> here to
'speak my joy' to--my happiness would be complete,
indeed.  I feel so light of soul--so hopeful of the
future--of our love and wedded bliss!--surely were there
clouds or tempests to darken our horizon--such is my
faith in Heaven's goodness--that 'twould be <u>felt</u> by me
today!--Your letter, with your several 'billets-doux'--
enclosed I received too--on this my 'natal' morn;--it
filled me full of <u>serious thought</u>--and tonight I will
give you the long 'wifely' letter--and the 'assurances'
you require: certainly I know all your 'fears'--did I not
write you, yesterday--that your 'nature was a book within
my hands'?  I will read it to you when you come; and lull
to rest <u>forever</u>--I hope--all your doubts, and strange
forbodings.  If you can comprehend and confide in the
holy preference, 'not of <u>Passion</u> born' which dwells
within my heart, for you, dear Edwin--the 'hideous
phantom' will be subdued and chased away.--
    Why I do not give my 'wifely' consel now--is that my
time is limited:  I have a long lesson on my mind--and
fear a 'scolding' if 'tis not 'au fait': en you will
forgive me darling, for a 'courte' birthday epistle--this
will be only a 'tiny' morning 'kiss'--and the <u>evening</u>
shall be all your own!--
    Direct your letters to Harry as usual;--he does not
mind playing 'post-boy'--I pay him ~~with~~ smiles, and
carresses. for his salery.  Tell me positively the day
you will be here--ah! how I long for it,--for if on
Thusday you come--I must give upon my lesson, on that
day--if on Friday 'twill not be necessary.  Your <u>choice</u>
will go--as the old adage says--'by contraries'.  I would
love to linger over the pages and tell you many
things--but my watch reminds me of the lateness of the
hour--and the necessity of mailing soon.
    --Pray be cheerful until you come to me--I have so
many pretty things to tell you, dear papa!--God bless
you--tonight or tomorrow--I will be <u>wise</u> and 'wifely'.

Adieu--God guard my darling safely to my presence.  My
love to your Mother.

                                        Your own
                                            Mary.




40: to Mary L. Felton (Players), 29 September 1860


Dear Mrs Felton.
     I delayed answering your kind invitation--which Mr
Booth and myself accept with great pleasure--until seeing
Mr Carey, who agrees with us in naming Thursday to visit          T
you.  Mr Booth desires me to proffer you his sincere
thanks for the little poem "Anne Hathaway", which he has
endeavoured for a long time, but in vain, to procure; he
is quite happy in the belief that 'tis a genuine effusion
of his 'favorite bard'.  I remain with great esteem Yours
sincerely

Boston Sept 29th/                           Mary Booth--




41: to Julia Nash (NYPL—TC), Winter 1860-61


                                    Sunday Evening.
Dear little Julia,                                                A
     Uncle Ned has just finished a letter to your
'papa'--and remembering that I owed a letter to his               T
little daughter--in answer to the pretty one received the
other day.
     I have only a short time to spend in writing--for I
have promised Edwin to read him some pretty stories--and
since Sunday is the only evening he can give me in the
week--I like to make him as happy as possible.
     We are living at the Hotel where we met you, last
summer--the 5th Avenue--and it seems as though you should        10
be here; whenever I see, or hear the little children
laughing, and playing in the halls, it reminds me of
'little Julie'.--You can't imagine how sorry I am that
you have been so ill!  but never mind--be a good child            T
a̶l̶l̶ and all ↑will↓ be right yet, I hope.
     It is so tedious to be sick, and not able to enjoy
life--but having a kind father and mother, to love and
care for you, it must content and make you patient.  You
are very young yet--scarcely 'fledged'--and there is time

enough for you to become accomplished and learned; books
are sweet things--but when forced upon us, when we are
ill--give head-aches, and all sorts of pains; but there
are plenty of other things, besides for you to learn--
that you will find happiness in: obedience and
duty--love, and remembrance of your friends--that will
give you a disposition gentle and lovable;--even though
you may know less of books than others these will cause
you to be dearly loved. But I'm sure you do not need
Aunt Mary's advice upon this subject--so now I will say a
word to you, for 'Ned'; his health has not been very good
this winter; he has worked too hard, for one so delicate;
I have to take as much care of him as though he were a
little child, but then you know I love him so very
dearly--and he is so good too--that I would rather have
him dependent on me, than not.--Now I will say 'good
bye'--for you see how little space I have left to say
much more. I hope that God will save our Union and keep
us fast friends, although it looks so very dark now.
Tell Mama she must bring you to see us next summer--and
give my best love to her.--to 'papa' also--
    Accept Uncle Ned's, and a kiss; I will let you have
one, though I would not part with it to any one
else--Adieu--your own
Write me soon.                                                 Aunt Mary.

42: to Julia Ward Howe (printed in *New England Magazine*, 15 [Nov 1893], 317),
    30 June 1861

My dear Mrs. Howe,--I met your sweet daughter Julia
yesterday, and told her that I should see you in the
evening; but I was doomed to a cruel disappointment! On
our way from Camp Andrew our bump of locality misled us,
and we found ourselves far from South Boston, and from
home too. The shades of night o'ertook us and confused
us further, so that when we arrived at home I was
fatigued and almost prostrated. Now I wanted so heartily
to see you and kiss you "good bye" before leaving for
Bethel--that we do to-morrow morning at 7 1/2; so I must
be content, I suppose, with sending this little note, for
to-day I am held prisoner by the dread packing of trunks
which stares me in the face. If we go to Europe, as we
hope to, our return in August will allow us a day at
least to go to Newport and receive your encouragement and
adieux. Has your prayer for Edwin been in vain? No, the
earnestness of your admiration, dear Mrs. Howe, has had
its effect, and I trust it may increase every day for
him. My kindest love to all "your pretty chickens and

their dam." Edwin begs to be kindly remembered; but that
I am sure he is. Adieu.
                    Your devoted little friend,
                                        Mary Booth
Sunday Morn, June 30.



43: to Emma F. Cary (Players), 3 July 1861


                                    Bethel--July 3rd

My dear Miss Carry
     We left Boston early on Monday morning--and your
note of the 30th has just reached ↑me↓ here. Had we but
known of the "presentation" earlier, we would certainly
have deffered our departure. On Saturday last we went to
the Camp hoping to see your brother; imagine then, our
disappointment, when after the parade, the Captains all
came forward to salute their Colonel and he was
absent!--I have not ceased reproaching myself that we
delayed our visit so long. Mr Booth has written him
'Good Bye'--and give him from me, our hearts' best wishes
for his safety.
     Thus far Bethel has been dull beyond expression--for
we have had nothing but rain--when more friends arrive we
hope to have pleasanter times. England absorbs every
thought for the present, in my mind--and if earnest
wishing will aid success, I may rest confident of seeing
you, in a very few weeks. Mr Booth joins me, in kindest
remembrances to you and yours. With great esteem and
regard believe me
                              Very truly Yours
                                   Mary Booth.
Eames's Hotel
     Bethel, Me.



44: to Emma F. Cary (Players), 30 August 1861


                              London August 30th
                                        1861.

My dear Miss Carry--
     After a most delightful voiage of only ten days we
arrived safely--and remained in the dingy town of
Liverpool but one day, our eagerness to see this great
city, outweighing all fatigue. We are now most happily

domiciled here--and I trust for a long residence. Not
being at present, in a "sight-seeing" condition, I have
been obliged to control my impatience, and rest content
with visiting those places of interest in our immediate
vicinity; the 'Abbey of Westminster' alone, has filled me
with content and produced such an impression that I care
not to have it disturbed; of course you have seen it and
realized the overwhelming thought it occasions.--The last
news that reached us from 'home', came two days ago--and
brought us the defeat of the 'Unionists' and the sad
intelligence of General Lyons death; we hope that this is
'report' only. The feeling against the North, here in
England, is very bitter; they seem to desire that ~~the~~
neutrality will be preserved, but at the same time
express the strongest hopes, that the "South may get her
rights." Has your dear brother been in any danger
yet?--how glad I am that <u>his</u> regiment, at least, are well
disciplined it ↑is↓ terrible to think of the thousands of
precious lives, under the command of those who through
ignorance sacrifice them: but you are surrounded by so
much that is sad--that I will spare you in this, and try
to give you a little intelligence that will prove
gratifying, I am sure to you and yours.

Mr Booth has not 'appeared' yet the proper season
being October--and he will then have the appreciative and
genuine audience to play before. An unbounded success
has been predicted for him, since our arrival here, on
all sides, but he is very nervous and anxious about it
himself; if he should fail, the disappointment would
almost crush him; I feel confident, however that he will
succeed. Immediately after his first appearance, I will
write you everything regarding it--knowing how much
interest you take in his progress.--Before leaving
Boston, I could not find a leisure moment to acknowledge
the pleasure, that the pretty presents of Mrs Felton,
Miss Sallie's and yourself, afforded me; I prize them
all, dearly, and long most anxiously to welcome the
little stranger, that is to 'don' them: my health being
excellent, I have no reason to think that happiness will
come to me, before the early part of November. You will
write me soon I hope--a letter from you, would bring to
me, so much cheerfulness,--for there is a sense of
friendlessness, steals over one, in a strange country,
that naught but communication with the 'loved ones at
home' can quite dispel. Mr Booth joins with me in the
kindest remembrances to all your family circle--and
accept yourself, my hearts best love.

        Your friend affectionately
          Mary Booth.

P.S.
  Is baby well--and Mrs Cary too? remember us to her,
especially--and kiss the baby for me.
          M.B.

<u>No</u> 15, Bedford Place
   Bloomsbury Square.

54  Letters

45: to Emma F. Cary (Players), 1-2 October 1861

                                London: Oct 1st
My dear Friend
     Your kind letter reached me yesterday--upon the very
eve, of Mr. Booth's debût--and the heartfelt wishes it          A
contained for his success, made its arrival at that
apropos moment, doubly dear; and I was so anxious to
communicate the verdict of the public to you, that I
could scarcely have patience to await the issue.
     As the evening drew to a close, I tried to 'spirit'
you away, from your quiet home, and take you with me to
my box in the theatre--needing sympathy--in my anxiety
and feeling that you above all others, would afford it          10
me; so remembering that you once told me, you never
suffered from sea-sickness--I felt no scruples for thus
'willing' you to cross the "inexorable deep" and sit
beside me:  allowing this to be a thing <u>possible</u>, I do not  T
think you would blame me for my treachery unless indeed I
detained ↑you↓ <s>to</s> 'til this morning, when you would have
found yourself in one of these unearthly, bewildering
fogs, that are only indigenous to the soil of 'merry
England', I believe or rather London; added to which
several of the morning journals--fortunately of ↑but↓           20
little account or consideration, to any, save to thier
editors--came out, in the most unkind censure of
'Shylock' at the Haymarket'--the part Mr Booth chose for        AT
his first appearance not daring, after so long a rest to
task his strength with any character, requiring more
physical power.
     The 'Times'--the journal of most consequence, did
him some justice but still its praise was 'luke-warm' it        T
however said nothing--it may not recall in the future.
This tone of criticism, certainly could not fail to             30
chill, and depress, one so sensitively organized as my
dear husband--but he knew there was against him,
pre-existing <s>predjdudice</s> predjudice--and saw before him a
very high-hill to climb; that he will reach its summit, I
trust and hope, but he certainly has much to contend
against.  The enthusiasm of the <u>audience</u>, was
unbounded--and as far as he could judge of <s>their</s> its
pulse--it beat with him, and of course it is the approval
of the public--and not that of a few newspaper critics he
will strive to win.--Your comment upon 'English nature' I       40
have found true, thus far, in almost every instance; it
is astonishing how ignorant they are of the manners of
other peoples!  There is not a magazine, ↑or↓ periodical
of any description, now being published here, which does
not contain at least two articles, upon the "American
Crisis"--and to the great surprise of every honest
thinker--written in direct contradiction to truth and
<u>facts</u>.  N' importe,--time, will I hope remove the sad
clouds which now hang over, and threaten us with
dissolution--and prove to 'these Englishers' the fallacy        50

of their darling wish, to see the Union dissolved.--By
the same mail which brought your letter, came one from
your dear brother; cheering Edwin, with the kindest
words, his warm, friendly feelings could suggest--to make
a grand success. He gave, us glowing accounts of the
improvements in our army and wrote evidently in as quiet
and cheerful mood (although I'm sure, with less comfort)
as though his camp were his home, and, where fear or
danger, dwelt not;--how happy this must make his wife;
I don't know whose courage, I most admire; his or hers:
facing cannon balls, is not more dreadful, in my eyes,
than the deprivation of the sight of those I love.
                              Thursday Morning.

    I left my letter unfinished, that I might inclose a
word to you of the impression made upon the public by
Shylock's second appearance;--Mr Booth had more control
over himself than on the first night, but the novelty of
his position--surrounded as he is by entire strangers--
will not, for some little time, wear away, and until it
does, he will hardly, 'feel himself'.
    I have yet a few lines to send your sisters, in
reply to their warm expressions of regard--so will close,
by entreating you to write me often. The journals of
most interest, and <u>conscience</u> I think--are the weekly
ones; these I will <u>mail you</u>--as soon as they come out.
With kind love to your Mother--beleive me yours sincerely
and affectionately
                              Mary Booth.
Kiss little Georgie for me--and tell Mrs Cary, I will
write her in Mrs Felton's letter a 'private word'.
                M.


46: to Emma C. Cushman (FL—BTM), 4 October 1861

                              London Oct 4th
My cherished friend
    Your letter, longed for most impatiently by me--came
duly, 'per Arabia';--no doubt you were prompted by some
good spirit, who watches over ladies in my condition to
keep me no longer, <u>longing</u>, but to send instantly,
without waiting a further summons, news of your sweet
self, and husband.
    By the same mail, my letters from Cambridge
arrived--from my dear friends there--and all strange to
say (for good news seldom comes when most needed) on the
very day, the eve of which Edwin was to make his debut;
of course they cheered, and made me feel, less a stranger
in a strange land. He opened in 'Shylock'--and made

quite as great a success, as we could have wished--with
the larger audience assembled--but the next day the
morning papers came out most unkindly in their
censure--at all of which he 'snaps his fingers' for
really their criticism is not worth the perusal; however
I fear he has a hard hill to climb, for there seems to be
a pre-existing predjudice against him; of course the
press might have been <u>secured</u>, but I am happy to say, Mr
Booth has too much dig<u>nity of</u> character to buy praise.
'Shylock' was perhaps the worst part he could have chosen
for an opening--but he dared not trust his strength in
any more powerful character, after his long rest, and
absence from the footlights; but I have confidence ~~that~~
in the public--whose approval only an artist should look
for--and that eventually the press will do him justice.

   How I should love to have spent that <u>one</u> <u>day</u> with
you at Mrs Howe's--although, you tell her for me, I feel
myself forgotten by her--she has not written to me, since
our departure.

   I am writing, dear child, in the quiet of my room,
<u>alone</u> and by gas-light--Mr Booth being at the play; quiet
<u>did I</u> say? ah, word <u>incommon</u>, in London--a horrid
organ-grinder begins, as I pen the words, to mutilate,
beneath my window, some lovely operatic air!--In the
daytime I have all the disposition to write, but the
atmosphere is so smoky, so fogy, and bewildering, that
really I yearn for the day to close, that I may shut
close the blinds, and revel in artificial light. They
tell me, I have nothing <u>now</u> to complain of--and promise
that I shall see Joys in November, that penetrate and
sourround one completely! No wonder the English are so
un-progressive, so thoroughly conventional; all that I
have met, know a great deal more of <u>English</u> nature than
of <u>human</u> nature. My dear baby, my looked for blessing,
is to be born here, however, so I must not be too severe,
though I shall never look upon the little darling, as
indigeneous to this soil; no, an American <u>he</u> must be!
You see I have fixed upon the sex--if I am disappointed
now!--My health continues excellent would that yours were
better than you lead me to beleive it is; of course your
whole constitution received a terrible shock, that in
time only you~~r~~ will recover from; you must be most
prudent--and guard yourself well from the cold and damp
of Boston; their winters are frightfully trying to those
unaccustomed to them.

   I promise that you shall be apprised as soon after
as possible, of the forthcoming of my expected little
treasure--I endeavour not to think of the suffering I
must inevitably bear, but look only on the bright
side.--London is terribly dull, the season has not
begun--everybody out of town they say--and the only
objects worthy of notice--are the <u>shops</u>; they are truly
gay, and most beautiful: England was aptly named--"a
nation of shop-keepers" for ~~b~~ in beauty they surpass
ours--in fact the people seem wholly devoted to and
occupied with this department of the social system.

Dress of every description is very much cheaper here--and
I long for the period when I may indulge ↑in↓ my favorite         70
passtime--money-spending.--
   We are deeply interested in everything pertainting
to our country now, and await with anxiety every fresh
arrival; I am constantly in ill humour with the press
here--who agravate, but give no sympathy.  There is not a
monthly or periodical of any description now being
published in London--but contains at least two articles
on the "American Crisis"; the writers of which, are not
only ignorant ↑on↓ the subject--but deny, with an
effrontery unparrelled, established and incontestable            80
facts.  I can only hope, that the strength of the
American people, will soon be so well confirmed by
success--that the darling wish, of a vast number ~~of~~ on
this side the water, will fall to the ground--and the             T
fallacy of a dissolution of the Union decided upon
forever.  A letter from Captain Cary, at Maryland now,
intimated to us, that a great battle, and a decisive one,
was not far distant--and assured us at the same time of
the efficiency of our army; so before this reaches you I
hope the day will be ours.--You no doubt have received           90
accounts of the loss of the G. Eastern; but you will be           A
glad to hear that 'twas not total;--the great strength of
the monster, withstood the terrific shock it received in
the storm--and it found after days of suffering to those
on board safe harbour.  This last disaster will I think
effectually cure people, ~~from~~ ↑of↓ a desire to voyage in
so vast a ship;--I'm sure I would not like to trust
myself in her.
   Your Aunty is ere this I presume at Rome--where no
doubt cherie would like to be too; although I'm sure that       100
you will find in Boston the right kind of society, as
well, as earnest friendship; I have great faith you know
in everything 'stamped' Boston.--Your Grandma was to have
accompanied me to the Theatre on Monday but I received a
note from her, urging sickness as an excuse, so I was
deprived of the pleasure; she is not very strong--yet I
hope will grow better.
   I must wait until Spring before visiting the
Continent--where I long with all my soul to wander; we
will be joined there by friends of ours--the Grahams of           A
New York; they are now in Edenbourg--where Mrs Graham was       111
sent for her health--to be under the care of Prof                 A
Simpson; if you don't recover shortly you must come and
test his skill; although I doubt, darling if you care for
the present--to be cured, as my friend hopes to be.--Mrs
Felton of Cambridge is so solicitous in her letters to
me--for a 'carte' of myself--that after a great deal of
deliberation and many times viewing myself in the
glass--I have concluded--that I may be taken en neglegè--
and in my next, you shall have one.  I will close              120
now--having prolonged this to a tedious length--and I
fancy you impatient for the end.
   Give my kind regards to Mr Cushman in which Mr Booth
joins--with the same to your little self.  Please give my

58  Letters

best love to Miss Smith--tell her she shall hear from me
before 'the event'.  Write me soon darling and believe
me, very sincerely and
                         affectionately yours
                                   Mary Booth.

Best love to Lucy--
         I have written her.



47: to Josephine Graham (PSU), 1 November 1861

                              London--Nov 1st 1861.

My dear Mrs Graham
       What shall I say in praise of the "wee blanket"
wrought by your hands--and which was safely delivered to
me yesterday morning?
       I was prepared for the receipt of it, by Mr Graham's              A
letter--and your kind thought for the 'little stranger' I
hope soon to welcome, touched me deeply.  The beauty of
the precious little covering I prize dearly now--and its
utility shall be proven hereafter; although Mr Graham
gave it, as his opinion to Mr Booth, that it was "too
small" for any practical purpose.  Long ere this I hoped         10
to have seen you in London; am I to believe, that you are
recovering less rapidly than you anticipated, under Dr
Simpson's treatment?  I trust not; however you must be
patient; a slow effectual cure, is always to be preferred
before a rapid and unsafe one--and if you can only await
the "getting well" I have no doubt that you will be
restored to the full enjoyment of health again.
       Miss Graham is well, I hope--and not home-sick as
she feared she would be.--As you ↑will↓ be coming to town
soon, doubtless, perhaps it would serve you, to allow me,        20
before closing this--to give you, just an idea, of how,
and where, I think you would find the most comfortable
residence.
       This morning, I rode out with a lady friend, as far
as Brampton--four miles ~~about~~ from town--to inspect
with her a house, she had previously engaged.  'Tis a
Villa beautifully located--with large gardens--and
thoroughly furnished inside, with the sole exception of
plate and linen; the place has every comfort and
convenience--stabling ect--for the reasonable sum of six
pounds, per week.  But this is a much larger house than          31
either your family--or mine, would require;--for half
that sum, smaller and equally elegant cottages may be
had.  The luxury of home--suggested to me, by this casual
visit--has made me wild with impatience, to be the happy
mistress of a similar abode--and this morning, my

precious husband has gone in search of one.  During the
Exhibition 'twill be next to impossible to procure
suitable apartments--so if you conclude to reside any
time, amid the bewildering joys of 'Lud's town'--let me
beg you, to locate yourselves as I advise; and if in any
way we can aid you, do not hesitate to call upon us; we
should be most happy to be of service.  In these
furnished Villas--modest conservatories are almost always
attached--well stocked with "gorgeous planets" and you
will be visited there by sunshine--rarely to be purchased
in the city.
    Mr Booth joins with me--in kindest to yourself and
Miss Graham;--give her my love--and pray don't let the
Doctor keep you in Edinburgh too long; come soon to
London.  With affectionate regard beleive me--very
sincerely Yours--
                              Mary Booth.


48: to Emma F. Cary (Players), October 1861

My dear Miss Cary.
    I have written your sister, as full an account as I
have been able to make, in the short space of time that
has elapsed, of Mr Booth's success:
    I think it will be commensurate with his pains--if
not immediately in the course of his engagement, when he
has had time and opportunity to produce his plays.
    A letter from your brother gave us excellent
accounts of himself and 'our cause'--and was most gladly
welcomed by us;--I hope and pray, he will have no reason
to change the tenor of his future correspondence and that
he may remain cheerful until the end--which it seems to
me, cannot be far off.
    With what joy you will welcome him back!--Will you
please express to Mrs Felton the great gratification her
letter gave me--and signify my intention to have written
her particularly by this steamer, but must delay it--the
time approaching now, when this must be sealed.--Tomorrow
I am going to have taken some cartes-de-visite of
myself--and in my letter to her will enclose some;
perhaps they will be as acceptable, as those taken in
Boston, though I am extremely sorry, the man Silsbee,
should have refused them.  Mr Booth so feared a liberal
circulation of them on his part--and as that would have
been very annoying, he requested that he should only give
them upon an order from me.--My health continues
excellent--but my hoped for blessing, fills me with
constant longing.  With Mr Booth's kind regards and my
own best love beleive me ever Yours
                              Mary Booth.

## 49: to Edwin Booth (NYPL—TC), 22 November 1861

A

Friday Morn.

Dear papa--I fancy I kept you company this morning--not having been up very long--and 'tis now getting on towards noon!--The reason of my laziness--that, all last night I lay awake and ↑was made↓ dreadfully nervous by the 'warring of the elements' outside.

At first, I fancied the noise was over my head, alone--and I lay trembling with fear--then, by the time I had convinced myself--that there were "no ~~ghosts~~ ↑spirits↓ stirring"--I was too wide awake to go calmly to sleep again:--besides I felt so anxious about you, darling--and by the light of~~from~~ the lamp--I could see distinctly from my bed--papa's dear dressing robe and cap I fixed my eyes intently upon them--and they seemed to quiet me, and afford protection.

Now this morning came your kiss--and that told me, that my darling had been ill while writing! this accounted to me for all my misgivings!--I hoped so to have been told this morning--when you are coming--but from your playing two peices on Saturday, I may make up my mind that I cannot see you before Monday, I suppose. Well, I will try and patient--for I am only too grateful that you can come to me then: for somehow I fancy--that 'my time' is not far distant; the nurse will come to me on the 8th--. I do not want her here, the first week you ~~were~~ ↑are↓ home. I will send you by this mail--the morning paper; to read a critique upon the 'Strand'--and also a vicious, malignant article (leader)--upon America. I only hope the North will assert properly her dignity in this last instance--the seizure of Slidell, ect.--ah! for some great and wise statesman, now! is'nt it lamentable what a derth of genius--in politics--there is in our country now. A Cabinet council' of H. M. ministers was called yesterday to look into the case of the San Jacinto--the papers all cry for war to the knife--but of course the heads of the states will act more deliberately.

I am going to write home now--perhaps for the last time, ere I become a 'little mother'; for I grow more and more fatigued every day.

I will leave the rest, my own papa--until we meet; this is the last letter I will have to send--and I hope earnestly to hear, that you may reach London ~~?~~ Sunday. God bless you dearest--and bring you safely to my heart and home.

Your longing and
expectant baby-wife.--
Mollie.

10 T

T

A
20 T

A
T
31
T
A

40

50: to Emma C. Cushman (FL—BTM), 13? January 1862

                              5 Stamford Villas
                                    Fulham
                                    London.

My darling friend
    I am so happy that I am again enabled to sit before my desk and reply to the kind and anxious solicitations of my dear friends across the sea. First letter of all that meets my eyes, and prompts a <u>first</u> reply is yours dear Emma. It came during my illness and Mr Booth withheld it, until the nurse said there was no longer fear of head-ache--and I assure you its pleasant contents did me real good.--You heard from Lucy I suppose upon her receiving Mr Booth's <u>funny letter</u> of my safe delivery and the dear treasure given me--in the form of a darling <u>daughter</u> however, not a <u>boy</u> as I so wished and hoped for. Shall I say that I suffered disappointment? no, cherie, I have forgotten that I ever felt such a pang--or ever desired aught beside what I possess.--
    This is the fifth week now, since my little blessing came--and from the hour she was born 'til the present one I have (thanks to our Heavenly Father) no unusual suffering, nor unnaturel pain to recount; all has gone thus far well with me--and my former strength is rapidly returning. My only trouble has been my breasts--and they are always so I am told with the <u>first child</u>. I can only nurse her from one side at present, but have used such care, that I have avoided that terrible affliction, "a broken breast".--Of course you would like to know how the "enfant" looks and to whom she bears resemblance.
    You know how very camelion-like they are the first month--so you would smile, I am sure at any attempt of mine, to define her features. I can only safely vouch for one beauty she has--and that is, a pair of large & splendid eyes!
    I fancy I can trace too, the likeness of her loved papa, upon her little infant brow--but another month will better decide that hope of my heart, for me. I am yet too feeble to write at any great length--though I have a thousand things to say to you, darling.--I am most anxious to know if the hope you expressed about your dear self, in your last--is indeed to be realized; oh, do take care of your health--you cannot appreciate the unmeasurable joy that awaits you--hope for it, pray for it.--Have I written you since I took possession of my little villa? I think not. Tis a cosy little nook--just big enough for Edwin, me, and the baby!--I have no trouble having excellent servants--and we are so happy and comfortable, that but for the dear and cherished faces 'on the other side', I should have no present wish to return. As it is there is no likelihood of such a thing--for Mr Booth plays again in London in the Spring

(the only proper season) and after that will make his provincial tour.  I was very much annoyed at receiving a Boston Post' with a comment upon Miss 'Edwina Booth'.  I cannot imagine who could have given publicity to such a private matter; they knew little about it--to say 'born in Manchester'--Edwin had been playing there--perhaps they meant him--could "nature so err"?  Boston will ↑ever↓ continue to recognize gossip that's certain: well we must forgive it, for all the good it otherwise does.

I have seen your Grandmama but once, since I moved to Fulham--but hope for a visit from her soon.  We have American friends--the Grahams of N. York--in London at present--and we have them a great deal with us, which renders it very home-like and delightful for me.  They go soon to the south of France--and were it not for our having taken 'til May this little Villa, we would go with them.  Next winter, if all goes well, I shall try and pass ↑it↓ there--for London is a tomb in Winter time.--I cannot allude to politics without getting very prolix and as that would seem '<u>bleu-bas</u>-ish' I will confine myself to the simple expression of my delight at the happy conclusion of the Trent affair, although the 'Times' and several other of the leading papers here still continue to misjudge the people and Government of the North--and will insist upon them being all 'unmannerly beasts.'  Oh, it is too much to bear, their insults; why, I assure you that every day in their preaambles about town, Mr Booth and Mr Graham are attacked upon the question, sometimes in a most rude and uncalled for way.  Mr G-- though he bears letters of introduction to the best people of London--fear to present them, while the present bitter feeling lasts.  I pray that all may go well with us and our cause--but as I read and ponder, at this great distance I can judge more calmly than while at home--and I must say, that I tremble for the future.--Chere amie, I have not alluded <u>particularly</u> to your health for, I trust by this time you have no cause for complaint:  what a long tedious time of suffering you must have passed--let us hope that the future may restore you, and give you additional strength--as the trying period I have just gone through often does, you know.

A little voice from my nursery falls upon my attentive ear--it has grown familiar even in this short space--and warns me to make haste.  Often now I am called from Edwin's side to minister to the wants of the little helpless one--and he bears it, as he should.  I once thought it would do harm--but I find the contrary-- leisure hours when we find ouselves alone--are more precious than ever;--see, if <u>you</u> don't find it so, darling.

Adieu, I will write Lucy soon--so tell her.  Follow my example in your next--and tell me all about yourself. Cherish and love ever, your affectionate friend
                                          Mary Booth.

My kind regards to Mr Cushman--whom I hope is in the enjoyment of health and happiness.

M.

51: to Mary L. Felton (NYPL—TC), 14 February 1862

Feb--14th/62--
London--

My dear Mrs Felton

Since my recovery we have received two welcome greetings from you--and from your dear sisters also. They should not have remained so long unanswered but that I have suffered up to the present week--with my right breast, rendering my arm too, helpless.--Aside from this I passed through no unnatural pain--and remember only my gratitude to our Heavenly Father for his watchful care, during that the most trying period, my life has ever known. My precious babe is now within two days of being ten weeks old, and though I do not pretend to have <u>yet</u> felt the full depth of maternal, love I experience already joy enough to assure me that a priceless treasure has been added to my store.--I can only nurse her from one breast--which of course is not sufficient to give proper nourishment: this was such a sad disappointment to me at first, but finding the 'feeding bottle' to agree perfectly well with her--am partly consoled for the deprivation.--Since her birth she has not taken one drop of medecine--does not this prove her health?--I would attempt--if I thought I could give you the least idea of the truth--to describe her form and features; but you know what cameleons, babies are--and perhaps before this reaches you she will change to something totally different.

The first month I was bewildered by the many colors she changed to--and from; she is fair now with the <u>bleuest eyes</u>, you can imagine; but I doubt if she is yet <u>settled</u> enough to tell you to whom she has resemblence.

I <u>will</u> have her like her papa--and the nurse agrees with me that she is; so I rest satisfied that 'tis so.--The 'Trent excitement' has all but ceased here; the tone of Parlament at its opening, assured the people that America had acted justly though tardily; but 'tis the currant belief that unless something be done by the armies of the Potomac <u>soon</u>--that England will break the blockade. The feeling against Americans is very bitter; we have friends here from New York--who were in <u>Edinburgh</u> at the commencement of the Trent business and though previously most constantly entertained--were <u>dropped</u> immediately, after that occurred. They have met with the same cold receptions here--and will not present their

London letters. I enclose you a photograph of the bust of Hawthorn, executed here, and to be paid for by subscription, begun by the English, and presented to Mr H-- as a testamonial etc;--It is now in the artist's studio waiting the small sum of five gunies to complete the amount. This 'American difficulty' came, and the most eager, lost their interest. Sir E Bulwer & Charles Dickens refused "under existing circumstances" to subscribe! this I had from the artist himself--so may rely upon its truth. I presume the feeling at home is almost as bitter.--The seeming stand-still of McClellan' army tortures us; we await the arrival of every steamer to hear the cry of Victory; and every week disappoints us.--Your brother's letters give us great pleasure, when they come; so full of hope and confidence in his Commander. May it all be fulfilled--and be he returned soon to his brave little wife, and loving friends.
    Our kindest regards to Mr Felton--and your family.-- The kindness and anxiety you have expressed for my safety--is deeply appreciated by us--and the dearest wish we entertain--is that we may live to return, and see your brother restored to his quiet home,--then pass more of those delightful days in Cambridge--which we often live over again in memory now.
                    Yours most affectionately
                            Mary Booth.
P.S--Your description of Mrs Kemble was highly amusing; but I beleive with you, that under that, too theatrical manner--is much to be esteemed and admired.


### 52: to Emma C. Cushman (FL—BTM), 26 February 1862

                              Feb 26th/62.
                          5 Stamford Villas.
                                Fulham
                                London--

My cherished friend--
    A week has passed since the receipt of your last--so full of kindness, interest, & fondness, for me.
    I have read it again & again--feeling redoubled confidence in the precious friendship I had formed, through that most magnetic, of all sources--Charlotte Cushman--your dear Aunty.--Yes--at this great distance I think I have a right to boast of the deep sympathy engendered not a year ago, and steadily on the increase. Oh, cherie, how my heart craves to unfold to you, all it feels for, and desires to impart to you!--The new and precious interest I have in life--you are about to share; and while sitting talking over, and fashioning, those

tiny <u>garments</u>--I would tell you how wonderfully dear will be to you the treasure they will enfold.  For you cannot realize <u>now</u> to the full extent your future bliss.

You complain that I did not in my last say more about myself during that short period of indescribable suffering: well I thought it best not to pain you by a recital of what awaited you; but now let me assure you that I suffered much less than I expected--and if I may judge by the weakness ~~of~~ which followed after your <u>misfortune</u>--last Spring--can safely assure you that you have gone through worse.

But pray, darling--take my advice--and I entreat you to receive it as the best that can be offered; take plenty of exercise--even up to the last hour--if possible.

I know perfectly well the scrupples that will prevent you--"I look such a figure" &c;--but never mind what 'people say'--ride out of town, and then <u>walk</u>, <u>walk</u>, <u>walk</u>!--The result of out-door exercise with me--~~has been~~ ↑was↓--a natural birth--and the most healthy little babe, a fond Mother could wish for.  Since her ~~coming~~ 'arrival' here one drop of foreign substance has not passed her lips; is not this a proof of her health?--If you are careful <u>now</u>--sleep well--eat well--and regularly--beleive me, dear, <u>she</u> will do the same.--My precious is almost as regular in her <u>habits</u>, as a grown person; and she never cries unless she wants something!  now is'nt <u>she</u> an Utopian baby.--Did I write you of the trouble I have had with my breasts?

the one affected is not well yet; though I suffer none, now.  My sad regret is that I could not nurse her. I told you ~~perhaps~~--I think, that I had milk in one breast: well, about a week since, she refused to take it and fought vehemently (very un-Utopian then I assure you)--and I was obliged to give up in despair, my attempt to <u>keep</u> my milk; so she feeds now entirely from the bottle, and is better for it the Dr says.  My darling friend I have no doubt that you are warned 'to do this,' and 'to do that', to your breasts <u>beforehand</u>: beleive it not dear Emma: I <u>did</u> <u>everything</u>.  If you have no nipples now--there must naturally be difficulty until the baby draws them.  I hope you may avoid all this; but I could not help writing you of my utter disbelief in all <u>preventatives</u>--for my credulity was so dreadfully imposed upon.--I see you or fancy I can, clearly--in your cozy library sourrounded by all sorts of delicate fabrics--your husband in the evening, with his anxious heart, full of joy in the future--overlooking you!  But when little <u>Charlotte</u> comes--ah, then--like a tale--↑though↓ no more--"to be continued" fills him with painful expectancy--the <u>romance</u> is not ended--no, just begun--beleive me.  A wife does not really appreciate the holy tie--until she is a Mother; and I speak from what my ↑own↓ heart has convinced me.  But you will soon know it all--so, I will not anticipate what it is impossible to describe.--I would like to give you a full account of my

'nursery proceedings'--but I fear to weary you; not so
much by the "twice told tale"--but I have some little
consideration for your present health--and to read much
of my miserable writing would I fear, task too much your
patience.--But I have a deal to say yet--so bear with
me.--I spend all the day in the nursery ~~with~~--and the
evenings with Mr Booth down stairs. this prevents a
great deal of jealousy as you will find when the time
comes.

    Not nursing her gives me more freedom than most
Mothers have:--perhaps 'tis fortunate, for you know how
much Edwin craves of my time; and I should be sorry to
deprive him of his sole companion.--He is very fond of
our baby as you might suppose but is so afraid to 'handle
her' lest, as he says, he should 'break her'. We have
beautiful gardens around our cottage--and every day the
nurse takes her out. As soon as she is big enough to be
photographed--you shall see her as she is!--Don't fancy
dear, that I bore all my correspondents as ~~unp~~
unmercifully as I have you with 'baby progress': no, I
am almost selfish in my joy--for I scarcely ever show her
to visitors--unless pressed to do so--and for a young
mother--that is something unusual.

    But you are interested now, I know and everything
pertaining to what you are soon to enjoy--will I'm sure
be welcome.--I have been quite anxious about your Grand
mother, I sent her a note after my recovery--but have not
heard from her since. Miss Cushman, I am glad to know is
better: will she be in London, do you know in the
Spring?--The Exhibition is nearly completed: I can see it
plainly from our windows. London is pretty full and
since my illness, I have gone about a good deal. The
feeling against Americans is softening gradually.--On the
22nd a large breakfast was given by the Americans in
London;--Mr Booth was there, and was agreeably
entertained.--I enjoyed so much the news you gave me of
what was going on in Boston. Be sure and write me how
successful the private-theatricals were; especally Mrs
Sandford's.--Do you like Miss Field? is she very
clever?--entre nous all this.--Boston--how I long to see
it--but 'twill probably be some time before we return.--

    I have left almost to the last--the acknowledgement
of your little present to baby. Beleive me 'twas not
through forgetfulness--but simply, that I have so much to
say--that I hardly knew when I commenced this letter--how
or where I should end.--<u>You</u> give such sweet and clear
expression to your thoughts and interest for me; but <u>I</u> am
conscious of the confused and 'jumbled' style of all <u>my</u>
epistles. The tiny chain of gold I put immediately on
her neck--and she shall be taught to lisp 'Aunt Emma' &
to love her too.--I will probably have an opportunity
soon of sending over a little parcel to 70 Pinckney St.
It will contain, darling, only a few <u>useful</u> little
things--which I do not beleive you can get on the other
side. Now that a mother's <u>care</u> is before a mother's
<u>vanity</u>--I can appreciate and recommend the <u>useful</u> as well

as the ornamental--Your little ↑knitted↓ shirts--were
used immediately; the smaller ones: and they are ↑so↓
cunning on her. I must write Lucy by this mail:--she
sends me such confusing, funny letters--just like
herself--full of frolic.--
    I shall want to know constantly of your welfare.--    130
April will soon be here! may it bring all the joy and    T
more than you can anticipate. My regards to Mr
Cushman--I hope he is with you again ere this. Accept my
warmest love and sympathies for yourself darling and
write me all you feel and think about the approaching
time.
    Mr Booth sends his kindest remembrances to Mr
Cushman--and yourself.
                    Ever affectionately yours
                          Mary Booth.


## 53: to Edwin Booth (Players), 28 February 1862

I try so hard to write                                      T
plain--can you read all I            Friday Morn.
write?--God bless.                        9 P.M.

    Two letters from you this morning, dear papa! how    T
loving & kind in you to write after the play--as fatigued
as you were too.--Every day I am more & more convinced of
our wisdom in taking this little house; and as it is
about the only wise thing we can boast of ↑having done in
England↓--I continue to expatiate upon ↑it↓ you
see.--What folly it would have been for me to have gone    A
with you. I must not be like Mrs Davenport--who follows    A
the example of Ruth (of biblical fame) to the letter: but
with a more jealous eye, I fancy than that most pious and    10
confiding lady. I will await your return to my bosom,
darling with all the patience that your truth & fondness
deserves.--I sent off your things yesterday, with a
'petit baiser'--Just as your telegram came--a carriage
stopped at the gate--& to my great surprise the Grahams    A
walked in! a party on the tapis at Mr Mowett's caused    T
them to wait over--& they came to take me to the
Horticultural Gargdens. I had ordered a cab to take me    A
to town & it was at the door; so that I was completely
confused (that's very bad English, I know)--& could not    20
exactly make out what you meant by 'getting a
basket'--'til 'twas too late to procure one. I did not
go with the Grahams--for I had several little things to
do--& they never think of anyone but themselves, so I
declined. They expect me today to say 'good bye'--but
'tis too cold & I shall do 'the polite' by a note. I
will send the 'four Georges' to day by mail--you will    A

have to read on Sunday. I finished it last night. There are some curious pictures there: and ↑when↓ we compare the wonderful improvement in men & manners since George the fourth's time in England--with the frightful degeneration in America, since the truest & most nobe George's time--in patriots & loyal men--it is heart-sickening is it not?--Thackery is a splendid raconteur;--if Badeau could only write like him.--I purchased yesterday two other books: one little "book of ballads" by Thackery: I wanted to learn for your darling some verses which Horace Mayhew sang to a valse tune, at the Mathews's. "The old mahogany tree" they are called: & will just your humour I know.--The other was ↑is↓ a most useful book:--every french noun--in english as well--& illustrated all through. It will serve my baby after she grows up--& is just what Mama need now.--Then I bought some beautiful songs to learn for you, & what do you think? I have the piano in the dining room! oh, it is so pleasant for me now. I got a little Swiss clock too--& paid £,12 for it: don't think me extravagant papa dear--for I have not had to get scarcely anything for the house. Ann says it is much cheaper living than having Mrs Andrews here--& I am of her opinion.--How remarkable must be the sympathy between? us dear Edwin: what was my surprise to read in your letters this morning things that I have already written you: for instance--your back paining you.--I sent you that complaint yesterday:--then your fears about baby--and in the same letter yesterday I beleive, I told you how confident I felt in her little life being spared to us. Our dreams too are troubled--& I have told you some of mine. Is'nt it strange? isn't it all because we love so well?--I don't think you need regret much the loss of the Provences: you would only lose money & strength. How happy I am that your leg is better: do pray be careful of yourself--for the sake of the dear ones in Stamford Villa. I went into Mrs Duflux's yesterday about the gas bill: found her as pleasant as usual--and her father will attend to the bill for me.--

I was up, & dressed the baby this morning!!!--this I am going to continue--for I find Nurse a little careless: but we can't find then perfection--& my only plan is to do for the darling myself.

I have nothing to tell you about the little blossom, except that she is well & grows dearer to me every hour. Ah papa she is the holiest tie we could have--for you even seem dearer, since she came.--I have learnt such a sweet song: loved for its appropriateness now: "I'm alone, I'm alone"--from the Lily of Killarney-- --
 "All things round me seem to say
That I am sad, & so are they;--
But could I see my heart's delight
His smile would cheer the gloom of night
The shade on my soul would be cleared ↑away↓
And my heart would leap to the glorious ↓day."↑

Eily sings it, & 'tis so mournful & pathetic.--I
have seen no one--of our few friends--since you left:
Macnair I suppose will be here on Sunday. Are you
going to wait for Captain Anderson to send home by? if
so let me know for I should like to send Emma Cushman
that little parcel I spoke of.--I must write a
congratulatory letter to John--and in it say what I think
of his kindness etc.--We have had no squabbles Ann nor
I;--she came to me yesterday for: £2-6 for the ring she
lost; I told she must pay for it herself: just as a
lesson. I will make it up to her though before we leave,
if she behaves well.--I long to see you that I may tell
you more than I can write about the Mathews's. 'Twas so
dull to me--that I looked over books of his the whole
evening. She asked if I was not terribly bored; I said
no, of course--but took the opportunity offered--of
saying how you would have been had you been there; how
you hated society etc. So do I--said she--"we live
almost entirely alone." I took everything in that I
might retail it to you.--They wanted me to go there--
either the Teusday or Thursday of this week--but I
thought it more prudent to stay away. In fact I
regretted exceedingly--going ther without you on Sunday.
I made up my mind firmly--never to go any where again
without my darling husband.--God bless you my own: I
can't write again--for you to receive it--before Sunday:
so take from this double comfort--double love--& a heart
full of tender thoughts for you. Kisses from little
Totty--kisses from me--per dozen.--The pain in my back is
better--I hope yours will be.--I will send you money as
soon as I receive the check.
    God bless again & again.
                                    Your fond little wife
                                          Mollie.
P.S--
    Play a strong bill for your benefit: you may get
enough to bring you home. Poor baby, don't be
discouraged.




54: to Edwin Booth (Players), 2 March 1862

                                  Sunday Afternoon

Dearest Edwin mine--
    I have read the weeks reviews--dressed myself & now
sit down for a little chat with you: feeling much more
cheerful even in my loneness than I did this time a week
ago--with the sorrow of parting from you before me. This
time next Sunday I hope to see & welcome you home. Can
you leave on that day?--Miss Corbyn was here to dinner

with me yesterday: I called there & she came back with
me.
    I was astonished by Mrs Corbyn's account of Avonia
Jones. "Is it not disgraceful, that a fine girl like
her, should be publicly <u>living</u> with such a man as
Brooke".--Edwin do you think it can be true, that she is
so guilty? Of course it is just as bad in the eyes of
the world--as though she really did. Macnair called last
evening: full of delight about the 'Post' notice. He
wrote to the 'N. Y Post' ~~last~~ yesterday--& quoted the
best part of the article. Also made mention of the
'Breakfast'--& gave Boughton & Kuntzie 'a word,' each.
    Papa dear, I heard something yesterday which I know
not, whether, will comfort or discomfort you: but I have
already made-up my mind to chance the former from it. It
is of 'my lord William' then: it seems that he was the
young sprig of nobility who married & was soon after
divorced from--Miss Peyton, the actress--afterwards Mrs
Wood the singer.--Miss Corbyn--who seems to know
everything & every body--spoke of "that ugly nonce Lord
Lennox": and for the moment I never thought to question
her; but I did a second or two after: "ah, he is a horrid
old wretch," said she--only associates with theatricals,
& goes to Cremorne three nights out of the week." Of
course I was silent upon <u>my</u> ever having seen him: but it
made me 'boil with anger', at Mrs Mathews, & her 'Sunday
night'. She told me herself that <u>Horace Mayhew</u> was a
"great villian": which I took to mean rouè: and I was
obliged to insult him two or three times during the
evening--to hush his compliments etc (insults I looked
upon them ↓as).--↑Now this dear papa--I never intended
naming to you: for fear 'twould make you unnecessarily
~~unf~~ uncomfortable--for you know how well I can take care
of myself--& that I would not allow of any undue
familiarity from any person. Though, understand me
darling, <u>none was offered me</u>: only Mr Mayhew is that kind
of man--whom you would have me never meet if possible--&
if it could not be helped, <u>polite</u> only. <u>Now</u>, for the
<u>comfort</u> to be derived from <u>this</u>: I will see Mrs Mathews &
tell her that I have heard since of the character of her
guests that Sunday--& I am astonished that she should
have invited me to meet such people: especially allowed
me to be there without my husband. And, that having been
betrayed <u>once</u> into such companionship I will never trust
again. I will say too, how ingignant <u>you</u> are about it.
Would that be the best way to <u>get</u> rid of them?--I enclose
Kuntzie's letter--I forgot it yesterday also the
photograph.--Oh, darling, how I did miss you, this Sunday
morning: no one to be cross with--& then kiss & make up
to! aren't you glad--that I'm paying penance for all my
late misdemeanours?--In the papers this week, there is an
evident change in the tone towards America. You have
read I suppose that Earl Russel considers the blocade
"sufficiently effective": this, together with the most
favorable accounts from the North--is beginning to prove
how earnest is the cause they are struggling for.--The

people at home are clamouring for 'heavier taxation' is
this not the greatest proof of their loyalty? ~~of~~ There
was a long article in the Telegraph yesterday--about the
morbid taste for the 'sensational' in Theatricals at
present: which for your comfort darling, I wish I had to
send you--Macnair told me of it. All complain of the
same bad taste; won't you rejoice when the "Boucicault's"
are 'ousted'. I see the Florences names on the bills at
the Princess's again. The Keans have begun again; but
the papers say little or nothing of their performances.--
I think the Grahams are gone--for I have seen, nor heard
nothing from them.--Mr G. told me that Boughton found the
most fearful anachronisms in Macnair's play: & told him
of them. For instance--'Calconery' is spoken of--and
there was no such thing known in Athens. So they advised
him to 'Athensanize' his play--or he would be treated
unmercifully by the critics. Mr G, ? advised him to go
to the British Museum, where he could find all the
authorities he wanted--and sent him his ticket for the
reading-room. This kindness Macnair told me of--but
never named having read his play to our friends.--
                            After dinner.

Mutton & Jerusalem artichokes:--but such a dull meal! I
hope you are not alone to day--darling: isn't it
miserable? God knows what I should do if away from you
long, papa.
     Your scarf & 'Raphael' hang in the hall--looking so
like you--that every time I go out--I fancy you near
me.--I must tell you of a newly discovered likeness to
you, in our little precious darling: last night--playing
with her--we saw her scalp move just like yours:--now
isn't she papa's baby! and your likeness that I
wear--she looks at for hours (or minutes) so intently--&
coo's so prettily to it--that I cannot but think she
knows it. Now papa is not that a precious recompense,
for all my world of thought of you, before she came to
bless & smile upon us.--
     The Nurse's "young man" has just come from the
country. She confided to me the fact that he was
'a-com'in' & that has not seen him for four months; so I
have allowed him to go up stairs to see her. I suppose
I'm shut out from the nursery for a little while now--so
will go on with my French--which I have studied
constantly since your absence. Will you 'Licher mei'
when you come home, dear?--If you can possibly reache
here next sunday--you will do so won't you? (Any home
letters that come, I will send immediately.
     I think you were wise about Hudson playing. I have
enough money to last me--til you come--but you had best
write a check for me to draw for you. I hope you will
make your expenses before you leave anyway. My letters
are necessarily uninteresting forgive them--for the love
they carry with them. evr your little love.
                                Mollie.

55: to Mary L. Felton (Players), 22 March 1862

>London. March 22nd
>1862.

My dear Mrs Felton--
    The last steamer brought us your sister Emma's letter announcing to us the sad, irreparable loss, you have suffered. The unexpected intelligence smote us with the deepest gloom. But the tone of your dear sister's mournful missive, expressed so much resignation & Christian fortitude, that we are assured you bear with becoming sorrow the deep affliction with which God has been pleased to visit you. Surrounded in that hour of trial by the most tender, loving sympathizers we hope that you were upheld & strengthened.
    Fortunately the journals did not reach us 'til after one had spoken to us from the very heart of your sorrow; she told us all; & need I say how truly we sympathize with you in your grief.--The illness of your children too must have surely tasked you; but I pray they may be entirely recovered ere this reaches you, and prove to you, in the future, that blessing & comfort which they cannot fail to be.--I will tell you something of my precious baby now, for whom you have expressed so much anxiety & delight. Her large bright eyes, & cunning look--would win your smile, I'm sure, could you but see her now. She has just been vaccinated & has recovered finely from it. Her first protection against the ills of life. I am making her pretty short frocks now, & next month will have her likeness taken & send to her Cambridge friends.--Mr Booth writes regularly to your brother Richard. We expect soon to hear of the movement, of his camp; & no doubt he will rejoice--for it must be extremely tedious to a soldier to remain so long inactive. The last message from the President has filled all our hearts on this side with hope that the terrible strife will soon end. London is dull & we grow very tired of it. We will go to the Continent soon & greet with thankful hearts a sky somewhat like our own.
    We long to return home, but Mr Booth must accomplish what he came here for; though 'tis difficult for them to overlook, & forgive him for being an American.--The Spring is quite upon us here: the lilacs in my pretty garden, are all in blossom & the tiny spring violets begin to peep from out their beds.--We live ~~beyond~~ ↑out of↓ the sickly air & smoky streets of London--& have the sun oftener to cheer & enliven us.
    I will not intrude longer upon your time & patience, my dear friend:--give my kindest love to your children--& accept the heartfelt wishes of myself & husband for your comfort & happiness.
    I wrote you some time ago--& fear now that it went to ↑&↓ met you in the midst of your grief.--I would not for the world that it should have intruded at such a

time.  I shall be most anxious to hear of your welfare &
the childrens.  With kind regards to all your family &
believe me dear lady--
                    Yours with deep sympathy
                              & affection
                                   Mary Booth.



56: to Emma F. Cary (Players), 26 March 1862


                         London--March 26th
My dear friend
     I thank you sincerely for imparting to us the sad
intelligence ↑of the loss↓ you were so unexpectedly
called upon to suffer.  By the last steamer I sent a few
lines to your dear afflicted sister; but they carry but
feebly the deep sympathy with which our hearts run over.
We read your account of his illness & suffering before
receiving any of the journals.  Your resignation under
this heavy affliction was most consoling to us & lulled
into partial quiet the deep anxiety the first
announcement caused in our breasts for Mrs Felton.
     We trust now to the love of her children & the
precious care sure to be lavished upon her by you & all
who cherish her--to find her restored again to happiness
& comfort.--How sadly your brother Richard will feel to
find the 'vacant chair' when he returns.  I presume his
stern duties forbade his being at home with you during
the time.  He valued & appreciated Mr Felton as well as
loved him.  I know from all that I have heard him say to
Mr Booth.--Your anxiety for <u>him</u> has just begun in
earnest, has it not?--for we read that on the 22nd the
army was to march!--You cannot realize our impatience on
this side to know the result.  England has quite softened
in her tone towards the North--but their recent victories
alone have caused the change;--at a defeat now I think
they would rejoice.--The only wish I have now to remain a
little while longer in London--is for my darling babe to
get strong enough to bear the tossing about, she is
likely to get--in travelling about.  She continues to
improve every day--& every day, aye, <u>every hour</u>, we
discover some new beauty; to descant upon, or some
trifling movement, that produces <u>wonder</u> & <u>astonishment</u>
from her papa & myself.  Her deep blue eyes are full of
expression: you remember I wrote to you my hope that
they should turn out <u>black</u>; but now I am satisfied to
have them as they are.--The first week in April I shall
have her photographed & send her to Cambridge.
     Mr Booth was in Paris for a couple of days--last
week: & was enchanted by the magnificence of all he saw.

We leave here to go there for the month of May--unless he
should decide upon acting here again which he has in
contemplation.  Of the many theatres in London only <u>one</u>
receives tragedians & there Monsieur Fechter is engaged
permenently.  The public here have surely eaten of the
"insane root"--for the taste for legitimate acting is
woefully perverted.  The press unanimously protest
against the introduction of sensational peices--but with
no effect:  The actor leaps from a precipice, or jumps
head-long into the water--& the people go & applaud &
enjoy.  No doubt they would like it much better if in
reality the person should lose his life.  If the morbid
taste increases nothing less will satisfy them I'm
sure.--I enclose you the photograph of a head, sculpured
by a clever artist here, of Mr Booth.  I am more pleased
with it than any~~thing~~↑one↓ ever taken of him.--I shall be
most eager to hear of Mrs Felton's & the children's
welfare & rely upon your goodness to let me know.
    Spring is with us here, & the gardens are beginning
to look lovely.  You know how beautiful the flowers in
England are.  Excuse I beg this poor letter: I have
procrastinated, until I am forced now to make great haste
for the mail.  Our kindest love to all, especially to Mrs
Felton:  will you please say to Mrs Cary I will write her
next week all about my baby.  Is little Georgie well?
Kiss her for me.
                    Ever effectionately Yours
                                    Mary Booth.




57: to Emma C. Cushman (FL—BTM), 12 April 1862


                                    April 12th/62.
                                    5 Stamford Villas
                                            Fulham
                                            London.

My darling friend
    May I yet greet you happy Mother?--I have been most
anxious about you ever since April began; & would have
written sooner, but I have had so many letters to write
to our friends in Cambridge upon the death of Prof
Felton--that the sad task--quite unfitted me for writing
upon so joyous a subject as the one now in question.  I
hope by this time you have your little treasure in your
arms; but in case my wish be unfulfilled, rely dear Emma
upon my deepest sympathy in your hour of suffering.
    In my last I mentioned my desire to send you some
'useful little articles' for the pet: but meeting with a
lady friend from America who said, "why my dear Mrs Booth
those things are to procured at home"--I abandoned my

cherished proposal:--for I know that you have in
readiness everything for use & comfort--long perhaps
before mine could reach you.  Paris ~~then~~ now must furnish
'quelque chose jolie' for our little one.
  How I do yearn now to go home to see yours & to
introduce to <u>her</u> my precious babe.  The 1st of May ~~he~~
↑we↓ leave here for Paris; there to remain until we are
tired; a period not likely soon to arrive--after the
wretched dullness of London.  Tomorrow the great event
will be inaugurated of my baby in short clothes.  For
several weeks her nurse's hands & my own have been busy
preparing for it--& I have the satisfaction today of
seeing all in readiness.  The weather is mild enough &
they thrive so much better out of long clothes.  On
Tuesday she is to be photographed--so by the next steamer
you may expect Miss Edwina!--There is a boat-race between
the Oxford & Cambridge students today & I can scarcely
concentrate my thoughts--for the turmoil in the road; for
we live close to Putney Bridge--the scene where it will
take place--& the Fulham Road, you know is the great
outlet from London.
  I have not heard from Lucy for some time; is she
well?--About a week since I drove over to see your
Grand mama; but to my great disappointment she was in
Liverpool.  I shall go again, however before I leave.
Your Aunty will be here for the Exhibition I suppose: if
so I shall see her.  Our Country has no space allotted
them--& all at Rome exhibit in the Roman department.
  The American artists here are dreadfully annoyed by
the neglect of our Government.  They are now trying to
collect from the Americans in London a £1,000 for the
purpose of ornamenting the small space, which the English
have very kindly allowed them--from their own.  I cannot
bear to give up my pretty cottage, just as the flowers
are coming & the pleasant weather.  But Mr Booth went to
Paris for a couple of days, & came back so enchanted with
the place--that we are eager to get there.--I heard
Dickens read the other night; & was most sadly
disappointed: for to hear him, had been always, the
dearest wish of my heart.  But I blame those who
described him so enthusiastically rather than him: for he
is certainly over rated.--The Operas are in full
blast:--& I see Miss Kellogg will soon appear.  She has
much to contend against--so if she succeeds, her credit ?
will be all the greater.  They wisely do not announce her
as from America--for that would surely have ruined her:
the feeling is so bitter against the "'orrid Yankees."--
The news of our glorious victories at home however, will
I earnestly hope, clear their minds completely of the
misapprehensions regarding us--which they have so long &
so <u>willingly</u> laboured under.  John Bull is ever on the
side of the successful ones--& the 'Monitor' has quite
astonished them & woke them too to a sense of their own
danger.
  How are all ~~my~~ ↑our↓ friends in Boston?  <u>you</u> are
their especial charge now I trust: & if none of your

nearer & dearer relatives are with you--I have no doubt
but you will find in the warm friendship of those around
you, every sympathy & kind attention.--Dear child--even
while I write you may be suffering! for your health
threatened to be so delicate.--Be very careful, cherie, &
don't get up too soon.  I am so well & have never had the
least trouble--all owing to the good nursing I received
Now as soon as you can--write me all about yourself--&
'little Charlotte.'  Adieu my darling friend.--Give my
kind regards to Mr Cushman whom I trust is well.  Tell
him how admirably Mr Booth could sympathize with him were
he near him now.  Remember us kindly to all our friends
who are yours & let me hear from you very soon.
                    Beleive me your anxious
                         loving friend
                                    Mary Booth
P.S--
     Im trying, most foolishly to separate the sheet--you
see I have torn it.  As I am pressed for time please
pardon it.  per
(Bankers) M. Adreess.  Care of ↑John↓ Munroe & Co--5 Rue
de la Paix--Paris: we will be there in two weeks.



58: to Emma C. Cushman (FL—BTM), 11 May 1862


   I have blotted this      our address--Care of Munroe & Co
& am almost                                         Bankers
ashamed to send                            5 Rue de la Paix.
it.  I hope you will
excuse the untidy                        Paris--May 11th/62.
appearance.

My dear friend Emma--
     Every day since my arrival here--& even before
quitting London--my firm intention has been to sit down &
send to you, cherie, my greeting: for ere this you must
be a 'Mama' & let me hope, a happy one.  That you cannot
fail to be--if your own health has not suffered too
severely.  Is it not worth all the pain--to hold in your
arms the little one?  oh! I am so anxious to know what it
is!--but believe me--you will love it just as well--if it
is a boy--as though your wish for another Charlotte to be
born, had been fulfilled.--
     I have thought of you every day for weeks past; &
said to Mr Booth a dozen times a day--"I wonder if Emma's
baby has yet come"!  We are in the gayest capital of the
world now; but I doubt very much if anything I could tell
you regarding it would interest you or engage your
thoughts for a moment, away from home; made so recently a
new world to you.  How I should like to have seen

you--the day after! I am writing now with my heart full
of ↑the↓ hope--that you came safely through. If so, you
will be convalescent when this reaches you; & as soon as
you are able, I hope to hear from your dear self, all
about the dread & anxious time; from the beginning to the
end.--I left stupid old London--with a mixed feeling of
sorrow & gladness.--My little villa just began to assume
a more cheerful aspect. The gardens looked so
inviting--& I had become thoroughly innitiated into the
deep & uninteresting mysteries of housekeeping; which was
very <u>Dora-like</u> at first I assure you.
    Here, everything is 'toujours gai' you know: but I
was so fearful of changing my darling baby's food; which
in London was so excellent. But I lost no time here in
procuring the very best milk--& I am happy to say--she
thrives just as well--as in her little nursery at
Stamford Villa. Mr Booth's parental affection increases
rapidly.--to be best accounted for, perhaps--by the
fact--that the little pet never cries--but is ↑as↓
smiling & happy as a little bird--the live long day.
Pray, my darling friend--avoid all the old fashioned
ideas of dosing for colic = etc: which most nurses
imagine the sole cause of a crying spell. 'Tis the
continual giving of what is termed soothing
syrup--&c--that worries the child--& brings on all sorts
of disorders. Nature is the best nurse. Are you able to
nurse, yourself?--if so you know that everything depends
upon yourself.--The change of air from London--gave my
Edwina a slight cold: being the first she ever had--I
was alarmed; but resisted my desire to give her "a
'little something". for it. The next day--her little
bowels were slightly disordered--<u>for the first time</u>,
<u>also</u>; but I waited to see if all would come right again;
& my patience was fully repaid: for by the evening--her
cold had disappeared & all. Nature requires no urging.
    I had a note from your Grand mama, the other day.
She was not well enough to see me before I left. She
spoke of you--& expressed her hope that she was a Grand
mother.
    I wonder if your Aunty will pass through Paris, this
summer? As yet--we have seen but little, of this
wonderful place. We don't like making a toil of
pleasure--& as we are likely to remain here two months at
least--we enjoy ourselves leisurely. The Theatres of
course will be attended to all in due time. We were
fortunate enough to see Le Maitre--the actor in his great
rôle of Don Ceaser:--the poor old man--has lost almost
the power he once possessed: but there remains still all
the grace of action--& the most of his great
originality;--so, that made up in a great measure--for
what younger men possess; voice & elasticity of action.
Ristori, I expect will be here; & we await her appearance
with anxiety. Yesterday we spent a delightful day at
Pere la Chaise. You know the great interest it
possesses; so I will not offer any ↑superfluous↓
description.--

I find here all that I could hope or wish for, in the shape of baby clothes.--You will be ready to look at & enjoy them--when I return; for by that time you will have your darling in short clothes.

They look so pretty--when that time arrives.--Lucy has quite neglected me of late: although I expect every day now a letter from her, announcing to me your condition. I shall be annoyed, most dreadfully if I don't hear soon.--We are worse off here for news--than in London. Mr Booths ↑can↓ only see the journals at his Banker's; & after a long walk there--before breakfast--arrives to find every one taken up--by anxious absentees like himself.

We have not yet made up our minds when to return.--At all events Edwin has no thought of acting in England again. Tragedy is dead there. Next season all the old standard Theatres change hands: for there are all losing money. Except Mr Sothern who is very successful in 'Lord Dundreary.' That speaks well for the taste of the legitimate. Mr Booth has no ambition to act for nothing--and to make any money now in England is out of the question. The prejudice against Americans is very great--at this present time.

I have had one letter from dear Mrs Felton of Cambridge, since her husband's death. She is resigned & more cheerful than we expected.--I long to get home again. My only anxiety now is to secure here a good french nurse. Have you a competent one? Tis a difficult thing to find in America.--Now, dear child--I must close.--Let me hear soon from you--& pray be generous & tell me <u>all</u>; for I shall not rest satisfied 'til I hear from yourself. The photograph I enclose is very bad of <u>me</u>: but pretty good of the baby. I took off her little shoes--& you see how her feet look. Don't imagine I look as hidieus as the in the picture. 'Tis only a Mother's anxiety that overshadows my face. I shall sit here & send you a better one.

My love to all & a thousand kisses to it.

      Evr your affectionate
       friend
         Mary.

59: to Mary L. Felton (Players), 13 May 1862

The photograph I enclose--is
very bad: but I have promised
so long to send it--that I will
ask you to accept this, until
I have a better one taken
which I will have here.           Paris--May 13th--1862
    Baby's toes--are the
most prominet feature!

My dear Mrs Felton.
    On the 1st we bade farewell to our cosy little Villa
in London.--Not without a pang of regret neither--
although I was about to visit, this most charming
capital.  There my little one first saw the light: &
↑there↓ my first initiation into the duties of
housekeeping took place.  Very Dora-like it was at the
beginning, I assure you.  But I kept constantly in mind
the fatal experience of the poor little 'child wife'--&
avoided in consequence many of the deceipts, so
successfully practised upon her.
    Paris, I like very much; but the two months which we
have made up our minds to pass here--will thoroughly
content me.  Our desire is, of course to travel; but I
fear for my little one.  'Tis so inconvenient to carry
with me, just the proper food for her & still more
difficult to find it--while travelling.  Thus far she has
done well enough; better than I could have expected,
after so great a change, as from London.  She is the
dearest comfort we have ever yet known on earth.  God
grant, I may be permitted to take her safely home.--This
glad return--will take place in August--we think:  Mr
Booth is tired of everything connected with his
profession in England.
    The Theatres are all very badly supported & Tragedy
especially--droops her head.  'Tis much to be regretted
that he came here just at the time he did.  The
predjudice strong against the 'Yankee'--& the public
surfeited with Shakespeare.--He has borne up bravely
under his disappointment, however--& the experience has
benefitted him wonderfully: so, on the whole, we ought
rather to rejoice than complain.--
    My heart leaps with joy at the very thought of <u>home</u>.
My earnest prayer is that no ↑other↓ sad~~der~~ change ~~?~~
↑shall↓ take place in the homes of those so dear to us.
    We look with intense anxiety--at each day's account
of the war at home.
    Do you hear often from your brother?  Mr Booth
writes him, as usual--but cannot expect, now that we
suppose him to be in action, any reply.
    Your account of his dear little wife's health, quite
alarmed me.  I trust nothing serious is the matter.  Her
anxiety must be torturing.--Ah, when we return--I indulge
in the hope--that we may be able to have the little home

near yours, that you speak of in your letter.
    You will be very happy in your new home--I hope. In every letter I have intended asking of Mrs Shaw's little baby. Tell me of it--I am so interested in the little ones now.
    Your own dear children are all well, I trust & your own welfare what my heart desires it should be.
    I beg you will pardon the lack of interest in this: but really our pleasures & persuits here, are so ~~eff~~ ephemeral--they are not worth the reading. 'I have but one desire now--that is to get through the 'sight seeing' toil as soon as possible--& return to our dear home across the seas. Give my affectionate regards to <u>all your family</u> & Mrs Agassiz's. Mr Booth joins with me & begs that you will let us know any important news which concerns your brother & his friend. Ever affectionately yours
                                    Mary Booth


60: to Mary L. Felton (NYPL—TC), early September 1862

My dear Mrs Felton
    I will go to you tomorrow--but cannot say wheather Edwin can or not--for he is still asleep.
    I think it probable that he will however, unless business prevents him. I am very anxious to see you: this weather makes me dull & sad. I could smile though if I were at Cambridge.
                            Affectionately Yours
                                    Mary Booth.
Monday Morning


61: to Mary L. Felton (NYPL—TC), 10 September 1862

Fifth Ave Hotel.
                                    New York Sept
                                            10th
My dear Mrs Felton
    Your letter giving us the particulars of your brother's death, reached us yesterday. Upon our arrival we went immediately to Philadelphia, & not until our return to New York did we learn of the brave spirit that had fled! Mr Booth wrote the same day to the darling wife; but he could not express to her or to anyone his

sorrow for the loss of the precious friendship he was
permitted to enjoy. Your brother's influence & advice
had great effect upon my husband's life. His
encouragement & appreciation he bestowed upon Edwin when
he stood in need of both & I know how much it did to
soothe & brighten his troublesome path. I was the first
to break the sad news to him--& he wept like a child.
But soon his face brightened--& he said to me--"I wonder
if it was not a p happy releif to Dick he must have been
so weary".
    All that you wrote us was very comforting--for we
could ↑learn↓ nothing of the manner of his death. But
from all sides--the same reply to anxious enquiries--"he
suffered & died nobly". The valiant never taste of death
but once; & for him the bitterness is passed. There
remains to you, his loved ones--the consciousness of his
bravery & noble sacrifice.
    Mr Booth will write you himself today--℮ & give you
directions for the letter you have for him--that it may
reach him safely.
    My little one has been ill & my time I have had to
devote to her constantly since my arrival. You will
pardon the brevity of this, & the poor expressions of
sympathy it contains. I wish I could write all ↑which↓
our loss suggests, & my heart prompts.--Give my dearest
love to Mrs Cary. What comfort & solace she must find in
her little daughter now. We will visit Boston as soon as
we possibly can.
    I long to see & talk with you. Mr Booth joins me in
kind remembrances to all your family.
                                Yours ever sincerely
                                    Mary Booth

## 62: to Mary L. Felton (Players), 22 September 1862

                                New York--Sept. 22nd
My dear Mrs Felton.
    Your letter enclosing the one of your dear brother,
Mr Booth received. It was begun in May. He had been
performing the most arduous duties, but his brave
enduring spirit breathed throughout--No wonder ↑his↓
Colonel & men loved him. It was hard for us while
perusing his letter to beleive that the hand was forever
stilled which penned it. It terminated abruptly, making
the precious relic doubly sad. Your sister Emma wrote me
the mournful particulars, related by Mrs Cary's brother.
They must have given some comfort to her poor grief
stricken heart mournful as they were. Her letter to Mr
Booth breathed the sweetest patience; her courage under

the heavy sorrow, must set an example to you all.--Poor little Georgie & her innocent questionings about 'papa'! She will hear the answer with pride one day, when she can appreciate the noble sacrifice of that dear papa.--Many thanks for the photograph you sent me; it delighted me very much. Is the likeness as great to Professor Agassiz in reality, as in the picture. We remarked it immediately.

It is so strange that the likeness of the Grandfather will reappear in the grand child. My little pet has always resembled Mr Booth's father: & each day grows more like him. Poor little one her teeth cause her considerable pain: they are coming along so fast. She has six already. I do long so to have you see her; she is beginning to get very cunning, & her pretty ways do so distract & charm us.

Her wants give me just occupation enough to make me feel the responsibility resting upon me. Thus far I have had no reason for any anxiety about her: her strength is something remarkable. My heart is completely filled with her.--The death of Major Dwight is a very great loss; such men as he & your brother we cannot replace.

The proclamation of the President this morning is a most important one. God grant it may put an end to this vile rebellion. I should be very sorry to see however--anything short of an entire demolition of the Southern Confederacy. Too much brave blood has been spilt--for anything save a complete restoration of the Union.

We hope to visit Boston in November & pass many a pleasant hour with you. I hope your children are all well: give my love to them & to all.
                         Yours affectionately
                              Mary Booth

63: to Elizabeth Stoddard (NYPL—MD), October 1862

My dear friend
Edwin has just come home (I hope you have too) sick with cold. The Dr recommends a vapor bath--nothing to eat--& bed until tomorrow night. A part of the disagreeable programme he will perform; so we shall miss seeing you tonight, as I have done all the week. Will you & Stoddard come up tomorrow evening: we would go down

to you but Edwin had better remain within doors--for as
he feels this afternoon he could not get through the
first act. of Hamlet. Did you pass an agreeable time in
the country?
    I hope you won't go away again.  Do come tomorrow
evening.
                        Affectionately Yours
                              Mary Booth


64: to Mary L. Felton (Players), 31 October 1862

                                     New York--
                                       Oct 31st
My dear Mrs Felton
    The receipt of the letter you addressed me at Paris,
must have surprised you very much.  The postal
regulations there are certainly very wonderful.  I wish
we could have such system introduced with us here.  The
account of the Winchester fight is painfully interesting
to us now: we would have read it with joyful hearts at
the time you wrote it.  We have few regiments like the
one he helped to make perfect:--the scale would have
turned in our favor long ago, I think had such men as
Gordon's been numerous in the field.-- --
    There seems to be a lull now of all excitement: &
judging from the appearance of this city one would
scarcely believe in the existence of such a thing as war.
As much gaiety & extravagance as in happier times.  We
will be in Boston about the 23rd of Nov.  I want so much
to see you & to have you see, my little one.  She stands
alone now & does so many wise & cunning things to delight
& amuse us.  She is a real comfort to Mr Booth. says,
'Papa' & Mama, & ↑makes↓ many other attempts at
words--which if we could interpret her baby language
would be very startling I have no doubt.  She has gained
her independence so far, that she can slide from my lap &
cross the floor to any point that may attract her & is
more trouble now than a month ago.  My health has not
been very good since my return: I feel a part of my
husband's fatigue perhaps.  He has been acting five weeks
& must continue two more before he can rest: he is very
tired indeed.  I will enclose in this a 'card' of him:
the most like him of any I have seen.  Do you find him
changed in appearance at all?--his hair is much longer.
    All that you tell me about little Georgie proves her
a gentle meek child.  Poor babe, poor Mother, your own
grief must have been partly drowned in their greater
sorrow.  I hope she is well & that resignation brings her
content.

My kind love to all. I owe your sister Emma a letter which I must repay. She is very lonely--is she not? Her acquaintance I cherish in my inmost heart.

Mr ↑Booth↓ joins with me in kind remembrances to you all.

        Ever affectionately yours
         Mary Booth    T


65: to Emma C. Cushman (FL—BTM), 10? November 1862

My precious friend

Two or three evenings this week I determined within myself to shut myself away from everything & everybody & devote to you. Both evenings were stormy so some of my persevering friends who never find me 'at home' threw out a net on the nights in question to catch me. Denials were useless on such occasions & I quietly submitted myself over to be bored--instead of greeting my 'little one' so very far away from me. I don't know how it is, or why, but ever since you went away I have had bubbling up constantly in my bosom--a real sentiment a yearning for you I might say--which I never experienced before. I know if your husband saw this, he would call this silly & me along with it; for he does not beleive in woman's love. And for the most part, I think he is in the right:--but do you not think there is something in the breast of every woman, no matter how fondly she loves--which aches to pour itself into the worshipping bosom of a woman friend?--When I pause sometimes to count the days you & I have been together--I wonder & try to explain to myself the cause of the sympathy ↑& deep seated love↓ between us. The only answer I get is--"she is lovable beyond all other things" & I fancy my heart beats a little faster when you are near me. I have <u>enjoyed</u>, & you have <u>suffered</u>, in the maternal development & since that I know, I grasp your nature--& would still, if I could, its every throb of pain or doubt.--

I hope darling you are by this time in the full enjoyment of your new home. We leave for Boston next week: how dull & sad it will be without your loving, welcome embrace! But I will see Lucy often & talk of <u>you</u>, to our heart's content.--as we always do, when we are together. You know what New York is: I have a great deal of company & am forced to go out a great deal. I long for rest I am so weary of the constant wear & tear of this excitement.

Enclosed you will find my baby--not very good, but a reminder. When I have one done I will send you one of myself. Do pray, enclose one of yourself to me. I have you in your bridal robes only. When you write tell me

something of your Aunty--her whereabouts, etc. It is now
very late & I must close--but hope you will answer
soon--that I may have a pretext to write you again & at
greater length. Do not forget me--hold me in your loving
heart. I will give you all the news I can glean from
Boston, although your friends keep you well posted, I
have no doubt. My little babe is strong & well. & a
greater comfort than ever. My husband has been playing
Sir Edward Mortemr & Don Ceaser--it seems to me for two
weeks.
    The public crowd to see them every night. My love
to your husband & my husband's to you.
               Ev'r yours
                  <u>Mollie</u>.


66: to Helen S. Cary (NYPL—TC), 25 November 1862

My dear Mrs Cary.
    I thank you very much, for your kind advice
regarding baby.
    You were right in guessing that I should receive ?
it all like love. After I left you yesterday, I thought
very seriously, over what you had said to me. & came to
the conclusion, that I had thoughtlessly neglected to
compare our climate, with that of England & determined
that my little one, should run no further risk, but be
en relaxed, immediately as you suggested. Georgie's
little chemese she shall have put on tomorrow--& I hope
will prove a talisman. I shall prize the two you sent me
very much: in rememberance of your affection for Edwina
& for the sweet darling they have before enfolded. Will
you please express to Miss Emma Cary, my regret at
missing her today. I took advantage of the fine weather
to ride out with baby--thinking it probable, she would
not be over before tomorrow.
    I will remember hereafter the promise I gave to be
at home after 10 P. M. & hope to see her very soon.
                            Yours affectionately
                                Mary Booth
Tuesday Evening

67: to Elizabeth Stoddard (Players), 7 December 1862

                                                Sunday Morn.

My dear friend
        You are with 'Dick' to day, I trust. All day
yesterday I followed you, with my thoughts: & by 9
o'clock in the evening, I was almost as much brain-sick
as though I had been with you in the cars.
        I miss you very much--& so does Edwin. We went to
Mrs Howe's--but saw no one worthy of particular note. It
was a fashionable conversatizone (is that the way to
spell the word?) I had a trying time to get Edwin
started--as I anticipated. He fell asleep after the
play--& it was like being dragged to the infernal
regions--he said, to go to meet a set of d-- fools.
        Mrs Howe asked for you: she was very agreeable & the
evening was a pleasant one on the whole. The Field's'
were there--as patronizing as usual.
        With a bad pen--& miserable ink I will not make this
as long as feel inclined to. I will show you some ~~l~~
mercy & spare you the torture of ~~deep~~ a lengthy scrawl.
        I did intend when I sat down to write--to enclose
the key of the trunk you are to send: but remembering
that Perry the servant at the Hotel--can get the
carpenter or locksmith of the house to lock it--I have
changed my mind.
        I am afraid you will have much difficulty--in
getting them ready. But I rely upon the willingness I
know you feel to get them off as soon as possible. I am
ashamed to send ↑you↓ this miserable sheet--but I had no
other--& I feared to delay--lest I should be interrupted
& prevented from saying, "How d'ye do," today. My love
to Dick: tell him that Edwin has made nearly $5,000 in
the two weeks. The house yesterday was crowded. Adieu
love.
                        Affectionately Yours
                                Mary.


68: to Elizabeth Stoddard (NYPL—MD), 13 December 1862

                                    Boston <u>Saturday</u>

        I have been waiting the arrival of this writing
paper, which I ordered several days ago, ~~before~~ to answer
your sweet letter, my dear Elisabeth (or "Lisabeth").
        I have a great deal to write you about--& it would
have been wiser had I kept an account of each day's
work--for now I fear, my memory will fail me. In the

first place--after you left--the party at Mrs Howe's came
off. I wrote you that there was no one there of any
particular note--but nevertheless it was a real ovation
to Edwin.
   All Beacon St was invited and all Beacon St was
there: but you know us both too well for me to affect any
delight at such a gathering--'twas tedious and perhaps
heartless. I love Mrs Howe though & love her more than
ever before, for what she said of you. Now comes the
test of memory; I must try & remember all. She described
her feelings when she first saw you sitting in the room
at Whipple's: thought she never could go forward & speak
to you: your eyes repelled her: not ~~through~~ ↑from↓ any
disagreeable impression--↑they awoke↓ but that you seemed
drawn within yourself. I bluntly asked her--knowing her
to be a woman of the world & one who could face a
legion--if she was not exaggerating the state of her
feelings a little. She declared not a whit!--She was
delighted with you, after she had spoken with you--but
still thinks that you are very difficult to get
acquainted with. What pleased me most was her great
confidence in your power as a writer. She has heard
everyone, who has read 'The 'Morguesons', say that it
possesed immense talent. She knew the cause too why
Field had refused to notice it in the 'Atlantic'. The
same that Mr Whipple gave you.
   A great deal more was said by us about the fair
Lisabeth--which I will relate in full when we meet.
   And now I am come to the point dearest to us all, I
think.
   A few days since I called in a celebrated ~~Dr~~ M. D.
here to examine into my case, which I felt certain
was a serious one. From the symptoms he could tell
nothing~~s~~--so I was obliged to undergo what I have most
feared & dreaded. I was right my case is serious: but
not alarmingly so--& four months of secl~~l~~usion & perfect
repose will cure me. But as I must have local treatment
I am advised to <u>remain here</u>. You remember our jesting
with you--on the subject. it is, I am afraid, going to
be a sad truth. Dr Miller is at Dorchester--& there I
shall be obliged to reside.
   If I can get a furnished house with good established
servants--as there is some probability of my getting--
the case, though the saddest & drollest prospect
awaits me, will not be so tedious. You may rest assured
that unless I had found it absolutely necessary for my
well being in the future--I would never have entertained
the horrid thought--of giving up all the joyous, pleasant
entertainment of my friends in New York & above all the
sweet companionship of youself & Mr Stoddard.
   I am wretched too thinking of Edwin's absence--for
he ~~1~~ must leave me part of the time.
   I was going to write you of pleasanter things--but
began this subject too soon--for now I am unfitted. And
so you will be I think--won't you? Strange--how
completely you have entered into ↑our↓ life & thoughts.

The first words we uttered after the cruel decision was--what you & Dick would feel!!
  But do try & bear it--if it really comes to what I fear--& think how much I need your sympathy.
  Let us say no more about it.--I meant to break it gradually--but after all I have been cruel. You see how egotistical I am: but love like yours has that effect.
  Write me soon & tell me everything about yourself. Edwin got your letter this morning. My love to dear old Dick.
                    affectionately yours
                           Mary Booth
Edwin had an immense crowd last night. He will clear $7000 by this engagement




69: to Emma C. Cushman (FL—BTM), 13-16 December 1862

                                    Boston--Dec 13th

My darling
  Can you forgive your friend for so long neglecting to answer the sweet reply, to her most poor faver, sent you from N. York.
  My heart was fully satisfied by the affection you expressed in it. Ever since my stay here, my love for you has been fed, by intercourse with mutual friends. We have had a great deal of attention paid us--but of this I will only speak inasmuch as it will interest you.
  You are really missed from Boston. Dear little heart, I would have no patience with them, if so sweet a flower could be transplanted & not be missed.
  There was a large party given to us, at Mrs Howe's last week. All Beacon St was invited & all B. St was there. But it was tedious to me--perhaps heartless. I am wrong to say so--but society wearies me now, for I am not well: & it is of that more than anything else I wish to speak to you in this.
  To you I can pour out my heart & find sympathy--am I not right?
  For months past I have been suffering where almost all women suffer, but only a few days ago I thought seriously enough of my case to call in a physician. Hearing, that Dr Miller was very skillful, I saw him & from the slight symptoms could tell nothing: so I agreed to undergo what I have always loathed & dreaded. He found it to be more serious than it gave evidence of but, thank God, no dangerous, nor incurable. He advises me to remain here, either four or six months which I have decided upon doing--& at the end of that time he is sure I will be better than ever before.

I have heard of a furnished cottage at Dorchester,
near the Dr; & when I am quietly domiciled there you may
expect to be inundated with my scrawling epistles. I
shall crave your affection & attention more than ever,
for Mr Booth is obliged to go to Brooklyn to fulfil an
engagement already entered into. He seems pleased that I
am forced to take some rest--for I am wearing myself out
very fast.--I have seen Mrs Sandford only once: she
brought Kate Field to see me. She expressed great regret
at not having seen you, but for my part, I was rather
glad that somebody had suffered as well as poor little
me.--If you were only here now! ah, it is too
provokingly sad to dwell upon--How I did long, when your
letter came to put my arms around your neck. I want you
to write me, just as you would talk if you were here.
There is something sweeter in you to love, Emma, than
↑in↓ anyone I ever met; any woman, I mean.

Can't we have something arranged for communication,
between the Cottage at Dorchester--& your home in St
Louis this winter? It would be pleasanter, & much more
consoling for me, than to wait long intervals to hear
from you & would be a blessed thing for you not to be
obliged to read my miserable, uneven scrawls. Shall we
ever meet & hold each other in a warm embrace again,
darling? When we experienced that pleasure, we scarcely
appreciated it--for we were new friends then. "Now are
you my leutenant"?--Why precious, I have rattled on, &
said not a single word about my lovely little daughter.
Oh! Emma she is a real comfort to me. The 9th of Dec saw
her one year old. We tried to make it a fête, her papa &
I. Silver presents lay spread upon the table & we fully
realized what a blessing had been given us. Sweetheart!
don't despair; I feel assured that you will yet bear as
fair a blossom as your soul has ever dreamed ↑of↓ or
craved for.

But pray be careful: you must get thoroughly strong
before that "consummation devoutly to be wished" can come
to pass.

<u>Tuesday</u> <u>Morn</u>.

I was interrupted, darling on Sunday but will
resume, although after perusing the sheets already filled
I am tempted to "tear them all to peices" & begin afresh.
But I will try & full up the sentences & make them
intelligable, for I am far from being well & writing
fatigues me 'trop'.

I have not yet heard whether I can have the cottage
at Dorchester but will know to day. Shall we not hold
sweet converse then?

I want you to write me all about yourself, just as I
have done. Lucy comes often to see me, yet not so often
as I desire she should: she has a heart of gold. It is
strange how many noble hearts, just like Lucy's are left
to pine away in solitude, while corrupt & heartless ones,
triumph.

My little baby all but walks Emma; she stands alone
& imitates everything & every body. She pulling now at

my dress, & trying to reach my hand--so I must leave off
to play a little with her. Remember me to your
husband--& write me very soon. The only direction I can
think of at present to give you--is to address me in care
of Orlando Tompkins, cor of Washington ~~etc~~ & Winter
Sts.--As soon as I decide to take the house, I will write
again.
   With much love believe me, most lovingly yours
                    Mary Booth.


**70: to Elizabeth Stoddard (NYPL—MD), 16 December 1862**

                 Boston
               Tuesday Morn

My dear Elisabeth
   Your letter came & was just what I expected--for I
was not explicit enough in ~~describing~~ ↑writing↓ you of my
case. Edwin in his, gave you perhaps a better idea of
the state of things. That I need immediate treatment, is
beyond a doubt--& ~~that~~ I must remain quiet ↑as that↓ is
the very first thing towards getting well. The physician
I named to you--Dr Miller is very celebrated in this part
of the country for this kind of desease & he has inspired
me with a great deal of faith. If I went back to New
York & placed myself in the hands of Dr Sims (I believe
that is the way they '<u>spell</u> <u>him</u>') it would cost at least
three times the amount for his visits & I would still be
living up 'four pair', where I could have but little
rest. So that economy, & profit both point to my
remaining where I will be almost secluded from everybody
& can devote myself to getting well. Everything is in
favor of my being away--excepting <u>you</u> & from the first
moment it was proposed, I hesitated on your account.--But
remember it will only be for a few months & the Dr says
very likely I will be able to go on with Edwin in
Feburary. I have talked to a great many persons of the
skill of Dr Miller & they all agree in saying that he is
<u>wonderful</u>! Now dear heart, don't take on, but try &
think as I have done, that it is this very best thing I
could do.
   I will enclose the Dr's statement of my case, to
Edwin, that you may know exactly in what condition I am.
You will see there that Mrs Pike was right. This is
Tuesday & we have not yet learned what house we can have
at Dorchester. I must not remain in town at a Hotel, for
then I should be as badly off as in New York, where God
knows I would greatly prefer to be.--Edwin will be
low-spirited enough without me, so pray do try & comfort

him.  Do you think he could get a room at your house, if
so I think he would be happier to be with you.  I have
not dared to think of parting with him--you know well
enough how I will suffer.--The dearest consolation you
could have sent me, is your promise to come to me, if I
need you, for be assured I shall.  I have preferred to
keep ~~to~~ quite secret, my intention to remain here, so                40
that with ↑but↓ a few exceptions I shall be free from
intercourse.--I beg & intreat of you not ↑to↓ look upon
us as lost forever; you can come on & pass some days with
me & the months will pass by ~~to~~ almost unheeded.  Edwin
will only play three nights in Brooklyn so the other                     A
three he can pass with you.  I shall rely upon you to
keep him cheerful & the thought that he ~~will~~ ↑may↓ date
his letters to me from your rooms, takes away half the
grief of not being there myself.
    I must not close without repeating what Stuart (who          A
came yesterday) said of the 'King's Bell'.  That it was                 51
as great as the best poem of Tennyson & that in England
it would without doubt create a sensation.  Are we not to
have it?  I am quite disappointed in not receiving it
before.  I will enquire today, if it is to ↑be↓ had here.
Mrs Whipple brought me "Mrs Trench's Remains" and they                   A
have given me much pleasure.
    Did I tell you that they ↑(the Whipples)↓, with Mrs
Howe & her daughter took tea with me the other evening.
We afterward went to the Boston & W, was delighted with                 AT
Sir Edward.  Edwin still draws crowds, but I fear the                   61
golden apples will cease to fall after he leaves here:
for Brooklyn I doubt very much.  How is Mr Stoddard?  is                 T
he going to miss poor little me too?  tell him how much I                T
love him & tell my Elisabeth how much I love her too.  I
shall be most anxious to know what you think of my
remaining here, after you receive this--so don't delay
answering me.  Tell me too whether you are really in
earnest about coming on.  God bless you both.
                  Ever Yours
                    Mary Booth                                         T


**71: to Richard Henry Stoddard (NYPL—MD), 20 December 1862**

My dear Mr Stoddard.
    What can I say to you, about your 'Bell'?--I had but
one impulse & that was to call together all whom I knew
in Boston & demand they all should read, this most
exquisite poem.
    We read together in bed, last night--& will it
please you to hear, that we shed tears over, Felix's                     A
death?
    You have been perfectly successful I think.

Is it strange that I should love you more after
reading this work of your genieus? Certain it is--& I
cannot help it--that while perusing it, I could not but
ask myself has this poet ever walked with me, talked with
me? no I could not have been so fortunate. Edwin will
be with you tomorrow evening if possible & tell you all,
with which my heart is running over.
        Yours
          Mary.
 Give to my love, my poet.
      M.B.


72: to Elizabeth Stoddard (Players), 21 December 1862

               Sunday.

My dear friend
 Our affairs have cried such haste, the last two
days, that I have not been able to write you.--The
arrangement for going to your house, Edwin will have to
give up, & for this reason. He will be forced to go to
the Hotel to pack my things & cannot well do this without
taking on rooms there for a day at least. He will arrive
there about the same time you did, as he leaves by the
same train, you did & he will take a peep at you just
before going to bed. He says he will feel lonely, so you
may expect him tomorrow night.
 I must tell you how fortunate I have been about my
house. I go in on Tuesday. Everything is cosy & 'at
hand' & there is every prospect of my getting better, if
only in consequence of the perfect quiet I shall enjoy.
 Pray write me often;--the only pang I feel while
reading them, & afterwards too, is from my intense desire
to see & talk with you. Edwin has promised you shall be
sent on, while they go to Fortress Monroe.--If you come,
you can write all day & in the evening meet, just one or
two to take tea: or no one if you so desire. I forgot to
enclose the Dr's statement, but will do so today. Edwin
has just refused to see James T Fields--& the card
returned with a request to see them at their house
tonight; a 'regret' is already written. How I hate such
hypocracsy: they don't care for us, & yet put themselves
so much out of the way to invite.--I have a great deal to
write--but I will defer it, 'til I am fairly settled in
my cottage at Dorchester.
 Dear heart, if I had paused or even now did pause,
to think over the lonely, bleak hours I may pass there, I
would grow heart-sick.--But I know what I need & my good

sense, bids me bear the isolation.--Edwin will tell you
more.  Do look after him as much as possible--& love ~~him~~
me through him.
                              Yours lovingly
                                   Mollie.



73: to Mary L. Felton (Players), 22 December 1862



My dear Mrs Felton
     I do so much, regret that I shall not be able to go
to Cambridge today.  I will be deep in the mysteries of
the Grocer & Iron-monger 'til a late hour this afternoon.
Tomorrow I leave for Dorchester but many days shall not
pass before I visit you.  The former proprietor, Mr Ives
has found me a competent servant, or so she is
represented.
     I may as well try her as any other.
     I hope you are better.  This is favorable weather
for us.  Everything points or seems to--towards a              10
confortable time this winter.  I shall woo peace, 'avec
tout mon coeur'.
     Accept a kiss from baby & much love from her Mama.
                              Ever yours
                                   Mary Booth        T



74: to Elizabeth Stoddard (Players), 24 December 1862



                                   Wedensday Morn
Dear friend
     I have just finished a long letter to Edwin & I am
pretty well tired--but I must send you a Christmas kiss.
"May we never pass another one apart"--you may add that
to the toast you propose to offer in the goblet tomorrow.
How I shall wish to be with you!  But it may not be--so I
must content myself with Dorchester.
     "An excellent place to study the Sanscrit
language"--a lady friend told me at Mrs Howe's the ~~1~~
other night.  She is a daughter of Rufus Choate has a          A
great deal of humour & lives two miles from me, out            10
there.
     I would welcome you with all my soul next week: but

I think with you, that you had better leave it until you can come to stay.

I shall follow your remedy & cultivate the warte that lies a little way from my mouth. I anticipate the sweetest repose: providing I can keep Mrs Howe & others like her, at bay. Even now, this morning, she was in to know when I could visit her again. She is the most importunate of her sex. I have made up my mind to get well & anything that conflicts with my ideas on that subject, will be indignantly rejected by your humble friend.

Dear Elizabeth, who knows better than we do your hard pressed struggle for existence; you know too, that it is a subject sacred to us. We would share with you--but what is the use of such offering to your proud souls. The only thing we can do, is love you & regard your wishes in respect to extravagance: & for your dear sakes lay by something to purchase joy for you & ourselves in books & pictures.

Mrs Howe has just been telling me how amazed all were by Edwin's performance here on Saturday. Fields was thunderstuck by his power. He has been one of the unbelievers, but was converted on Saturday. Tell Edwin this. I know now why J. T. F. sent his card on Sunday

Strange, but lately I have felt that same heating in the abdomen, that you complain of. I wish you had nothing worse than I have to be got rid of. It is the beastly complication of disease that is so difficult to cure. Dr Parsons is reading the 'King's Bell'--he read from my copy, last night a page, aloud & thought it great. He was glad he said to see another poem in heroic verse.

I am more & more charmed with it--it rings in my ears--in fact I have it in my hands more than half the time. Give my love to Richard & my blessing with my love to Edwin.

I shall dine alone on Turkey tomorrow think of me the while.

         Ever yours
            Mollie.


75: to Elizabeth Stoddard (Players), 30 December 1862

My dear Elisabeth

Tompkins brought me out your & 'Dick's' letters on Sunday. It partly consoled me, but it destroyed the last hope I had been foolishly indulging in--that Edwin would defer the visit to Fortress Monroe 'til February.

Poor darling, I know he is tired to death--& needs rest more than anything else. I have not written since Saturday last not knowing where he would be. I hope he

did something towards relieving the sad Christmas day,
for such a one it must have been to you. I am going to
send you a book--that cannot fail to bring comfort to
your grieved & lonely heart--if you read it. I recommend
you to begin ↑at↓ the second part--the first will be
meaningless without--for I consider the last part, the
key to the first. It is so clearly, so exquisitely
written, that the heart must indeed be dead to
consolation, that cannot find it there.--I think too--now
that you have begun your book--that your mind must be
clear, unfaltering & beleiving.--
    I have thought ever since I met you, that your
genius was struggling to get t into the daylight: I
beleive too, that if accomplish this time something which
satisfies the craving restless spirit within you, that
will be better: better in health as ↑of↓ body as well as
mind.--You know I live with genius; am forced to bear the
ills & restlessness of his untaught mind, his undefined
purposes: & I know, how dreadful it is to suffer as you &
Edwin suffer.--I like my house so much; there is freedom
& independence which I enjoy. I saw my Dr for the first
time yesterday!--no I will tell you nothing about it; you
have gone through, what I must & perhaps think more
reasonably about such things: but for me, I am weak &
cowardly.
    All my courage is gone--I pass half my time in
tears.
    Dear heart, your letter has just come, telling me
all.--I knew Edwin would leave his affairs to the last
moment. I have counted time as well as I know how--& see
no possibility of a letter from me reaching him; so must
wait his return as patiently as I know how.
    I am late for the mail & must close. Adieu
                                    Yrs ever
                                        Mollie.
Teusday Morning.




76: to Mary L. Felton (Players), 1 January 1863


My dear Mrs Felton
    I had arranged to see you yesterday, but the storm
blasted that pleasure & too my poor little one was ill &
is so still from teething. She has considerable fever,
but I do not feel at all alarmed about her.--I like my
house very much; have been most fortunate in my servants
too, as far as I have tested them. The time drags slowly
along, however until Mr Booth returns: which will be
tomorrow or Saturday. He has gone to Fortress Monroe.
    Dr Miller, has only attended me once, as yet; but I
have the most earnest conviction, that all will go well.

I know that I have done exactly what I ought to have done.--This has been a busy week I presume with you at Cambridge. I earnestly hope you were able to take part in all that interested the children. I look forward with anxiety & pleasure to my babe's first Christmass!--I may see you before the end of this week, it will depend upon how soon the baby gets bright again. My kindest love to all & best wishes for your improved health.

           Yours affectionately
            Mary Booth

Dorchester.
Jan 31st

---

77: to Elizabeth Stoddard (Players), 7 January 1863

           Wedensday Morn.

My dear friend--
  Edwin was greeted & welcomed with my warmest embrace on Sunday last, as you know ere this. All the day was passed in telling me of his delightful visit to the Fortress.
  It is something accomplished, tell Mr Stoddard, to produce any pleasureable sensation in him. He has been full of the trip ever since.
  The day before yesterday, after a visit from Dr Miller--I was taken very ill; but in the morning rose quite well; though I am weak, still.--I hope to go on in Feburary if the Dr thinks it advisable.
  Edwin is enjoying so much our cosy little house; but suffers from neuralgia dreadfully.--I have had a visit from Mrs Howe: she took from my table "The Morguesons" to read. I have only been twice in the city since I moved out here.--I want to tell you a secret: I would not live in or near Boston for the world; <u>reasons</u>: they pay attention to everyones business but their own. I have heard since I have been here, the most ridiculous stories about us. that we were unhappy--going to be divorced &c. I think New York is the only place, away from Paris for liberal minded people to abide.--I do want to see & hear you talk again!--Edwin's goblet is most beautiful & the book too: you have such beautiful taste, both. Edwin has told me so much of your brother Wilson that I am almost in love with him. I am tired & can say no more. See how my pen 'wriggles'. My love to my poet.

            Lovingly Yours
             Mollie.

78: to Mary L. Felton (Players), 7 January 1863

Wedensday Morn

My dear Mrs Felton.
   Your welcome note reached '<u>even</u> in Dorchester.' My husband came home on Sunday last--very much fatigued but delighted with his visit to Fortress Monroe.
   The day before yesterday after a ~~letter~~ visit from Dr Miller, I was taken ill: it was very serious for the time being, but after a night's rest I rose in the morning, quite recovered. It has made me quite cowardly, & I shall dread more than ever the Dr's coming.
   Baby is better too; Mr Booth found us both unwell, but he is very happy now & enjoys the rest & calm of this little house very much.
   As soon as I am strong enough I will go to you.--To reach me, you take the Grove Hall & Dorchester cars, they pass the door & I think the conductors all know now where 'Mr Booth lives'. My love to all.
                    Yours most affectionately
                         Mary Booth


79: to Richard Henry Stoddard (Players), early January 1863

My dearest friend--
   Edwin has the table & I am writing on a 'french dictionary'. I require its support very often. We were so glad to get your letters to day; we are always glad when they come. Ed thinks with me, that the country is good for folks morally as well as physically. We see very few people--& forget as much as possible that we are near a great city. Its shadow we are tired of--How we talk of & long for you & Lisabeth!--But we have many pleasant things to remind us of you. There is the 'goblet' & the 'flower & fruit dish' on the side-board of the dining room. Songs of Summer--my pet--my King's Bell, & The Morguesons (absent now) on the table of my sitting room--sweet letters in my desk--& your precious love enfolding us. Are we worthy of it? we will try--we can do no more.--I thought I had sent a letter to my Lisa yesterday--but I was mistaken. I will send it with this.--I have an advantage over her in one way, & it is so much comfort to me. When I am ill & weary, I can lay on my sofa, close my eyes, & let my soul travl to her cosy room. see her pale, sweet face bending over her work, & think the while, how happy I am in having such a tender loving friend.--Write us long, sweet letters--'til

we meet.  If I go on in Feb--'twill only be for a few
days; & I want very much to arrange to be there, at the
time of the Artist's Reception if I can.
   This is a cosy little home, & I am very well
content.  We live for about $20 per week--isn't that
nice?--Dr Parsons praises very highly your new poem.  He
is a strange being--I will tell you all about him--as his
wife confides in me--when we meet.  Dear poet--you are
not the only one who struggles.--I wish I could send you
some of the good milk our cow gives;--it is making me
fat.  (poor me, I wonder if I will ever be well &
strong.)  God bless & guard our loves.
   Kiss Lisa for me.  I long to know what her new book
will be.  I will write her soon again.  Yours ever
                                             Mollie B.


80: to Richard Henry Stoddard (Players), 15 January 1863

                                         Thursday night

My dear friend--
   Edwin having left a little space--&, I just happening
to meet a likeness of myself, I & remembering the promise
I gave to send one to you--it shall go along with the
'entry'.  How we do miss you & Lisabeth:--we sit--E. & I,
& talk about you & have concluded, that we are so much
richer, than we were last year, in having your love, that
we ought to be content.
   Write us often.  A kiss to Lisa.  The scent of
Tuber-roses only reached me yesterdy  I will write her
of it.
                                             Mollie
                                                   B.


81: to Elizabeth Stoddard (Players), 19 January 1863

                                           Monday Morn.

My dear 'Lisabeth'
   I have only one sheet of paper & you shall take it.
I want you to see how very 'smart' I am.
   Dr Miller has only been gone 3/4 of an hour, & I am
at my desk, feeling pretty well.  He says I am very much
better & will be perfectly cured even before the time he

thought.  Certainly my general health is better: but that
is no doubt, owing to the 'cuisine' of my own house.  You
have no faith or seem to have none, in local treatment.
tell me why.  I know <u>nothing</u> of internal deseases; but it
seems to me, that it <u>is</u> the only way to remove conjestion
& inflamation.
   Edwin has gone to town after some cigars;--he is <u>so</u>
<u>happy</u> here; acts just like a child.  You may imagine what
pleasure it gives me to see & have him comfortable.  I
look with dread & horror upon the four weeks separation
that must ensure, but I try & find consolation in the joy
he will feel, at returning to his <u>home</u>.  Besides I expect
that <u>you</u> will come & see me for a <u>little</u> while; leaving
Dick to Edwin.  I never felt so much the direct need of
you as I do here.  Do you know that you ~~are~~ & Richard,
are as much bound up in our hopes & desires for the
future, as though you had been "twin'd with us"!--We know
how secure you feel in us--how entirely you depend upon
us, to love & cherish you.  No doubt, that you will have
to suffer the most poignant grief on our accounts, at
times; for Edwin--well you know the demon that persues--a
noble, ungoverned spirit like his.  He is so gentle, so
yealding, so <u>abstemious</u> now: & I advise with him & he
promises that the victory shall be his.--How differently
you & I are placed.  Richard is ↑so↓ perfect a man, so
free from human vices--so true to ↑his↓ better nature:
<u>you</u> are the turbulant, ↑the passionate↓ one.  I have read
your 'Tuber-roses'.  It is full of ~~of~~ charm, of thrilling
beauty.  I understand your work, better now than when I
read 'The Morgensons'; for I know you better.--You must
be courageous--as you will be successful.  How much has
been taken from your life--none but your own hearts know.
And yet I feel, that if I could replace for a single day,
that tiny one, who was the life of your lives--I would
sacrifice years of my own.  Could I do more to show how I
loved you?--Tell me when you ↑write↓ what you think of
Lillie's interest for Aldrich.  I have hated to ask the
question before, wanting all that you wrote to be of your
dear self.--I have not written them, nor any body else,
for I am not strong enough to sit long upright.  I keep
my sofa--half the day.  Baby is well now, thank God.  Oh,
how I long to have you visit me.  Tell me if it is true
that you will come in Febuary.  If you do I would go
on--if not I shall go on for a week.  My heart's best
love to Richard--keep it bright in your memories.
                      Mollie B.

82: to Elizabeth Stoddard (Players), 20 January 1863

                                  Dorchester
                                  20th Jan.

My dear Elisabeth
    Your last gave us a great deal of pleasure. I wish I could find enough to make a worthy answer; but this rural life of mine, enforced upon me by desease & suffering--shut me away from everything that might prove interesting to you.
    Last night Mrs Howe gave a large & fashionable dancing-party; I was the first invited--but prudence kept me at home. It was given for her daughters; everything now she does, being for their advancement & benefit. Her maternal love is strong--& therefore she ought to be good. I am writing on a book--seated or rather lying on the sofa. The Dr has been here--he finds me much better, & I know there is improvement going on.
    About my going on the 1st--Edwin & I have only referred to the subject. I think he would be glad if I gave up all idea of the visit--but of course it rests with me to decide. I did not intend--before your letter came--to go with him--but follow after; say, in a week or two:--thereby breaking up the tediousness of his absence. I would like to be there for the Art Reception--but above all things to see your brother Wilson. Edwin is quite sick to day--we had a long ride yesterday & got lost; the fatigue & all together has made him ill.--Poor Dick--is he too "under the weather"? Oh, if you could only come on here & bring him for a couple of weeks, you would at least be refreshed. If he only had a position on some paper that paid as well as his present one--& was less confining, how much better it would be. Has he no plan in embryo--that our Edwin could help him to bring to light. You know how anxious he is to make you comfortable. There is nothing to be done--but for us to have a house together. You ought to see how quietly & without annoyance I manage my little house now & if I grow strong as I hope to--you would have no care or trouble resting upon you from it. It is the only rational thing for human being to do--"lord of all you survey" is my motto for the future.--No matter then what I decide upon doing as regards going to N. York--it will in no way prevent your visit to me I trust. That is the bright spot I look forward to now--in contemplating the miserable isolation Edwin's absence will doom ~~&~~ me to.--Tell dear Dick, that I got all the notices & papers he was thoughtful enough to send me. Boker's notice was very fine. Write me often & tell me all you do & who you see; it is the next best thing to being with you. My love to Dick--Edwin joins with me--says he loves you &

all sorts of things besides.  He will write tomorrow.
Love me better than all the world.
                                      Yours ever
                                        M.B.
P.S.
    I will write you <u>definitely</u> in a few days, what date
I shall be in N. York.




83: to Emma C. Cushman (FL—BTM), 22 January 1863

                                    Dorchester Jan 22nd

My dear Emma
    I can give you no more sufficient reason for my long
silence than the natural horror I have of writing.  I
talk about you to Lucy & think of you enough when I am
alone--but my thoughts remain unwritten, until my intense
desire to hear from you, forces me to this most
uncongenial mode of expression.--I presume Lucy has told
you how pleasantly I am situated here; everything goes on
as merry as a 'marriage bell', & the sacrifice I made, in
giving up all the pleasure & entertainment, ~~of~~ promised
me in New York this winter, had I remained there, ↑I↓
will be more than compensated for; for my health is being
restored & I am much better in every way.  Although so
near Boston, I see only a few people, my desire being to
keep as much away from excitement as possible.  Dr Miller
is very skillful, & his family very kind & attentive to
me.--My husband enjoys so much too his respite from his
profession ↑& the pleasures↓ of his home here.
    Last night we went to see J Wilkes B-- for the first
time.  We were very much pleased with him--but he has a
great deal to learn & unlearn.  Just think how short the
time is, before you will see your Aunty!--how happy you
must feel.--Mrs Howe gave a large dancing party, on
Monday last & though ↑one↓ of the first invited, prudence
kept me at home.  Her great ambition now is for her two
daughters--everything she does, seems to be for their
advancement.  Julia is very handsome & very bright.  Mrs
Howe is a wonderfully clever woman--don't you agree with
me?--She is the sort of woman--who, if she gave her mind
& heart up to the cause--could work wonders by the
influence of her pen, at this time.--Boston is just as
dull as usual--a few parties--~~a~~ theatrical performances,
a little better than the general--plenty of abolition
fanaticism, "the rest is silence".
    Mrs Sandford I have never seen but once--it is a
day's journey to her house, else I should have seen her
before this.

I want very much to see your sister, can't you send me, dear a photograph of her? I hear she is so lovely. If there is anything I can do for you here, darling, let me know. Poor Lucy, I know gave up her visit to you with a struggle--but she thought it best for her to remain here, as she was situated. She is a dear girl, I love her better than any one around me here.

    She told me she had written you of our precious baby. My heart is all devotedness to my pet. I hear her little footsteps now, in the chamber above my head--& my heart beats faster as I think & write about her. All that is said or done, she imitates, as well as can; & her nurse does everything to encourage her. Parden this stupid effort of mine--I am not very well. My dearest love to you & yours--my 'hubby' joins with me
    Write me <u>very</u> <u>soon</u>.          Yours ever
                                           M. B.

## 84: to Elizabeth Stoddard (Players), 29 January 1863

                                         Dorchester
                                                29th
My dear Lisa
    If we do not hear from you every day or every other one, we complain most bitterly.
    I was 'scolding' the other day just as one arrived. How we should have enjoyed your tea-party! Ludlow wrote E-- in the Custom House, before going & mentioned the fact.
    I want to explain to you, so that you may understand all about my proposed visit to New York.
    E-- got it into his head, I don't know how--that I wanted to go & stay during his entire stay there. This arrangement he very justly thought an extravagant & foolish one--for we cannot afford to keep up two establishments. <u>I</u> had long ago decided not to go--or if I did ↓only↑ for a few days; but <u>he</u> did not so understand & after a good deal of talk of the silly matter--<u>I</u> indignantly refused to go at all; giving as my reasons, that he did not seem to appreciate my natural wish to go on & see him for a few days--in doing which, I fancied I would be giving him great pleasure & content. The 'sorry child' then begged me to hold to my original plan & assured me how much happier he would be to have me there. But I have not relented yet & I must be coaxed a great deal more before I yeald.--Stuart has been on & releived Ed considerably by arrangeing everything for his engagement satisfactorily. He will not begin 'til the 9th of Feb. Edwin's hobby now is--what d'ye think? Stoddards poems! All night & day he reads them. He is so natural so much himself when he is away from the

Stage--that I almost lament he is ever forced to assume
the "sock & buskin." But we must not say so to him--for
he is already too much inclined to idleness & looks with
horror upon his approaching engagement. I have laid all
my plans for a home next winter in New York & for the
cottage where you & Dick will come for the summer. I do
nothing all day but lay out bright visions for the
future; it pleases me, beyond all things to dream
thus--but experience has taught me that it is all folly.
We are not masters of our destiny only to a very small
extent.--
    I am so much better & am getting so fat you would
scarcely know me. Every day I stand before the glass &
pinch my cheeks to feel if they fuller grown. You would
pardon my weakness if you knew how often I have been told
"go get thyself in flesh". I beleive thin folks, like
you & I--are generally avoided or only pitied at the
best--the world like Ceaser--"hate lean & hungry men". I
have longed for you this past week on several bright days
we have had. Now if Elisabeth was here--I have said--we
would take a carriage & together scour the country.
    But you have promised me you will come & my heart is
impatient for the time. Everything shall be done for
your pleasure & convenience.
    Edwin sends love. Mine to 'Dick'--we love you so
much, not an hour of the day, but we mention in some way
your dear names.
    Write as often & lovingly as you feel. God bless &
guard you dearest friends.
                                              Yours ever
                                                  Mollie B.


85: to Matilda Woodman (HU—MD), 29 January 1863

                                          Dorchester
                                          Jan 29th
My dear Mattie.
    A thousand thanks for your kind thoughtfulness about
our comfort when we arrive in New York; but Mr Booth's
engagement is now prostponed another week--& I have
decided not to go on at first with him. I prefer to
leave it--if I go at all--to the middle of his engagement
thereby breaking as much as possible the tedious absence
of my "kind lord".
    Your pleasant letter satisfied entirely my love of
gossip--& was most interesting. The affair with the
young ladies, & Mr Booth--we could not guess. Were they
the daughters of Rufus Choate--the vamping Mrs Pratt &
Mrs Bell?
    Boston is a fearful place for small talk. They have

divorced us & had our darling baby dead a dozen times.
As for me--I am according to the seers of 'hub town'
living in a state of misery (conjugal) the like of which
is unparrelled in modern times. Poor human nature it
must vent its spite & spleen; & even so unoffending a
little woman as I ↑am↓ cannot escape. I write this
supposing from your letter that the story of the
'treatment' had some such coloring.--I continue to grow
better: baby walks & almost talks. She is our heart's
delight. I have just finished a long letter to Mrs
Stoddard (whose sweet & mournful face I hope you see
often) & am tired, so you will excuse brevity. I must
ask you another favor. Will you get for me the book
entitled "The Married life of Albrecht Durer" or the
Artist life--I forget exactly which & send it by mail. I
enclose in this, what I hope will be sufficient to pay
for it. If not you may add the rest & I will settle
afterwards with you. My dearest love to all. Mr Booth,
babe & Marie join with me.
                            Yours ever
                                Mollie B.

P.S.--
    I thank you for the ↑books of↓ Ruy Blas they came
safely. The bill I enclose is a Boston one. If it will
not pass send it back & I will wait til Mr Both goes on.
            M.B.


86: to Edwin Booth (Players), 9 February 1863

                                    Monday Morn.

My darling
    I pray that you may have arrived safely. We are
very very lonesome. What do you think of your little
daughter? This morning she came into the room as usual,
but stopped short at the door & fixed her eyes steadily
upon Lucy who occupied your place. I could not coax her
to come farther, until Marie came & brought her to me.
Lucy attempted to speak to her but she screamed & said
"no, no, no"; poor darling missed you & thought perhaps
you had been transformed. This morning I had a letter
from Rose--she regrets she cannot come. Mother has so
much for her to do. I forgot to give you a part of the
sponge but will send it with the shirt for Ruy Blas.
Give my love to the Stoddards & find out when she is
coming. Write me all about your opening. How you are
received & ↑how many↓ the familiar faces you see around
you &c. Today is as warm & pleasant as yesterday--but
the sky threatens a storm. I hope you will have fine

weather to night.
    My dear Edwin I hope the cloud that gathered about
your pure soul is completely scattered--& that you think
of me as you have always thought.
    Be patient & courageous with your 'theatre troubles'
& don't let Jackson wrong you. Lucy sends love: I shall
hear from Orlando, perhaps today wheathe Henry went with
you or not. God bless you my dearly loved one.
                                                      M.B.


87: to Edwin Booth (NYPL—TC), 12 February 1863

                                              Thursday

    Your "after Hamlet" came yesterday darling, but not
until 4 P. M--Orlando says that I could receive them by
10 A M--if you send them to his care. So let us waive
the objection I had to having them sent there--for I am
so anxious every morning to hear from you.
    Yesterday I was only unhappy 'til your letter
came--then I felt such regret that I had said anything to
you about it. I shall try & be good to you, my dear
one--in the future, if you will only overlook the past.
Yesterday I had two extraordinary visits.--
    I have been interrupted by Dr Miller--& now it is
near the time for the mail to close & I must be
brief.--One visit was from two young ladies--strangers to
me; very elegantly dressed & both related to Mrs Ballow,
at the Tremont House. One of them a Miss Walden-- --came
she said to shake hands with Mrs Booth as ↑whom↓ she knew
as Mary Devlin; when I was only eleven years old at
dancing school in Troy. She told me how fond her
brothers & sisters were of me, & recalled or tried to
many things, which of course I could not remember. On
the whole the visit was a pleasant one. While they were
here. I had a call from the man we had carriages from at
the Winthrop House. Asked if I had not received a
bill--e. tc.
    I insisted that everything had been included in the
bill of the Hotel--He could explain nothing & sent the
man--the 'cocher' in the evening; who presented me the
items--which may & may not be correct. I shall send some
one to The Winthrop to enquire into the fact.--Last night
we went--Dr Miller--Lucy & The Tompkins' to see John. He
looked badly: for although he had a ↑good↓ costume & was
made up well for the part--yet he lacked character. That
is one great draw-back to his success, I think--he can't
transform himself. The combat was ~~the~~ strictly
'gladitorial'--the muscles of his arms--for his sleeves
were rolled up--eclipsing everything else besides. "Look

at his arm"--every one exclaimed--& highly delighted the
audience seemed at this exhibition.
  He was more melo-dramatic than I have ever seen
him--& no better--if quite so good--as Eddy & a host of
others I have seen in the same part.--The Goulds sat
<u>behind</u> me--& Daley the artist.  They talked with me
between the acts.--I am so sorry Mrs S-- has been called
to her brother's side on so sad an errand.  Will this
preclude the possibility of her coming on here?--My
dearest papa--write me all about yourself--& your
business at the Theatre.  I will write you longer
letters--after a few days, I have no news yet.  The snow
is falling beautifully to day: & the sleigh-ride you will
miss.  Babe talks of Papa--kisses his picture--& cries in
her pretty half complaining style--when we ask--"an
est-↑il↓ Papa"?  Is Launt T-- at work on you yet--have
you seen the Woodman's?--write me all that you do & hear
& above all things love me dearly!  Try & make yourself
comfortable & be happy.  What a fine show you had of
Monday night--I am anxious to know the result of
Tuesday.--God bless--Yours
                 Mollie

# NOTEBOOKS

Record Book (NYPL—TC), 4 October 1860

Encouraged by the quiet attention and most kindly comendations of my dear husband--on every occasion, when after 'the play' I have offered him my humble criticism, (suggested entirely by his beautiful impersonations, and not my own conceit,) I begin the following pages; which I dedicate with deep affection to his service.
 I tremble lest the too partial eye of love, may overcome and help to defeat my purposed wish; but since I am assured that his generous nature would not accept aught save ~~the~~ truth,--consience, shall guide me, and to it, heart must succumb. These "Records" will be seen, and read by his eyes alone, and from such a 'loving Judge', condemnation (if they merit it) will fall lightly on this 'devoted head'. In the grandest compositions shades are mingled--nothing real, is perfect; but the closely discerning, friendly eye, is, by the sight of one great beauty, led to discover another; of less importance and remark, it may be, but is, nevertheless, one of the subtle links, most necessary in preserving--what art would be lifeless without--unity; chefs-d'oeuvre are produced by observing it.--Audacious to my self, seems, my contemplated task; but certain I am that my efforts, will meet with no scornful rejection--though thir adoption may be kindly turned aside, at times. With this confidence in the tenderness, if not the approbation of the subject of it--I cheerfully prepare them for his perusal.

                                         Baltimore Oct 4th
                                                    1860.

                              Macbeth
Set 1st                                         Scene 3rd--

"Into the air"--
     The posture, expression and tone most admirable; the
'even emphasis' upon these <u>three words</u>--the long dwelling
upon each--~~in~~ and uttered in a <u>subdued</u>, though slightly
elevated voice, cause them to fall upon the auditor's
ear, as though they themselves were as vapory as the
substance which has just vanished before them.
     The effect is indeed--"as breath into the wind"

          "If good why do I yeald"--

     I have never seen it made sufficiently                      10
apparent--that the <u>murder</u> is <u>already</u> <u>conceived</u>. It seems
to me, that by some internal working the horrid thought,
should reveal itself to the spectator, in the expression
of feature at these words--"the greatest is behind"; at
least, the impossibility is more than half o'ercome--and
he begins to "yeald to that suggestion" which doth unfix
his hair.

          "To-morrow as he purposes"
     From this time until their exeunt it seems most
natural that he should avoid her penetrating glance.  he     T
could not have anticipated so immediate a detection by      21
his 'face' of the deed within and had he intended the
revealing of it <u>then</u>, would not have been so easily
disconcerted; and encouraged by the promise of his wife's
help--in a half inclining tone says--"we will speak
further"; a proof that his maner should be abstractd is
her last entreaty, and ↑gentle↓ reminder, that "to alter
favour ever is to fear".


                    "Hamlet"
     Of this play--Goëthe says "that Shakespere's            A
intention was to exhibit the effects of a <u>great action</u>,
imposed as a <u>duty</u> upon a mind too feeble for its
accomplishment"--; "an oak planted in a china vase" &c; a
view that to me seems the clearest and most comprehensive
of any that have been offered and thrust upon us by the
'<u>meddlers</u>' of our immortal bard.
     After reading their several 'commentaries' do we not
return to the work itself confused and unenlightened?
their endeavours to seek after and explain the truth,        T
leads them almost invariably into a mutilation of nature    11
that is unpardonable. All that has been said about
it--and written too, can never, to my mind--throw a light
comparable to that, that the intellectual and spiritual
power of an actor of <u>genius</u> can irradiate.  In the person
of 'mon cher ami'--we have an ideal of Hamlet--"the glass
of fashion and the mould of form" the closely critical,      T

and penuriously analitical might quarrel with an
estimate finding him too tame, too passionate or
conventional in such or such a place--but the musical and
poetic ones--will not allow their soothed senses to be
shocked by the material standard of these carping
critics. Who but those too entirely encrusted with
'mortality' to receive the images of ~~his~~ fancy--could
resist the pale, spiritual beauty of his face and form
when he first appears upon the scene; ~~a reluctant, shrincking--~~ There in the gaily assembled court, a
"reluctant member" shrincking from his place--yet obliged
as Prince to occupy it; the sombe drapery--fixed and
thoughtful, melancholy gaze--tell us that his thoughts
are with the past! other affairs of court dispatched the
'cousin and son' attract regard--and that sorrow that his
form so well discloses to us is questioned and
unveiled!--
   This 'opening' of the character is difficult and
almost impossible for the artist to portray
satisfactorily; we have had time during the previous
dialogue of the several personages to fully comprehend
the depth of ~~his~~ ↑Hamlet's↓ grief--with his listlessness
and abstraction--we are 'en rapport' and to hear broken
that silence, (by words)--that we ourselves ~~partake of~~
↑share↓ in for to us 'tis a prevailing woe--and we feel
nervous and tremulous for him who first breaks through
the cloud.


   [addenda on inserted leaves]

3    together with the facial expression perfectly
~~portrays~~ ↑definite↓ the idea--and produces ~~the~~ an
atmosphere wholly spiritual.--This or the scene following
are not always seizable--the ~~actor's mood~~ poet's here ~~and~~
is entirely under the control of the actor; his mood,
mars or makes true the ~~treasure~~ picture.
     'Hamlet reading'--
   How well assumed is Hamlet's madness towards old P.,
the meddler the tell-tale of the Court--yet therefores
seasoned with wisdom to further astound and confuse the
old cortiere who thoroughly appreciates the method in his
'madness'--
   look you this brave o'erhanging &c--
   Here Edwin goes to the open window and descants upon
the pestilent congregation of vapours" returning ~~to~~ ↑at↓
"what a piece of work is man" to his listeners and
addressing ↑to↓ them this universalism; now, the first
action I think truthful--but the last apostrophe ought so
to be delivered--that Hamlet, the theme--all should be
forgotten and the eyes of the auditors turned to inward
contemplation. for here Hamlet is the personifict of
Man--the reason the philosopher,
   --the players shall receive."--
   How singular that after this great desitive upon

Man--Rozencrantz ~~a superficial court tool~~--should
announce the player; an intended analagism of Shakespere
perhaps--for else where he calls man a 'poor player': a
reasoning which if true would argue more depth ~~than~~ we
superficial court tool--than we feel inclined to award
him.
   --"What a rogue am I'

4 the spirit I have seen--
as My dear Edwin utters these lines--'wonders are revealed'.


Journal (Players), 4-12 November 1860

                        Nov 4th

   ~~Str~~
   The keeping of a Journal--or a faithful record of my
daily thoughts and actions, has always been my intention,
and earnest desire. Before my happy marriage I failed in
this determination. the wild hopes, and strange emotions
of the fiancèe, eluded constantly my pen--and would not
be transcribed; they were indefinite though by no means
transitory, for I enjoy them now in their fullest
reality.
   I regret the non-possession of such a transcript of
the past, deeply! how much I should like <u>now</u> to read
over the joys and sorrows, comforts and discomforts of a
former time! how illy they would compare with my present
bliss--which is too great for my soul's compass. Such
memories--though they seemed generous enough at the time
I'm sure would look to my eyes most selfish, compared
with my present feelings every one of which, is shared by
and with my dear 'life's partner', and 'tis for his
benefit and service I begin this diary of my married
life. My new existance has dawned upon me, with many
cares and responsibilities; sometimes they seem great and
startling to me; I get confused and almost irritated
amidst them, and frequently feel the need a quiet little
corner where I may lodge my griefs and sore distractions,
that has no speech to answer me--my own hand giving the
only reproach and advice; encouragement too will be thus
extracted for the performance of my duty. My dear
Edwin's health--his moods and various humors, I will
endeavor faithfully to regard and here insert them; they
will prove gentle reminders and entreat my patience: for
dearly as I love him, my own selfish exactions make me
forgetful of his ailments.

Nov 5

Last night, and the greater part of yesterday was, ill and complaining; gloomy where there was no need, for my dear husband, gave me his presence the live-long day. He bore most gently my dullness and restlessness--at night a feverish longing, which his kindness failed to quell, possessed and made me unreasonable, and I know caused him annoyance--O, let me forget it--and this the only record be, of my folly--for such the calm reasoning of the present proclaims it!--This morning, he took his bath, and I assisted at it;--how fondly I love him when he admits me thus to be by him; he seems so like a child, and accepts I'm sure the attention my soul prompts me to give him with all the gratitude of his nature. But the breakfast that followed these playful moments ~~were~~ ↑did↓ not pass so joyfully; the coffee did not please (this was distraction enough for anybody) and I very foolishly but Heaven knows not wantonly, argued with him upon a trifling, silly, matter, not worth the words spent upon it; He is obstinent and persistent by nature--but a little kindly yealding on my part, will make him, see his wrong--when 'Mary''s committed; and I will by this womanly trait obtain a far greater triumph, than wifly 'holding out' would effect, even though truth sustain me. A husband is woman's only friend--she ought to cling to, and yet support him in all things--at all times, and never allow her own selfish desires to disturb or cloud their fair horizon. I ? must remember always his delicate frame--his beauty, and the supreme goodness of his heart--and never do aught to cause his faithful, confiding nature, a moment's regret. He took me for his companion, and helpmeet--I am full of error, and need restriction--he is all indulgent, and I must repay him by forbearing on all occasions, against--ill humor, fatigue--disappointments of the day--business &c &-- --

Nov. 6

Kept amiable to day, and had a rich reward; a long 'morning sleep', gave rest to my Edwin's tired brain--and produced a wholesome and a sweet temper. Morning is a very dangerous time to parley with a husband's humour--especially the strange being, God has given me to guard; having passions--different from 'the race of men'--his moods and dispositions vary, and I must school myself to adopt my conversation and wishes to them always. This is a trifling sacrifice and will be richly repaid--for his goodness will not fail to appreciate it. A wound has been inflicted upon me, severe and painful--one of the sweet and cherished friendships of my young life, rudely dissevered--I fear even to make this record of it, lest it prove true--or if false, will stare at me in reproach--

Had it been a breach of confidence--placed by me in some fresh young bosom, in all things my equal--and then to have been deceived--I might have cause to bewail it more; but <u>here</u> there was no such thing; the protection of a powerful mind--strong in the ways of the world as well as in <u>art</u>, I enjoyed and felt deep pleasure in--nor ever thought to question its sincerity or disinterestedness; I was mistaken and--no not, mistaken I hope--even my 'journal' shall contain no harsh thought against one that may yet be cleared. I have lost a deal of time today,--I must continue to economise, or my duties will be neglected. Work goes hand in hand with cheerfulness, I must presume that or I am lost. Good we must seek, but evil comes unsought!--Scarcely realizing--my position as <u>wife</u> I neglect or do things contrary to the calm reasoning of such moments as these; I must seize as many of them as time will permit--and by and by they will come uncalled and stand in readiness to serve me; thus will 'things' remain undisturbed ever--

Nov<br>7

This day let me never forget: Edwin and myself both ill from the suffering of last night; what torture I endured and inflicted; the cause, can never ~~be anything~~ will always bring us pains, so let it be buried ere further harm comes from it. My spirit has long forborne resentment--in yealding this and it was a crime, for which I was justly punished.

Edwin brought me a tiny gold necklace this morning, so opportune it came--when I was ignorant of his feelings--(for he was sick when he left me to go out) that it seemed like an embrace--and I prized it more for its significance--Before returning we talked of Art and its critics; though lively and animated, the conversation did not assume or approach the form of argument in any way. This was as it should always be: argument ever ends in obstinancy and what is more ungracious? between husband and wife. opinion should only differ when absolute truth is outraged and then, it should be gently held forth: A little variety is refreshing too--but let it never be so opposite in tone and expression as to give rise to that 'chose terrible'--<u>argument</u>. Yet I have been inclined to indulge in this with him whom I esteem and respect so above all human beings--I believe I have already confessed to these pages "A voice gentle and low and excellent thing in woman"!--

Tonight read in Goethe; "Elective Affinitie." I have not ~~caught~~ ↑seized↓ yet the aim or what it is meant to be proven by the book. These abstract metaphysical subjects excite the curiosity to follow them--but to a mind predisposed to follow only, natural and simple laws--they offered no satisfaction and fail to infuse into the intelligence that high order of spiritualism

that is their foundation.  But I will reserve my
judgement--until 'finis', gives me full liberty to pass
judgement.

Nov<br>8

No particular even to mark this day;--only a sense
of happiness and contentment distinguishes it from the
early part of yesterday:
My husband spent all day with me: was much better in
health than yesterday: walked out a little while--and for
the first time, met me on the street by accident!
I make note of it for we have both remarked the
oddity of our never meeting thus before.--The Theater I
have not entered for nearly two weeks, and begin to feel
an anxiety to see my darling on his 'throne' again.  The
"Fool's Revenge" has been a great hit; its sensation
effects have pleased the Philadelpheans; whose mediocrity
of appreciation is well established; they prefer it to
Shaks this is easily accounted for; the mass support the
Theater--and where they go--the 'select few' withhold
their presence; crowds always hear and see but it must be
something striking that will make them feel.  Listening
Shaks their brains are too much torted--Tom Taylor
thrills the blood and excites eagerness and anxiety for
the fates of his heroes--it mattering but little what
words they utter--so they be furious at times--at times
talkative.  One of the Journals say, Mr Booth has
elevated the play--and 'tis true--his genius is of a
higher order than this play will admit--but why ought not
a great actor sometimes condescend to stoop and lend his
talents to aid the success of an author who has labored
to please and his work fails through lack of
encouragement; the actor may portray truth and bring a
moral to light, where it may be appreciated--and
inculcate a lesson, by his power of producing--which the
author small too obscure.  11. o'clock has come I'll sit
and wait!--

Nov--<br>10

Went to the play tonight--saw "Fool's Revenge";
witnessed with delight the wonderful improvement in
Edwin's acting of the Jester; the first two acts are not
worthy of particular note; all wait for the deneument and
certainly 'twas ↑a↓ very grand dramatic tableau:  The
public throughout were held and entranced seemingly, but
yet I predict (although I desire my prophesy to fall
short of fulfillment) that 'twill never become standard:
This I only confide to you my journal--for Edwin's heart
is set upon it, and is convicted that it has merit of a
high order--that is for dramatic effects;-- ~~and~~ yet as a

quiet spectator I differ from him: success, elates the
artist ever and is apt to persuade him ↑his↓ work has
excellence especially when the rôle is new: it develops
resonances that he has not known himself to be the
possessor of, and novelity he enjoys. I almost feel
inclined to breathe a wish that he will soon lay it
aside, but would not dare say as much--lest I should
discourage his efforts; and they deserve better than
this.--

I hope he will make it succeed however--and gain the
applause of wiser heads than my simple, loving one, then
I will willingly draw a line across this page, and strive
to forget the predjices of to day; they were formed from,
and after reading V. Hugo's--Le Roi: I remember my wild
enthusiasm over that drama--how astounded I was--without
considering object or plot--nature or truth--and how upon
analysis, with my teacher, who had led me on to think it
gold--my admiration stood, staring at me a
reproach--heart had to give way before a saturnial
observer, of incidents of the fact's result. I am afraid
close criticism, makes me positive; ah, a hateful state of
being

I should alter myself then I'm sure and be looked
coldly upon by others

I must avoid it, and follow the natural promptings
of my heart.

Nov--<br>11

Read all day;--Edwin seated Pasha like upon the
sofa--poring over books--taking in by a cursory
glance--more I am convinced than twelve I's could have
done with attentive and close study. What a singular
mind he has; knows so many queer things that no one else
ever seems to have made any reconing of; these he hoards
up--or rather they seem to keep their place in his memory
better, than the knowledge that every body possesses;
this gives a tone of originality to his conversation; and
makes it intensely interesting at times; I have seen him
startle the ears of the best read people of the simple
relating of some odd occurrence that or queer fact that
has escaped their vigilant inquiry--

His intuitive perception of his Bard's works too,
are so clear and truthful--yet new to the close student
even--astonishes me at times--A 27, he seems to
understand human nature perfectly; whether 'tis more of
his innate knowledge of their dispositions--more than
from actual experience I hardly know; he has seen much of
life, but Fortune has been almost thrust upon him, and I
fancy 'tis with him as with those th who, seek by science
to know the man's misteries; they can only quess at the
other side: yet his opinions are not merely speculative,
they have good basis and you will find it difficult, to
entirely confute them

How strange how beautiful he is!--the deference I
used to feel towards him,--as fiancèe--has with marriage
almost entirely given way.--He is strong ~~and~~ in
individuality--yet at times I feel that I am required to
stand <u>alone</u>. At first, this affected me as I imagine a
drowning sensation would do--I looked around for
something to grasp--; but now I find a resting place when
driven to this strait; his nature craves my patience--and
fortitude--and 'twill strengthen me.

Nov--
12

Edwin plays Hamlet to night--his master piece ~~?~~ I
think; we talked long and earnestly before he left
me--gave me advice and consel--and although repugnant for
the most part to my feelings--I accepted and promised
obedience; but I am very happy now, upon reflection that
I acted thus wisely. The claim he holds upon is a sacred
~~repon~~ one--and a rejection of his rights is ~~even~~ very
dear to him:
Besides they ↑were↓ truthful and wise
suggestious--my conscience tells me this, and should
'remorse not sting me were the wrong followed instead?
[He likes] me to ponder well upon my past and [just] to
see when I am at fault--for ah! I feel that my duty,
though a difficult one, must be performed; and not with
reluctance nor tears neither, but cheerfulness; that god
of every household, of every bath in life.
Perhaps I ought not to consider so sensitively, what
must be done so lightly--but the struggle soon will have
passed away--'tis only the first few rods of the way that
seem difficult and wearsome--and the flowers unheeded
hitherto will appear brighter and more lovely as we
journey on--Let not fatigue ~~ore~~ over take us and the sun
will shine brightly before us to its setting:

Nov--
12

I turn awhile from the 'Informitive'--to convey a
few of the delightful impressions ~~of the week~~ made upon
me by this little work. ~~A few~~ Some pages just finished,
have filled me with ineffable peace, and sweet delight;
no doubt other thoughts and feelings will displace them
ere long, and I should so regret to lose all trace of
them; for perhaps with another reading--the same joy will
not be experienced--although their truth and beauty can
never escape me--
How the Author's own buffetings, and misfortunes
with the world breathes their complainings forth, through
the hero! Unhappy, <u>genius ever is</u> but when to this is
added unfortunate parentage poverty in the world's good,
and an absolute dependence upon the bounty of others it
is an unenviable lot. Does it not seem as though God had

endowed them with the genius power to sing their sad fate
alone?  'tis true that the voice frequently is hushed ere
it reaches the listless ears of the world--but its
utterings are not doomed to perish likewise: they live to
be a monument--and tears fall through them upon the
world's cold cheeck, at last.  In this little book of
Hans Christian Andersen's, how beautifully present joy
and past despair are blended!  Driven from his own land
by discouragement and ill health--his spirit was freed
under the soft genial sky of Italy; he saw Art loved for
Art's sake--for where so many assemble to worship the
shrine must be a holy one;--and he met with liberality
and generosity ~~when unknown~~ ↑held from him↓ in his native
land--and he began to sing.  Nature--there so golden--
took him to her bosom, and his whole being received new
inspiration; he forgave the cruelty of his native North
toward him--and produced a divine and universal work:
The moanings and lamentings ~~of~~ in his 'Impro'--are not

[third dateline]

the bitter and sarcastic out-pourings of the disappointed
poet; I can liken them to naught but the gentle sobs of
the innocent child--after the denial or refusal has
clouded its hopeful little bosom--and, sweet sleep comes
to refresh it; upon awaking joy beams again from its
eyes--resentment is forgotten--and hope and love return.
How thankful we ought to be to the bright land that thus
refreshed his thirsty dying soul--and gave his spirit
strength to describe its loveliness.  Italy--it is the
only home for genius!  beneath its fostering care, the
restless spirit grows calm and productive too; how I long
to see it:--This was once only a girlish craving--but now
for the sake of him I love the yearning assumes the form
of necessity and I pray that my desire to go there will
be answered.

# ANNOTATIONS

The text of these documents includes a wide variety of references to the people and events which contributed to shaping the lives of MDB and EB. Annotation is potentially unlimited. In general, therefore, the principle in this volume is to provide only that information which will make the context for the text understandable and useful to both scholar and general reader. Annotation is thus limited to identifying and making clarifying remarks about people, places, events, literary works, and other primary matters. Interpretive comment is carefully avoided.

Within this limitation, however, these notes aspire to be comprehensive. When appropriate, persons, places and events are not only identified but explained in detail, often by use of original materials in diverse manuscript collections. It is hoped that in these instances the notes go beyond simply annotating the text--that they point to additional (in some cases new) resources for study. As with the larger matters, snippets of verse and snatches of quotations, or paraphrases of them, have been identified when possible.

Furthermore, cross-references--to MDB documents or to annotations for MDB documents--have been liberally employed. This is based on the assumption that for many readers, this volume will ultimately be used for reference; that after an initial through-reading of all the letters, readers will often refer to individual letters in isolation. The many "see . . ." references among the annotations supplement the index and are more convenient and quicker to use than it is.

All annotations are presented following a "cue" word or passage from the text which in turn is followed by a colon. To alert the reader to the existence of each annotation, a symbol (A) has been placed to the right of the relevant line of the text. (A slight exception to this occurs on four occasions in the Record Book, where MDB wrote headings for newspaper clippings she pasted in. Because they are merely headings, they are presented only in the Textual Notes;

accordingly, since they are presented there, no symbol can be conveniently used to indicate the existence of an annotation for them, though annotations for the headings and for items in the clippings themselves do exist and are given in the present section.) Only one symbol has been used per line, even if that line has more than one annotation.

Letters

Letter 1 (Players)
    line 3: Capt Leitch: In a letter to Emma Crow from Europe, 14 July [1858], Cushman records using Capt. Leitch of the steamer *Europe* to carry her letter to Crow back to America (Charlotte Cushman Papers, LC--MD, Vol. 1, p. 78). See Annotation for Letter 2, l. 3.
    line 6: Mrs Davenport: Fanny Elizabeth Davenport (1829-1891), English-born actress. MD had been performing in Boston, with Mrs. Davenport and her American actor husband, Edward Loomis Davenport (1815-1877), as the headliners, since 15 September.
    line 11: Mr Pray: Isaac Clark Pray (1813-1869), American author, journalist and theatre manager credited with having brought Charlotte Cushman to the public's attention. His son, Frank W. Pray, married Emily F. Cutter on 29 October 1858.
    signature: "Juliet": MD played Juliet to Charlotte Cushman's Romeo during Cushman's farewell performance in Baltimore (26 April-8 May), Boston (31 May-12 June) and New York (21 June-6 July).

Letter 2 (LC--MD)
    line 3: "Pearls": In a letter to MD from London, 4 October 1858 (Players), Cushman records sending the "Roman pearls" she had promised. See Annotation for Letter 1, l. 3.
    line 6: Theater: see Letter 1, l. 6.
    lines 6-7: Mrs Davenport: see Annotation for Letter 1, l. 6.
    line 11: Mr Pray: see Annotation for Letter 1, l. 11.

Letter 3 (Players)
    lines 14-15: How ↑you↓ can act: EB was scheduled to perform in Buffalo in October.
    line 18: Paradise Valley: the Jeffersons' retreat during the summers of 1858 and 1859 in the Pocono Mountains in Pennsylvania.
    lines 29-31: Walter, Louise: Walter M. Brackett (1823-1918) of Boston was a painter, first of portraits and later of game fish, exhibiting in Vienna, Philadelphia, New York, Boston and at the Crystal Palace in London. He married Marie Louise Loring in 1850. His oil of EB as Hamlet was sold at the auction of Adam Badeau's art collection in

New York in 1901. Letters (1858-1864) from EB to
Brackett are at HU--TC and HRHRC.

Letter 4 (NYPL--TC)
line 1: Mr Baker: Benjamin A. Baker (1818-1890),
American actor who played minor roles with Junius
Brutus Booth, was a theatre manager, and was EB's
agent in 1856 when MD and EB first met and acted
together in Richmond. See Badeau's letter to EB
(Players), 21 April 1859.
line 2: Mr. Eddy: Edward Eddy (1822-1875), American
actor and theatre manager who was manager of
Niblo's Garden during MD's engagement there 29
June-30? July 1859 and EB's single night engagement there, 30 July 1859. See also Badeau's
letter to EB (Players), 21 April 1859. Eddy, who
was also from Troy (New York), had performed at
the Troy Museum while MD lived there. MD's first
known New York appearance (28 June 1855) was with
Eddy.
line 18: De Bar: Benedict De Bar (1812-1877),
English-born actor, manager, and theatre owner in
St. Louis.
lines 20-21: Mr. Spofford: Richard Smith Spofford
(1833-1888), American lawyer and politician, to
whom MD was nearly engaged in 1858. Spofford
became engaged to the American poet Harriet Prescott in 1860 and they were married on 19 December
1865.
line 22: Theater: Niblo's Garden in New York, where
MD performed 29 June-30? July, her final appearance.
line 23: Davenport: Adolphus Hoyt Davenport (1828-
1873), American actor.
line 23: very fine house: a reference to Davenport's
benefit, which was on 16 July 1859.

Letter 6 (Players)
line 14: "Dussoldorff Geallery": public picture
gallery located at 548 Broadway.
line 21: <u>Molly</u>: MD's pet dog.
lines 38-39: play <u>Richard</u>, every night: EB was to
open in Philadelphia in late August. See Annotation for Letter 10, l. 1. *Richard III* "was to be
the great feature of this engagement," but owing
to EB's illness and "the piece being so infernally
hackneyed, it ran only [the first] five
nights. . ." of the engagement (EB to "Walter," 12
September [1859], HU--TC).

Letter 7 (NYPL--TC)
line 26: Mr Sothern: Edward Askew Sothern (1826-
1881), English-born actor. He performed at
Niblo's sporadically between 22 July and 10 September 1859.

120    Annotations

    line 30:  Mollie:  see Annotation for Letter 6, l. 21.
    line 34:  officer of mine:  *Othello*, II.iii.249.

Letter 8 (Players)
    At head of first page, in pencil, in EB's hand: "Sept 19" and "Hoboken". In September 1859, when MD was in Hoboken, the 19th was a Monday, not a Tuesday.
    line 18:  <u>R. S. Spofford</u> Esq.: see Annotation for Letter 4, ll. 20-21.
    line 23:  Southern:  see Annotation for Letter 7, l. 26.

Letter 9 (NYPL--TC)
    line 44:  'Spiritualism': Since spiritualism was one of the most popular pseudo-sciences of the age, MDB was not the only influence on EB regarding it. She was the strongest and most direct, however, and her effect was undeniably powerful, even for some years after her death. In a letter dated 2 May 1864 (Players) EB wrote Badeau that he had conversed with three people via a medium after they were dead--his friend Richard Cary, his father, and MDB. Several of Badeau's letters to Harry Wilson (Princeton) reveal Badeau's amazement at the effect of spiritualism on EB. On 2 August 1864, Badeau wrote that EB "is wonderfully changed. I know no man more unselfish, more pure, more anxious to be useful, to be good, to do his whole duty to every one; more earnestly desirous to turn his natural gifts to account to the elevation or improvement of men. He has become profoundly religious, and . . . this is all through *spiritualism*." As late as 4 January 1865, Badeau wrote that because of spiritualism EB was a "consistent Christian" though he "has not united himself with any church."

Letter 10 (Players)
    line 1:  <u>Phil</u>:  EB was to open in Philadelphia at the Arch Street Theatre on 27 August 1859 (Saturday) but due to illness did not open till 29 August (Monday). He closed on 24 September. MD visited him from 9 September (Friday) to 12 September (Monday). See EB to "Walter," 12 September [1859], HU--TC.
    lines 18-20:  "Not mine . . . tire".: Tennyson, *In Memoriam*, CX, ll. 17-18.
    line 31:  Molly:  see Annotation for Letter 6, l. 21.

Letter 11 (NYPL--TC)
    line 13:  <u>Phil</u>:  see Annotation for Letter 10, l. 1.
    line 14:  <u>Louise</u>:  see Annotation for Letter 3, ll. 29-31.
    line 29:  Doc Holmes: Oliver Wendell Holmes (1809-1894), author and physician. His *The Autocrat of the Breakfast-Table* (1858) remarks often on New England language and speech.

line 31: Theater: see Annotation for Letter 10, l. 1.

Letter 12 (NYPL--TC)
Beneath MD's signature, in pencil in EB's hand:
        Dear, dear Soul!
            I was unworthy [of] so
        much goodness.
            Shall we ever
        meet again?

Letter 13 (NYPL--TC)
lines 3-4: trouble . . . N. J-- --R. R.: On 18 September 1859, two regiments of New Jersey State Militia were called to quell a disturbance by striking Erie Railroad workmen at Berger Tunnel near Jersey City (see Philadelphia *Public Ledger*, 19 September 1859, p. 1).
line 12: 'Niagara': EB and MDB did honeymoon at Niagara Falls as late as the date of a letter by Asia Booth Clarke (Peale Museum) which mentions the matter , 21 August 1860, and were accompanied by EB's mother and brother Joseph.

Letter 15 (Players)
line 22: 'Buffalo': EB performed in Buffalo 3-14 October 1859 at the Metropolitan Theatre.
line 25: brother's: perhaps Charles, 25, but more likely William H., 11, who would still be living at home.
lines 35-36: "Bertha . . . Helvetia": Bertha, daughter of Burkhard, Duke of Alemanni and wife of King Rudolf II of Burgundy. MD's reference is probably to Longfellow's *Courtship of Miles Standish*, viii, which refers to Bertha.

Letter 16 (Players)
line 6: Mr Clark: John Sleeper Clarke (1833-1899), American actor and theatre manager; schoolmate of EB. Clarke married EB's sister Asia on 28 April 1859 (see Letter 31, ll. 54-59 and Annotation for Letter 31, line 54). Clarke frequently performed with EB and with him co-managed the Walnut St. Theatre in Philadelphia (1863-1870), the Winter Garden Theatre in New York (1864-1866), and the Boston Theatre (1866-1867).

Letter 17 (NYPL--TC)
line 18: Boston: see Annotation for Letter 19, l. 8.

Letter 18 (NYPL--TC)
line 10: John Ford: John T. Ford (1829-1894), American theatre manager. During the mid and late 1850s, Ford managed Baltimore's Holliday St. Theatre, Washington's National Theatre and Richmond's Marshall Theatre simultaneously. MD performed at all of these "Ford Theatres." Her first

appearance with EB was at the Marshall Theatre in
November 1856.
    lines 23-25:  Shelley:  Percy Bysshe Shelley (1792-
        1822), English poet.  The lines referred to are
        from *Adonais*, stanza 31.  See Letter 19, ll. 43-
        45.

Letter 19 (NYPL--TC)
    line 1:  'Buffalo':  see Annotation for Letter 15, l.
        22.
    line 8:  Boston:  EB performed in Boston 17 October-12
        November 1859 at the Howard Athenaeum.
    line 11:  E. L.:  E. L. Davenport; see Annotation for
        Letter 1, l. 6.  Davenport was lessee and manager
        of the Howard Athenaeum; with Mrs. Davenport and
        daughter Fanny, he supported EB throughout EB's
        engagement.
    lines 43-45:  "Companionless . . . knell":  see Annota-
        tion for Letter 18, ll. 23-25.

Letter 20 (NYPL--TC)
    line 1:  'after 'Richard':  EB performed *Richard III* in
        Buffalo on 7 and 13 October 1859 at the Metropoli-
        tan Theatre.
    line 5:  Buffalo:  see Annotation for Letter 15, l. 22.
    lines 39-55:  Miss Bartlett's marriage . . . a full
        accout:  On 13 October 1859, Frances Amelia Bart-
        lett married Don Estaban Santa Cruz de Oviedo,
        Spanish "millionaire *de partibus*" at New York's
        St. Patrick's Cathedral, Archbishop Hughes of New
        York officiating.  The New York *Times* (14 October
        1859, p. 4) called it "The Marriage of the
        Season."  MD's "blue B's" refers to the Spanish
        aristocratic blue blood and "red B's" presumably
        to the American blood line.
    line 46:  Louise:  see Annotation for Letter 3, ll. 29-
        31.
    line 56:  'opening night':  see Annotation for Letter
        19, l. 8.

Letter 21 (NYPL--TC)
    line 7:  mad step, John has taken:  On 11 November, on
        the spur of the moment, John Wilkes Booth joined
        the Virginia militia to guard against attempts
        upon the life of John Brown (see Stanley Kimmel,
        *The Mad Booths of Maryland*.  2d ed. [New York,
        1969], pp. 155-156 and Charles F. Fuller, Jr.,
        "Edwin and John Wilkes Booth:  Actors at the Old
        Marshall Theatre in Richmond," *Virginia Magazine
        of History and Biography*, 79 [1971], 483).
    lines 15-16:  play of Taylor's:  Tom Taylor (1817-
        1880), British dramatist, editor of *Punch*, and
        professor of English at London Univ. The Taylor
        play referred to was probably *The Fool's Revenge*
        (1859), which became one of EB's favorites to
        perform.  See Letter 23, l. 43 and MD's Journal

for 8 and 10 November; also, Asia Booth Clarke, *The Elder and the Younger Booth* (Boston, 1882), pp. 152-153.
    line 19: opening in the Autumn in N. Y: EB opened in New York in 1860 on 26 November at the Winter Garden as Hamlet.
    line 26: 'well mouth': possibly MD suffered from fever blisters. See Letter 74, l. 15.

Letter 22 (NYPL--TC)
    line 9: 'Miller's daughter': "The Miller's Daughter," a narrative poem by Tennyson (1809-1892) published in 1832, first appeared in a gift-book edition in 1858.
    lines 43-44: "died . . . Keats: John Keats (1795-1821), English poet. The passage is from *Hyperion*, Bk. III, l. 130.

Letter 23 (Players)
    line 11: "Le Memorial": probably Émile Vander-Burch and C. Brainne, *Le Mémorial François*. Paris, 1855.
    line 43: 'Fool's Revenge': see Annotation for Letter 21, ll. 15-16.

Letter 24 (NYPL--TC)
    line 20: 'long journey': EB's lengthy southern tour from December 1859 to May 1860.

Letter 25 (Players)
    line 3: "Miller's Daughter": see Annotation for Letter 22, l. 9.
    line 8: Montgomery: EB performed in Montgomery, Alabama, 19-28 December 1859 at the Gaiety Theatre.
    lines 18-19: John's trouble: see Annotation for Letter 21, l. 7.
    line 47: H.'s new play: *Henry II*, by Gideon Hiram Hollister (1817-1881), American author and politician. See letters to EB by Badeau at the Players, especially those of 13-18 January [1860], 28 January [1860], 18 April [1860] and 8 May [1860]. EB performed *Henry II* 16-19 January 1860 at the St. Charles Theatre, New Orleans. In a letter to Hollister, 2 February 1860 (HRHRC), EB records his payment of $80 for the play and suggests necessary changes. He planned a New York opening for it and was so enamored with it that he thought someday it would stand at the head of American dramatic art. In a letter to Walter Brackett (10 February [1859]; HRHRC), EB observed that one act was "more telling--if possible--than the 4th act of Richelieu." Apparently Hollister didn't repair the play satisfactorily, however, so EB asked Badeau to "fix up" the script, which Badeau agreed to do (see Badeau's letters to EB of 18 April and 8 May [1860]; Players).

>    line 66: 'Alice': heroine of "The Miller's Daughter."
>    See Annotation for Letter 22, l. 9.
>    lines 83-86: "And now . . . heart!": "The Miller's
>    Daughter," ll. 195-198.
>    line 114: N.O: EB performed in New Orleans 2-22
>    January 1860, at the St. Charles Theatre.
>
> Letter 26 (Players)
>    line 4: N. O.: see Annotation for Letter 25, l. 114.
>
> Letter 27 (NYPL--TC)
>    line 8: new peice: Hollister's *Henry II*. See Annotation for Letter 25, l. 47.
>    line 11: 'W. Garden': Winter Garden, the New York Theatre most known for tragedy in the 1850s and 1860s. See Annotation for Letter 16, l. 6.
>    line 12: 'Lesbia': translation by Heron (see below) of five-act drama, *Les Noces Venetiennes* (Paris, 1855) by Victor Sejour.
>    line 13: Wallack: James William Wallack, Jr. (1818-1873), English-born actor.
>    lines 16-17: Miss Hernon: Matilda Agnes Heron (1830-1877), Irish-born actress who became the first great American Marguerite (Camille) Gautier, the heroine of *Camille*. MD had performed as Michette to Heron's Camille at the National Theatre in Washington, D.C. on 31 October 1855. See Letter 30, ll. 36-44.
>    line 18: Mr Jordan: George Jordan, New York actor.
>    line 27: accounted a failure: also Badeau's opinion--see his letter to EB at Players, 28 January [1860].
>    line 29: '<u>Camilles</u>': heroine of a dramatization of Alexander Dumas *fils'* novel *La Dame aux Camélias*, first acted in France in 1852 and introduced to American audiences in 1853 with the title *Camille; or, The Fate of a Coquette*.
>    line 29: <u>Medeas</u>: a reference to the heroine of *Medea* (431 BC), by Euripides (484-406 BC).
>    line 57: <u>Jules Thierry</u>: perhaps Jules Thierry who wrote on French architecture, but more likely Jacques N. Augustin Thierry (1795-1856), the eminent French Romantic historian.
>    line 66: 'Memorial': see Annotation for Letter 23, l. 11.
>
> Letter 28 (NYPL--TC)
>    line 18: '<u>Victor</u> Hugo: Victor-Marie Hugo (1802-1885), French poet, novelist and dramatist.
>    lines 22-23: 'Le Roi s'amuse': 1832 drama by Hugo adapted by Tom Taylor as *The Fool's Revenge* (1859). See Letters 21, ll. 15-16 and 23, l. 43.
>    lines 47-48: Mr Clarke: see Annotation for Letter 16, l. 6.
>    line 52: <u>Mobile</u>: EB performed in Mobile 24 January-14 February 1860.

line 62: <u>Louise</u>: see Annotation for Letter 3, ll. 29-31.

Letter 30 (NYPL--TC)
　　line 29: 'Cardinal': Cardinal Richelieu, title character in *Richelieu* (1839) by Edward Bulwer-Lytton (1803-1875), to become one of EB's most successful roles.
　　line 36: Miss Heron: see Annotation for Letter 27, ll. 16-17.

Letter 31 (NYPL--TC)
　　line 4: 'Titian': Tiziano Vecellio (1480-1576), Italian painter who excelled in the imaginative use of color.
　　line 54: your sister: Asia Booth (1835-1888), married John Sleeper Clarke in 1859. See Annotation for Letter 16, l. 6; and Asia Booth Clarke, *The Elder and the Younger Booth* (Boston, 1882), p. 157.

Letter 32 (NYPL--TC)
　　line 8: 'Memorial': see Annotation for Letter 23, l. 11.
　　line 53: <u>Memphis</u>: EB performed in Memphis 20 February-3 March 1860 at the New Memphis Theatre.
　　line 54: N.O: see Annotation for Letter 25, l. 114.

Letter 33 (NYPL--TC)
　　In upper right-hand corner of first page, right of datelines, in pencil in EB's hand: "Three years after this she died--Feb. 23' 1863--". Above MD's "Thursday" on first page in pencil in EB's hand: "1860". EB's memory erred about the date of MDB's death, which was 21 February 1863.
　　line 5: <u>Kate</u>: probably Catherine, MD's sister and wife of Henry Magonigle.
　　line 7: '<u>Cameille</u>': see Annotation for Letter 27, l. 29.
　　line 8: "No 1860": a reference to a letter from EB.
　　line 11: <u>Mdme</u> Le V--: Octavia Walton Le Vert (1810-1877), author, was at the head of fashionable Mobile society.
　　line 15: <u>Memphis</u>: see Annotation for Letter 32, l. 53.
　　line 16: Miss Nash: see Annotation for Letter 35, salutation.
　　lines 55-56: Mr Bader . . . mourning: a reference to the death of Badeau's brother (see letter from Badeau to EB [Players], 17 February [1860]).
　　line 59: <u>Miss Julia</u>: see Annotation for Letter 35, salutation.

Letter 34 (Players)
　　Upside down in upper right-hand corner of first page of letter, beneath date, in pencil in EB's hand: "The baby mentioned in this was <u>Sarah</u> Magonigle."

126  Annotations

    line 18:   'Mollie':  see Annotation for Letter 6, l. 21.
    lines 28-31:   Mr B--:  See Annotation for Letter 33, ll. 55-56.
    line 34:   <u>Memphis</u>:  see Annotation for Letter 32, l. 53.
    line 36:   Miss Julia:  see Annotation for Letter 35, salutation.
    line 40:   <u>Louise</u>:  see Annotation for Letter 3, ll. 29-31.
    line 49:   annoyance:  see Letter 11, l. 26.
    line 55:   strong-minded women:  a reference to assertive women; a notice in the Troy (New York) *Times* for 13 February 1853 (while MD still lived there) announced the appearance of a group of temperance women called "Strong-Minded Women" at Harmony Hall the next day.
    line 70:   'Miller's Daughter':  see Annotation for Letter 22, l. 9.
    line 79:   "the readiness is all":  *Hamlet*, V.ii.233-234.
    line 94:   <u>Alice</u>:  see Annotation for Letter 25, l. 66.

Letter 35 (Players)
    salutation: Julia:  daughter of Charles T. Nash, an accountant with the Crescent Mutual Insurance Company in New Orleans, and his wife, E. Adele. EB's acquaintance with the Nashes began as early as March 1857, during his engagement there that month (see letters from Nash and his wife to EB at Players). A decade later, EB's attitude toward the Nashes had become unfriendly, and he called Julia an "idiotic chick of a daughter" (see EB to John E. Russell, 24 January [1868], Univ. of Rochester).

Letter 36 (Players)
    lines 4-11:   'Royal Circus':  Cooke's Royal Amphitheatre.
    line 14:   <u>Memphis</u>:  see Annotation for Letter 32, l. 53.
    line 74:   John: probably John Wilkes Booth.

Letter 37 (NYPL--TC)
    On a slip of paper inserted, in ink in EB's hand:
    Ah dearer far ~~art~~ ↑to↓ me art thou
    Sweet faded, tiny violet wreath
    Than ~~all~~ the laureled one that decks my ↑brow↓
    Whose spreading leaves hide stems beneath.
    line 7:   <u>Charleston</u>:  EB performed in Charleston, South Carolina, 20 March-4 April at the Charleston Theatre.
    lines 30-31:   Hawthorne's last work on Italy: *The Marble Faun*. Boston, 1860.

Annotations    127

Letter 38 (NYPL--TC)
    lines 14-15:  'never . . . yours':  *Othello*, II.iii.249.
    line 18:  George Jordan:  see Annotation for Letter 27, l. 18.
    lines 62-63:  'discourse' of 'Cousin's':  Victor Cousin's *Du vrais, du beau, et du bien*. Paris, 1853.  See Charles Shattuck, *The Hamlet of Edwin Booth* (Urbana, IL, 1969), pp. 33-34, for commentary on what MD had in mind for EB's development as an actor when she cited Cousin.

Letter 41 (NYPL--TC)
    salutation:  Julia:  see Annotation for Letter 35, salutation.

Letter 42 (*New England Magazine*)
    Letter 42 was printed in "The Friendship of Edwin Booth and Julia Ward Howe" by Mrs. Howe's daughter, Florence Marion Howe Hall.
    line 4:  Camp Andrew:  "One of the camps near Boston during the war" [Florence Hall's note].  In fact, Camp Andrew was a Union training camp on Gurnet Point, nine miles northeast of Plymouth, Massachusetts.  See also Letter 43, l. 5.
    lines 19-20:  "pretty chickens . . . dam":  *Macbeth*, IV.iii.218.

Letter 43 (Players)
    line 5:  Camp:  see Annotation for Letter 42, l. 4.

Letter 44 (Players)
    line 15:  General Lyons death:  Nathaniel Lyon (1818-1861) was killed in action on 10 August near Springfield, Missouri.
    line 35:  first appearance:  see Annotation for Letter 45, l. 2.
    line 40:  Miss Sallie's:  Judging from letters by Helen Cary, Emma Cary and Mary Felton (Players and NYPL--TC), Sallie was a member of the Cary family.

Letter 45 (Players)
    line 2:  Mr. Booth's debut:  EB opened in London on 30 September 1861 at the Haymarket Theatre.
    line 23:  'Shylock' at the Haymarket':  EB opened his engagement at London's Haymarket Theatre (30 September-10 November) as Shylock in *The Merchant of Venice*.  In an undated letter, Cushman indicates she "seriously advised" EB not to open in Shylock (Charlotte Cushman Papers, LC--MD, Vol. 1, p. 332).

Letter 46 (FL--BTM)
    line 12:  opened in 'Shylock':  see Annotation for Letter 45, l. 23.

128  Annotations

> lines 91-98: G. Eastern . . . her: The passenger steamer *Great Eastern* was damaged in a hurricane two days out of Liverpool on 12 September 1861. In the light of MDB's feelings about the ship, it is ironic that a year later she and EB returned to the United States aboard it.
> line 110: Grahams: James Lorimer Graham, Jr. (1835-1876), art collector and, from about 1868 till his death, United States consul general in Italy, living in Florence. The Booths first met the Grahams in England.
> lines 112-113: Prof Simpson: see Letter 47, ll. 12-13.

Letter 47 (PSU)
> line 4: Mr Graham's: see Annotation for Letter 46, l. 110.
> line 38: Exhibition: The Exhibition of 1862, sponsored by the Royal Institute of British Architects.

Letter 48 (Players)
> line 21: Silsbee: perhaps Joshua Silsbee (1813-1855), American stage Yankee actor.

Letter 49 (NYPL--TC)
> In upper left-hand corner of first page of letter in pencil in EB's hand: "London Nov 23/61." 23 November 1861 was a Saturday.
> line 19: your playing two peices on Saturday: EB played Manchester's Theatre Royal 12-30 November 1861. On Saturday, 30 November, he performed in *Katherine and Petruchio* and *Romeo and Juliet*.
> line 29: Slidell: John Slidell (1793-1871), Confederate diplomat.
> lines 33-34: San Jacinto: On 8 November 1861, the Union ship U.S.S. *San Jacinto* intercepted the British mail packet *Trent* in the Bahama Channel and removed James Murray Mason and John Slidell, former southern U.S. Senators who were Confederate envoys bound for Europe to seek foreign assistance for the South.

Letter 50 (FL--BTM)
> lines 47-49: Booth . . . tour: EB did not play in London in the spring of 1862, but he did perform in Liverpool in February and March (see Annotation for Letter 53, ll. 7-8).
> line 53: Manchester: see Annotation for Letter 49, l. 19.
> line 54: "nature so err": *Othello*, I.iii.62.
> line 59: Grahams: see Annotation for Letter 46, l. 110.
> line 69: Trent affair: see Annotation for Letter 49, ll. 33-34.

Letter 51 (NYPL--TC)
    line 31:   'Trent excitement':  see Annotation for
        Letter 49, ll. 33-34.
    line 35:   armies of the Potomac:  From the disparate
        armies concentrated around Washington in July
        1861, General McClellan (see below) had formed a
        force of about 150,000 men known as the Army of
        the Potomac.
    line 43:   Hawthorn:  Hawthorne (1804-1864) served as
        United States consul at Liverpool from 1853-1857,
        having been appointed by his brother-in-law President Franklin Pierce.
    line 48:   Sir E Bulwer:   Edward Bulwer-Lytton (1803-
        1875), British dramatist and novelist.
    line 52:   stand-still of McClellan':  General George B.
        McClellan (1826-1885), Commander of the Army of
        the Potomac and, from November 1861 to April 1862,
        general of all Union armies.  Since late November,
        the notoriously indecisive McClellan had refused
        to attack the Confederates at Manassas.
    line 66:   Mrs Kemble:  Frances Anne (Fanny) Kemble
        (1809-1893), British actress.

Letter 52 (FL--BTM)
    line 98:   Exhibition:  see Annotation for Letter 47, l.
        38.
    lines 106-107:  Mrs Sandford's:  Judging from a letter
        by EB to Walter Brackett (undated; HRHRC), Mrs.
        Sandford was a medium residing in Boston.
    line 107:  Miss Field:  Mary Katherine (Kate) Field
        (1838-1896), author, actress and critic.
    line 120:  70 Pinckney St.:  the address of the house
        in Boston which Charlotte Cushman gave to her son
        and his bride upon their marriage in March 1861.

Letter 53 (Players)
    lines 7-8:  gone with you:  EB performed at the Royal
        Amphitheatre in Liverpool from 24 February to 8
        March 1862.
    line 8:   Mrs Davenport:  see Annotation for Letter 1,
        l. 6.
    line 15:  Grahams:  see Annotation for Letter 46, l.
        110.
    line 18:  Horticultural Gargdens:  in Hyde Park and
        part of the Exhibition (see Annotation for Letter
        47, l. 38).
    line 27:  'four Georges':  *The Four Georges* (London,
        1861) by Thackeray (1811-1863).
    lines 36-39:  little "book of ballads" . . . "The old
        mahogany tree":  Thackeray's *The Mahogany Tree*.
        London, 18[47].
    line 38:  Horace Mayhew:   (1816-1872) British author
        and editor.
    line 39:  Mathews's:  Charles James Mathews (1803-
        1878), English theatre manager and comedian.  From
        30 September-10 November, while performing at the

Haymarket (see Annotation for Letter 45, l. 23), EB had alternated with Mathews who was performing in his new comedy, *The Soft Sex*.

lines 49-50: Ann, Mrs Andrews: probably domestics, assisting in the Booth household around the time of the birth and early infancy of Edwina.

lines 76-82: Lily of Killarney: opera composed by Julius Benedict, libretto by John Oxenford and Dion Boucicault, based on the romantic Irish drama *The Colleen Bawn* (1860) by Dion Boucicault and first produced at the Royal English Opera, Covent Garden, 10 February 1862.

line 83: Eily: Eily O'Connor, pathetic heroine of *The Colleen Bawn*.

line 85: Macnair: Andrew Macnair published his tragedy as *The Painter of Athens* in Glasgow later in 1862.

line 89: congratulatory letter to John: John Wilkes Booth had been highly successful in his Chicago engagement, 20 January-1 February, where critics had praised him as the most brilliant actor ever to play there.

line 115: your benefit: EB played Mortimer in *The Iron Chest* and Petruchio in *Katherine and Petruchio* for his benefit on Friday, 7 February in Liverpool.

Letter 54 (Players)

line 4: parting from you: see Annotation for Letter 53, ll. 7-8.

lines 9-10: Avonia Jones: American actress with whom MD had performed in Richmond, 2-10 February 1857.

line 12: Brooke: Gustavus Vaughan Brooke (1818-1860), Irish-born actor, later married Avonia Jones.

line 14: Macnair: see Annotation for Letter 53, l. 85.

line 18: Boughton & Kuntzie: George Henry Boughton (1833-1905), English painter, and Edward J. Kuntzie (1826-1870), Prussian sculptor.

line 22: 'my lord William': Lord William Pitt Lennox (1799-1881), writer of miscellaneous works whose marriage to Mary Ann Paton in 1824 was dissolved by Scotch court of session in 1831.

lines 24-25: Mrs Wood: Joseph Wood (1801-1890) and his wife (neé Mary Ann Paton [1802-1863] were among the finest British singing actors of their time.

line 30: Cremorne: Grounds located at Chelsea along the Thames, once belonging to Lord Cremorne, were opened to the public in 1831. By 1860 these "pleasure gardens" had become synonymous with drinking and assignations.

line 32: Mrs Mathews: see Letter 53, l. 39.

line 33: Horace Mayhew: see Annotation for Letter 53, l. 38.

line 59: Earl Russel: Lord John Russell, first Earl Russell (1792-1878), English statesman who maintained strict neutrality between North and South during the American Civil War.
line 69: "Boucicault's": Dion Boucicault (1820-1890), Irish actor and dramatist, and his wife Agnes Robertson (1833-1916), Scottish actress, were performing at the Adelphi Theatre. MDB had acted with the Boucicaults in April 1856 in Washington, D.C. and Richmond.
line 70: Florences: William Jermyn Florence (1831-1891), American actor, and his wife Malvina Pray Florence (1831-1906), American actress. MDB had performed with the Florences in Richmond, 13-22 April 1857.
line 71: Keans: Charles John Kean (1811-1868), English actor-manager son of the actor Edmund Kean, and his wife Ellen Tree (1806-1880), English actress, were performing at the Drury Lane Theatre.
line 73: Grahams: see Annotation for Letter 46, l. 110.
line 109: Hudson: George Hodson, Irish comic actor who performed afterpieces during EB's engagement in Liverpool.

Letter 55 (Players)
line 2: loss: Cornelius C. Felton, President of Harvard, died on 26 February 1862.

Letter 56 (Players)
line 2: loss: see Annotation for Letter 55, l. 2.
line 42: Monsieur Fechter: Charles Albert Fechter (1824-1879), French actor who played in English and French in Europe and America, was performing at the Princess's Theatre.
line 44: "insane root": *Macbeth*, I, iii.84.

Letter 57 (FL--BTM)
lines 4-5: Prof Felton: see Annotation for Letter 55, l. 2.
line 39: Exhibition: see Annotation for Letter 47, l. 38.
line 56: Miss Kellogg: Clara Louise Kellogg (1842-1916), American opera and producer.
line 65: 'Monitor': Union's ironclad ship which had engaged the Confederacy's ironclad *Merrimac* in an historic four-hour battle on 9 March 1862.

Letter 58 (FL--BTM)
line 28: Dora-like: Dora Spenlow, the impractical "child-wife" of David Copperfield in the novel by Dickens (1812-1870). During the final engagement of her career, MDB played in the stage adaptation of the novel at Niblo's Garden in New York, 27 July 1859.

132   Annotations

> lines 63-64: Le Maitre . . . Ceaser: Antoine-Louis-Prosper Lemaitre (1800-1876), French Romantic actor. The role was the title role of *Don Caesar de Bazan* (1844) by Philippe Françoise Dumanoir.
> line 69: Ristori: Adelaide Ristori (1822-1906), Italian actress internationally famous for her portrayals of tragic heroines.
> lines 91-92: Sothern . . . Dundreary': see Annotation for Letter 7, l. 26. Sothern was best known for his role of Lord Dundreary in Tom Taylor's *Our American Cousin*.

Letter 59 (Players)
> line 6: Dora-like: see Annotation for Letter 58, l. 28.

Letter 62 (Players)
> lines 1-8: the one . . . doubly sad: In a letter (NYPL--TC) dated 7 September 1862, Mary Felton wrote the Booths concerning the death of her brother, Richard Cary, and spoke of a letter by Cary to EB which had been found unfinished among his effects after his death. Felton wrote that she would keep the letter until she could be sure of delivering it safely to EB. The letter, dated 20 May 1862, is at the Players.
> line 5: Colonel: see Annotation for Letter 64, l. 10.
> line 33: Major Dwight: Wilder Dwight, like Richard Cary of the Second Massachusetts infantry, was missing in action following the Battle of Winchester.
> line 35: proclamation of the President: The Emancipation Proclamation was signed by Lincoln on 22 September 1862.
> line 42: visit Boston in November: EB performed at the Boston Theatre 24 November-20 December 1862.

Letter 64 (Players)
> line 5: Winchester: town in northern Virginia, site of two important battles (23 March and 25 May 1862) which involved Richard Cary. In a letter to the Booths (NYPL--TC) dated 3 May [1862], Mary Felton transcribed long excerpts from Cary's letter home about the first of these battles.
> line 10: Gordon's: George Henry Gordon (1824-1886), soldier, lawyer and author, was colonel of the Second Massachusetts infantry regiment (Richard Cary's unit) and was a commander during the battles of Winchester. Among the books Gordon later wrote about the war and mentioning Cary is *Brook Farm to Cedar Mountain* (Cambridge, MA, 1883), which describes the battle of Cedar Mountain in which Cary was killed.
> line 15: Boston . . . Nov: see Annotation for Letter 62, l. 42.

lines 26-27: He has been acting . . . more: EB's first engagement after his return from Europe was at New York's Winter Garden Theatre, 29 September-15 November 1862.

Letter 65 (FL--BTM)
line 28: leave for Boston: the Booths left for Boston on 21 November 1862.
line 48: Sir . . . Ceaser: see Annotation for Letter 58, ll. 63-64. Sir Edward Mortimer is the lead character in *The Iron Chest* (1796) by George Colman, the Younger. EB played these two roles at the Winter Garden on 7, 8, 10, 11, 12 and 13 November 1862.

Letter 66 (NYPL--TC)
line 11: two you sent me: In a letter (NYPL--TC) dated 24 November [1862], Helen Cary wrote MDB about the proper dress for an infant and enclosed two flannel shirts for Edwina.

Letter 67 (Players)
line 2: I followed you: Elizabeth Stoddard accompanied the Booths to Boston on 21 November 1862 to help them get settled. She returned to her husband in New York on 6 December 1862, their tenth wedding anniversary.
line 13: Field's': James Thomas Fields (1817-1881), American poet, editor and publisher, was head of the publishing firm of Tichnor and Fields and from 1862 to 1870 editor of the *Atlantic Monthly*.

Letter 68 (NYPL--MD)
line 7: after you left: see Annotation for Letter 67, l. 2.
line 18: Whipple's: Edwin Percy Whipple (1819-1886), American lecturer and writer on literature and culture. In 1878 he co-edited with James T. Fields *The Family Library of British Poetry*.
line 31: Field: see Annotation for Letter 67, l. 13.

Letter 69 (FL--BTM)
line 35: Booth . . . Brooklyn: EB performed at the Brooklyn Academy of Music 23, 25 and 27 December 1862.
line 38: Mrs Sandford: see Annotation for Letter 52, ll. 106-107.
line 39: Kate Field: see Annotation for Letter 52, l. 107.
lines 56-57: "Now are you my leutenant": *Othello*, III.iii.479.
line 63: you will yet bear: Emma Cushman had a miscarriage in May 1862.
line 67: "Consummation . . . wished": *Hamlet*, III.i.63.

134    Annotations

>    line 90: Orlando Tompkins: An original stockholder of the new (1858) Boston Theatre, Tompkins became its manager in 1862. His first booking was the four-week November engagement of EB, whom he had known since 1857. Tompkins and his wife attended MDB in Dorchester after EB went to New York, and on 18 and 19 February 1863 Tompkins sent EB four telegrams (NYPL--TC) corroborating the letters Dr. Miller sent declaring MDB's condition to be stable or improving.

> Letter 70 (NYPL--MD)
>    lines 20-21: go on with Edwin in February: EB's engagement at the Winter Garden in New York was initially scheduled to begin 2 February and was delayed until 9 February 1863 (see Letters 84, ll. 25-26 and 85, ll. 2-3).
>    line 45: three nights in Brooklyn: see Annotation for Letter 69, l. 35.
>    line 50: Stuart: William Stuart (1821-1886), real name Edmund O'Flaherty, Irish theatre manager in New York associated with Boucicault, EB, Clarke and others.
>    line 56: Mrs Whipple: see Annotation for Letter 68, l. 18.
>    line 56: "Mrs Trench's Remains": *The Remains of the Late Mrs. Richard Trench . . .*, by Melesina St. George Trench. R. C. Trench, ed. 2d ed. rev. London, 1862.
>    lines 60-61: Boston . . . Sir Edward: EB acted Sir Edward Mortimer in *The Iron Chest* on Friday, 12 December 1862, at the Boston Theatre.

> Letter 71 (NYPL--MD)
>    line 6: Felix's: a reference to the hero of Richard Henry Stoddard's *The King's Bell*.

> Letter 72 (Players)
>    line 1: affairs . . . haste: *Othello*, I.iii.276.
>    line 22: James T Fields: see Annotation for Letter 67, l. 13.

> Letter 74 (Players)
>    line 9: Rufus Choate: (1799-1859), American lawyer and U.S. Senator from Massachusetts.
>    line 15: warte: see Annotation for Letter 21, l. 26.
>    line 33: Edwin's performance . . . Saturday: EB performed in *The Iron Chest* and *Don Caesar de Bazan* on Saturday, 20 December 1862, at the Boston Theatre.
>    line 33: Fields: see Annotation for Letter 67, l. 13.
>    line 41: Dr Parsons: Thomas William Parsons (1819-1892), American poet, translator and dentist. His poem on the death of MDB appeared in the Boston *Courier*, 25 February 1863.

Letter 75 (Players)
    line 1:   Tompkins:  see Annotation for Letter 69, l. 90.
    line 11:  grieved & lonely heart:  Elizabeth and Richard Stoddard's first child, a son, Wilson (born on 20 June 1855) had died one year earlier, on 17 December 1861, and in mid-October Elizabeth's brother Zaccheus had died in the Civil War.
    line 17:  begun your book:  Elizabeth Stoddard's second novel, *Two Men*. New York, 1865.

Letter 77 (Players)
    Centered at head of first page of letter, in blue pencil in EB's hand:  "<u>Keep</u>".

Letter 79 (Players)
    Centered at head of first page of letter, in blue pencil in EB's hand:  "--Keep--".
    line 11:  Songs of Summer:  Richard Henry Stoddard, *Songs of Summer*. Boston, 1857.
    line 25:  Artist's Reception:  An exhibition of paintings and sculptures held at Dodworth's Studio Building.  The first one of the season occurred on 16 January 1863.
    line 28:  Dr Parsons:  see Annotation for Letter 74, l. 41.
    line 35:  Lisa:  Elizabeth Stoddard.
    line 35:  new book:  see Annotation for Letter 75, l. 17.

Letter 81 (Players)
    line 39:  that tiny one:  probably a reference to the death of the Stoddards' first son (see Annotation for Letter 75, l. 11) who was, however, six and a half years old at death.  Perhaps a reference to the death of the Stoddards' second child, also a son, who died an infant in late July 1859.
    line 42:  Lillie's . . . Aldrich:  Lillian Woodman met T. B. Aldrich (1836-1907; American author and from 1881 to 1890 editor of the *Atlantic Monthly*) at a party at the Booths in the fall of 1862.  They were married in 1865.

Letter 82 (Players)
    line 20:  Art Reception:  see Annotation for Letter 79, l. 25.
    line 27:  his present one:  From 1860 to 1870 Stoddard was literary reviewer for the New York *World*. From 1853 to 1870 he worked in the U.S. Customs Office in New York, a position gained through the intervention of Nathaniel Hawthorne.
    line 43:  Boker's:  George Henry Boker (1823-1890), American playwright, poet and diplomat; intimate of the Stoddards' New York circle.  Boker's "notice" was probably either the one in the New York *World* (17 January 1863, p. 2), in the New

York *Times* (1 January 1863, p. 2), or in the New York *Tribune* (1 January 1863, p. 2).

Letter 83 (FL--BTM)
  line 8:  merry as a 'marriage bell': Byron, *Childe Harold's Pilgrimage*, III, xxi.
  line 18:  J Wilkes B--: Booth performed at the Boston Museum from 19 January to 13 February 1863.
  line 33:  "the rest is silence": *Hamlet*, V.ii.358.
  line 34:  Mrs Sandford: see Annotation for Letter 52, ll. 106-107.

Letter 84 (Players)
  salutation:  Lisa: Elizabeth Stoddard.
  line 4:  Ludlow: Fitz Hugh Ludlow (1836-1870), American author and lawyer, and member of the Stoddards' circle of friends in New York.
  line 23:  Stuart: see Annotation for Letter 70, l. 50.
  lines 25-26:  will not begin . . . Feb.: see Annotation for Letter 70, ll. 20-21.
  line 44:  "go get thyself . . .": *Romeo and Juliet*, V.i.84.
  line 46:  "hate lean & hungry men": *Julius Caesar*, I.ii.194.

Letter 85 (HU--MD)
  salutation:  Mattie: sister of Lillian Woodman. The sisters first saw EB on stage in the autumn of 1860 in Boston. Their family moved to New York a few weeks later just as EB began his engagement at the Winter Garden there, and they lived down the hallway from the Booths in the Fifth Avenue Hotel. The sisters became familiar with the Booths then and renewed the friendship in December 1862 when the Booths returned from Europe. Soon after MDB's death and again after the death of EB's second wife (1881), Mattie Woodman was rumored to be a candidate for marriage to EB (see Daniel Watermeier, *Between Actor and Critic* [Princeton, NJ, 1971], pp. 253, 254n and 255).
  lines 2-3:  Mr Booth's engagement . . . week: see Annotation for Letter 70, ll. 20-21.
  line 11:  Rufus Choate: see Annotation for Letter 74, l. 9.
  line 27:  "The Married life . . .": perhaps *Das Marienleben* (Berlin, n.d.), by Albrecht Dürer (1471-1528).
  line 32:  Marie: probably a woman hired to assist MDB.
  line 34:  Ruy Blas: verse drama by Hugo (1838; see Annotation for Letter 28, l. 18).

Letter 86 (Players)
  line 1:  arrived safely: EB went to New York for his engagement at the Winter Garden on 8 February 1863.

Annotations 137

　　　line 6:　Marie: see Annotation for Letter 85, l. 32.
　　　line 12:　Ruy Blas: see Annotation for Letter 85, l. 34.
　　　line 23:　Jackson: A. W. "Black Jack" Jackson, manager of Winter Garden for EB's engagements there in October 1862 and February 1863.
　　　line 24:　Orlando: see Annotation for Letter 69, l. 90.
　　　line 24:　Henry: Richard Henry Stoddard

Letter 87 (NYPL--TC)
　　　line 1:　"after Hamlet": EB opened his engagement at New York's Winter Garden Theatre on 9 February 1863 in the role of Hamlet.
　　　line 2:　Orlando: see Annotation for Letter 69, l. 90.
　　　line 30:　John: see Annotation for Letter 83, l. 18
　　　line 40:　Eddy: see Annotation for Letter 4, l. 2.
　　　line 41:　Goulds: Thomas Ridgeway Gould (1818-1881), American sculptor and author who was a member of the Boston circle that included E. P. Whipple and J. T. Fields. Gould sculpted a bust of EB's father in the early 1860s and wrote a brief biography of the elder Booth, *The Tragedian*, in 1868.
　　　line 43:　Mrs S--: Elizabeth Stoddard. On 7 February 1863, Elizabeth was called to Fortress Monroe to attend her brother Wilson, who lay ill there (see letter [PSU] from Elizabeth Stoddard to Lorimer Graham, 6 March 1863).
　　　line 52:　Launt T--: Launt Thompson (1833-1894), Irish-born sculptor and member of the Stoddards' New York circle.
　　　line 53:　Woodman's: see Annotation for Letter 85, salutation.

Notebooks

Record Book (NYPL--TC)
　　　Leaf 1 recto (see Textual Notes)
　　　　　Albion Feby 1861: see New York *Albion* (9 February 1861), p. 67.
　　　　　"Hamilton": a pseudonym of William Winter (1836-1917), American drama critic; later a personal friend of EB, collaborator with him in the publication of his promptbooks, and his first major biographer.
　　　Hamlet entry (see text)
　　　　　lines 1-4: Goëthe . . vase": citation is from *Wilhelm Meisters Lehrjahre, ein Roman* (Berlin, 1795-1796), by Goethe (1749-1832). Which English translation MDB read is not known.
　　　　addenda
　　　　　line 27: 'poor player': *Macbeth*, V.v.24.

138  Annotations

>     Leaf 62 recto (see Textual Notes)
>         "Stuart":  William Stuart (see Annotation for
>             Letter 70, l. 50).
>         <u>Tribune</u>:  commentary was published in New York
>             <u>Tribune</u>; its publication date is unknown, but
>             for a certainty it was not published during
>             the months the other clippings in this Record
>             Book were--September 1860-April 1861.
>     Leaf 82 verso (see Textual Notes)
>         Evening Post . . . 1861:  see New York <u>Evening</u>
>             <u>Post</u>, 13 February 1861, p. 2.  Article is
>             unsigned.
>     Leaf 90 verso (see Textual Notes)
>         Albion . . . 1861:  New York <u>Albion</u>, 15 December
>             1860, p. 595.

Journal (Players)

>     7 November 1860
>         line 26:  Goethe; "Elective Affinitie":  novel by
>             Goethe  published as <u>Die Wahlverwandtschaften</u>
>             (Tubingen, 1809).  Which English translation
>             MDB read is not known.
>
>     8 November 1860
>         line 11:  "Fool's Revenge":  see Annotations for
>             Letters 21, ll. 15-16; 23, l. 43; and 28, l.
>             18, 22-23; and Journal, 10 November 1860, ll.
>             1, 25.
>
>     10 November 1860
>         line 1:  "Fool's Revenge":  see Journal, 8 November 1860, l. 11.  EB was less bedazzled than
>             MDB thought.  In a letter to Lawrence
>             Barrett, 21 November 1860 (Players), he
>             wrote:  "The 'Fool's Revenge' was a tremendous hit in Phil<u>a</u>--ran it a week to crowded
>             houses--I'll make it 'howl' here--if I play
>             it--I'm rather afraid though--lest I should
>             get a sort of <u>Metamoric</u> or Meg <u>Merrilic</u>
>             reputation instead of '<u>Shakes</u>'."
>         line 25:  V. Hugo's--<u>Le Roi</u>:  see Annotation for
>             Letter 28, ll. 22-23.
>
>     12 November 1860
>         line 11:  'remorse not sting:  Shelley, <u>The Cenci</u>,
>             V.i.2-4.
>         line 16:  every bath:  see Journal, 5 November, l.
>             10.
>         lines 44-45:  little book of . . . Andersen's:
>             MDB probably read the popular translation
>             from the Danish by Mary Howitt of <u>The</u>
>             <u>Improvisatore</u>; or, <u>Life in Italy</u> (New York,
>             1861) by Andersen (1805-1875).

*just like a child. You may imagine what pleasure it gives me to see & have him comfortable. I look with dread & horror upon the four weeks separation that must ensue, but I try to find consolation in the joy he will feel at returning to his home. Besides I expect that you will come & see me for a little while, leaving Dick to Edwin. I never felt so much the direct need of you as I do now. Do you know that you alter & Richard, are as much found of in our hopes & desires for the future, as though you had been "twin'd with us". He knows how secure you feel in us — how entirely you depend upon us, to live & cherish you. No doubt that you will have to suffer the most poignant grief on our accounts, at times.*

Mary Devlin Booth's letter to Elizabeth Stoddard, 19 January 1863 (Letter 81), speaking of Booth's control of his drinking and of the similarity between his turbulent and passionate nature and Elizabeth's.

Courtesy Hampden-Booth Theatre Library at The Players

for Mwini — well you know the demon that Jealousy — a noble, ungoverned spirit like his. He is so gentle, so yielding, so at these moments more; & I achieve with him by his promises that the victory shall be his. — How differently you & I are placed. Richard is so perfect a man, so free from human vices — so true to his better nature; you are the turbulent, passionate one. — I have read your "Duke-coves". It is full of "charm, of thrilling beauty". I understand your work better now than when I call it "Moquours"; now I know you better. — You must be courageous — as you will be successful. How much has been taken from your life — none but your own hearts know. And yet I feel, that if I could efface from a single day that they

# Textual Notes

**Editorial Principles and Procedures**
   In this volume, the letters and notebooks of Mary Devlin Booth are printed in clear text which reproduces as nearly as possible their appearance in the manuscript. Manuscripts have been the copy-texts for all documents except Letter 42, which uses the form printed in *New England Magazine* in November 1893 as copy-text, there being no extant manuscript for it.

   It is impossible to reproduce in print with black ink on white paper the diverse and subtle strokes that MDB inscribed, usually with black ink on beige paper, in her delicate and often nearly illegible hand. Many judgments have been made about what to record and what not, what to regularize and what not. These matters must be explained.

   *Regularizations*. MDB followed no discernible pattern in indicating the beginnings of new paragraphs. Sometimes she began a new paragraph near the far right edge of the sheet, with only one or two words in the first line. On other occasions, the indentation is no more than the width of part of one character. Variations between these extremes are easy to find. In the present text, no attempt has been to reproduce these various widths of indentation; the relative spacing of the indentations has been standardized to conform to the typography of this volume. For the same reason, her dashes have been set at a standardized length and her underscores have been extended for the length of the entire word, except in the few instances when MDB clearly intended only part of a word to receive emphasis (e.g., lad<u>ie</u>). To preserve the appearance of the original, words underlined in the original have not been italicized but have been kept underlined. This includes the salutation of Letter 42 (for which the copy-text is a printed form using italics), the assumption being that underlining was used in the original. (Of course when quoted in print, words underlined here will usually be converted to italics.) A ragged-right format has been adopted since it too preserves the appearance of the original more nearly than a right-hand justified format would. The various ways MDB indicated cancellations and the degrees of emphasis for the cancellations have all been regularized by a single line-through. With rare exception, her practice was to indicate cancelled material with one or two line-throughs. Almost never did she obliterate her writing. Cancelled material which is undecipherable, regardless of its length, is indicated by a single cancelled question mark. Finally, the elongated *s* which MDB employed on a few occasions has been reproduced in the ordinary typographical form.

*No Record Made.* Occasionally MDB wrote the final portion of a letter crosswise, over a section of writing written earlier. No record has been made of this since position and location are textually unimportant. However, with such units of writing as postscripts and headnotes, position and location are potentially textually significant and for these the text and/or its notes record both. Among the letters, except for #42 all manuscripts are in ink, though no record has been made of the color used. The Record Book is also in ink, but the Journal is written entirely in pencil. Among the letters printed in this volume, there are no telegrams or messages on pre-printed forms. There are also no letters on printed letterhead stationery. No record has been made about MDB's use of writing stationery or of plain paper for her letters. No record has been made of the presence or absence of leaf or page numbers in the letters; however, for the ordering of material in the Record Book and Journal, a record of such details has been made. Often MDB employed a caret to indicate inserted material; just as often she simply wrote the material above (or occasionally below) the line without a caret. No record has been made of the presence or absence of a caret to indicate such material. Arrows are consistently used instead, and the placement of the inserted material above or below line is indicated by the sequence of the arrows, thus:

        ↑above↓           ↓below↑

In addition, no record has been made of raised letters, end-line hyphenation or superimposition. In the case of the first of these, MDB almost always raised the letters following ordinals, which usually occurred in the datelines. She rarely abbreviated, the most common occasion for raising letters among nineteenth-century writers. In all cases, letters raised in the original have been dropped to line level in the present text.

Regarding the second of these, when she needed to divide a word at the end of a line of writing, MDB's practice was to indicate that the word was a unified word (and not a compound) by a subscript mark resembling an equals sign (e.g., *poignant* in Letter 81, l. 25; see illustration following p. 138). On the other hand, when she was dividing a compound (e.g., *button-hole* in Letter 33, line 38), she used a single subscript mark like a hyphen. It is easy to know, therefore, when she intended a divided word to be unified or hyphenated. The present text follows MDB's indicators by re-unifying all words which were divided at the end of a line in the manuscript but marked by a subscript equals sign, and it has retained the hyphen in all compound words. The one exception to this occurs in #42, the one letter which has no extant manuscript. In the absence of authorial evidence, the one word divided in the 1893 printed text (o'ertook) is considered a unified word in the present text. Because a ragged right format has been used, no newly hyphenated words have been introduced into the present text; there are no end-line hyphenated words in it.

As for superimpositions, no record has been made of the times MDB wrote over her own writing. In the great majority of these, the superimpositions were merely to correct misspellings or to remedy grammatical errors or mechanical irregularities. In most other cases, what had been written underneath was simply impossible to decipher.

Finally, in about a dozen instances MDB absent-mindedly repeated a word or phrase usually at the beginning of a new line or new page. These have been considered textually insignificant; they have not been reproduced nor has a record been made of them.

With the exception of elements explained in the present section, the texts of the letters and notebooks--their scribal, syntactical and mechanical irregularities and the sequence and spacing of such parts as inside addresses, salutations, datelines, complimentary closings, signatures, and lines of verse--together with clarifications and alterations presented in Textual Notes replicate as closely as possible the originals. Only slips of the pen and stray marks have been totally ignored.

*Relationship between the Text and Textual Notes*
    This is an editorially unemended text (the two emendations, both in the 12 November section of the Journal and indicated by square brackets, are by MDB's daughter, Edwina Booth Grossmann). Thus, all snarled syntaxes and grammatical and mechanical irregularities and errors are reproduced literally. Notes providing alternative or corrected readings, recording textual data not displayed in the present text, and explaining miscellaneous textual matters are offered in the Textual Notes. Regarding alternative or corrected readings, only two categories of matters have received comments (in the Textual Notes section): errors so serious as to cause confusion to the reader (i.e., *not* such minor matters as ordinary comma faults, run on sentences, or obviously misspelled words); and errors likely to cause difficulty for scholarly quotation. Readers who wish a clearer form to read or to cite may refer to the emended version found in the Textual Notes. Either the unemended or emended version may be cited with full authority. To preserve the clear appearance of the texts no sub- or super-

scripts are used. All entries in the Textual Notes are keyed to the text by letter and line numbers.

Had MDB even dreamt that her letters would be printed, she surely would not have approved this procedure. She would have wanted a heavily emended text to be presented without textual notes, for she reveals in several of her letters that she was self-conscious about her lack of a formal education and about the resulting obvious weaknesses in composition, grammar, and mechanics. Her husband recognized these deficiencies and must have drawn her attention to them in his letters to her, so that she wrote in reply, "letter writing I'm most unhappy at, and I don't dare to read after having written, or I should not post one letter in the week" (Letter 15). Her fear of being harshly judged for these weaknesses was no doubt well founded in her own time but surely no such reason exists for modern readers, who pay attention instead to her gradual improvement in these matters (contrast the letters of 1858-1860 with those of the last year and a half) and who admire the concomitant development of her self-assurance and her perceptiveness when, as the wife of EB, she moved in increasingly well-educated circles in Cambridge and Harvard, developed close relationships with prominent literary people of the time, and expanded her influence on her husband during the formative period of his career. An emended text would not completely eradicate the evidence of this growth, but it would seriously obscure it. Furthermore, modern readers, especially those of informal documents like letters and notebooks, which were never intended for publication, are much more accustomed than their mid-nineteenth-century counterparts to reading such materials in their original form and are more forgiving of lapses. They might even respect such lapses in the view that "flaws" reveal the distinctive color and tone of the author's personality and mind. In truth, most of the peculiarities of MDB's style do not render the letters unintelligible. Rather, they make them intelligible in much the same way as the poems of Emily Dickinson are intelligible. Dickinson began writing in earnest the same year MDB wrote some of the last letters printed here (1862). Had Dickinson published her early poems during MDB's lifetime, MDB would have instantly recognized a kindred spirit, at least as far as writing style is concerned. Finally, emendations of form necessarily become changes in content. For these reasons, as literal a text as possible is presented here.

*Procedures.* The texts and the corresponding notes for all documents printed in this volume except the eight FL--BTM letters (for which the procedure was slightly different, as explained below) have been established as a result of four complete readings against originals (manuscripts for notebooks and all letters except #42) and numerous partial readings against both originals and facsimiles (photocopies or microfilm) to clarify specific textual matters. The following procedures were followed step by step for all the letters and the Record Book (but not for the Journal, as explained below). First, a clear transcript of each letter and the Record Book was prepared from a facsimile of the original. This prepared transcription, which was made and stored on a tape on one of Northern Illinois Univ.'s mainframe computers using the text-editing program SUPERWYLBUR, was then read aloud against the facsimile with a second reader. It was corrected and read a second time against the facsimile. During this process, work sheets for the Textual Notes were prepared in draft form. These treated such matters as questionable or flawed readings, undecipherable writing, and errors or irregularities in composition or mechanics. Because there was no manuscript for Letter 42, the procedure for it concluded after two more readings against the facsimile and appropriate revisions of the Textual Notes. For the other letters and the Record Book, the procedure continued with the first of two complete readings against originals, accompanied by appropriate revisions of the apparatus. Since these two readings were made during one visit to examine the originals, the first of them was made against a clean transcript and the second against a marked transcript. A fresh, clean transcript was prepared from these readings and used for the second set of two readings against originals, which again occurred during one visit to examine originals. During these final two readings, further revisions and refinements were made in the Textual Notes. During the interim between the two sets of readings against originals, the facsimiles were used when possible to settle questionable matters tentatively. A slight exception to this procedure was followed for Letters 85 (Harvard Univ.), 47 (Pennsylvania State Univ.), and 80 (Players). For each of these letters, only one trip to examine the original occurred, during which all four readings were made. A clear transcript was used for the first reading; a marked transcript was used for the others. Revisions in the corresponding Textual Notes were made at the same time.

For the eight FL--BTM letters, the procedure differed slightly. These received three complete readings against originals (manuscripts) and numerous partial readings against both originals and facsimiles (photocopies) to clarify specific textual matters. The first stage (establishing the prepared transcription) for these eight was identical to that employed for the other letters (except #42) and the Record Book, as explained above. For the second stage (reading against originals), however, these letters were treated differently. Franklyn Lenthall generously allowed these to be placed on loan in the Rare Books and Special Collections department of Founders Memorial Library at Northern Illinois Univ. This permitted the luxury of a second person to read against originals. The prepared transcript for each letter was read once against its original by each reader, accompanied by appropriate revisions of the Textual Notes. The marked transcript produced by this was then corrected. The clean, fresh transcript prepared as a result of these two separate readings by two people was used for a third and final reading by the two people together, one reading aloud to the other. During this reading, final revisions and refinements were made in the Textual Notes.

Since MDB's Journal is too fragile to be photocopied, the initial stages of the process of establishing its text differed significantly from that employed for the letters and the Record Book. An audio tape transcription of it was made first. A manuscript transcript was made from the audio tape and corrected against the original. A clear computer-tape transcript of it was made from this corrected manuscript transcript, then read against the manuscript transcript and further corrected. During this process, worksheets for the Textual Notes were prepared in draft form. At this point the state of the text for the Journal matched that for the letters and the Record Book; it was ready for the two sets of double readings against originals. The completion of the process was the same for it as for them.

This heavy reliance upon readings against originals was necessary in the interest of accuracy. It is hoped that this process warrants the statement that errors and peculiarities of the text are those of the original documents, not of the editor. After the corrections following the final reading against originals, the process of preparing the text was complete. The computer-tape original of the edited texts was used to drive a laser printer, which produced camera-ready copy. This process eliminated the introduction of new errors.

Upon the completion of the process of establishing the texts, final decisions about what elements in the texts needed attention in the Textual Notes were made by a complete through-reading of all texts. Textual Notes were then separately prepared on floppy disks with a microcomputer. The micro's own laser printer was used to produce camera-ready copy for this section so that no new errors were added here either.

These editorial principles and procedures are the foundation for the texts of the letters and notebooks printed in this volume. For the texts of the letters, each one is introduced by an editorial heading which includes the following, in sequence: a number, indicating the chronological place of the letter; the correspondent to whom the letter was directed; the location of the manuscript; and the date(s) of composition. On occasion the date(s) is different from that identified in the text of the letter; in these cases, internal evidence has been used to date the letter correctly and an explanation has been provided in the Textual Notes. Since there are only two notebooks, the editorial heading for the texts of each has been abbreviated to include only the title of document, its location and its year of composition.

## Notes

This section includes notes which either alter or explain the text. To indicate the existence of each textual note, a symbol (T) has been placed to the right of the relevant line of the text. Only one symbol has been used per line, even if that line has more than one note. (A special note regarding the Record Book should be made. On four occasions, MDB wrote headings for newspaper clippings she pasted in. Because these are merely headings they are not presented in the text of the Record Book; therefore, there is no "T" symbol to mark their existence, though the headings are in fact presented in the Textual Notes. Also presented in that section are notes concerning the arrangement of the text in the Record Book, but since there is no text these notes are necessarily also unmarked by a "T".)

For the notes to each document, a formal editorial introduction is provided which gives the document number (in the case of letters) and the repository where it now resides. Each note which provides an altered reading is preceded by two markers: a line number or other indicator (like "dateline") which indicates the place in the text that the note refers to; and the abbreviation for *id est*, followed by a colon. In some cases, explanatory material is included, set apart from the altered reading by square brackets (see, for example, note for Letter 19, l. 35). In a few instances, an alternative altered reading has been presented in a note. These are marked by "OR". Questionable readings are followed by a question mark within square brackets. When necessary, in the textual notes to the Record Book and the Journal asterisks are used to indicate material presented in facsimile within the note and a vertical line is used to indicate a line break. Obviously misspelled words (Wednesday, Feburary, beleive), words which have acceptable alternative spellings (honour, yeald), minor grammatical lapses, and common punctuational flaws have not been noted unless they cause confusion for readers or pose problems for scholarly quotation. Alternative readings have been provided only when necessary, and then they are made to conform to MDB's style and usual practice whenever possible. For example, when an alteration involves quotation marks and a comma or a period, the alternative reading has the punctuation outside the quotation marks because that was her usual practice. Similarly, when an alternative reading requires some punctuation where there is none in the original, a dash is used whenever appropriate rather than a full stop, which would also be correct, because she often used a dash in place of end stop punctuation.

On the frequent occasions when MDB employed a dash to imply continuation in a situation where most writers would make a full stop and begin a new sentence, no note has been made. Examples of this occur in Letter 29, ll. 33-39. This means that in general, MDB's use of the dash provides one of the unique characteristics of her text. What Thomas Johnson said thirty years ago about Emily Dickinson's poetic use of the dash is also true of MDB's use of it in her letters:

> Her use of the dash is especially capricious. Often it substitutes for a period and may in fact have been a hasty, lengthened dot intended for one. On occasion her dashes and commas are indistinguishable. Within lines she [often] uses dashes with no grammatical function whatsoever.[1]

As with capital letters, commas and even colons (which are also occasionally used as full stops), her use of dashes was dictated more by mood than by standards of mechanics in composition. MDB would have preferred to be able to write in a more standard, educated manner. She had a low regard for her ability in this matter and certainly did not sense any particular expressiveness to her manner. "I often reproach myself--that I do not talk differently than I do, when writing you--but very frequently I am deprived of this great joy--by lack of time . . . ," she wrote in Letter 31, ll. 19-22. She was being truthful--for her to write better would probably have meant writing a draft or two first. Nevertheless, this text preserves the expressiveness of her writing. Whenever possible, her text has received no alteration by way of a textual note.

MDB's eccentric mechanics raise another point meriting special attention. Often within a paragraph she caused confusion by going only half way in ending one sentence and beginning another. That is, she either put in full stop punctuation and no capital or she did the reverse. Occasionally, she made a variation of this by using a comma and a capital. In a few instances, she did not go even halfway; she did nothing and so created a run on sentence. These definitely require notes and are treated in the following manner. When she went half way, the text does too--end spacing (two blank spaces) is placed between the two sentences (easily permitted by the ragged-right format)--and the textual note clarifies the text by bringing it into conformity with standard punctuational usage. That MDB would have consented to this practice is illustrated by comparing l. 11 of Letter 1 with the counterpart passage of Letter 2, for which Letter 1 seems to be a draft. For run on sentences, only those which are so egregious as to cause confusion for many readers or to pose difficulties in quoting have merited a note. In this, the point of view of MDB's first (and only intended) reader has been kept in mind as far as it can be surmised. If an instance is clear enough within the context and style of that particular letter (her style in some letters did change from her usual one), it has received no note. These instances should not be confused with the frequent occasions when she used ques-

---

[1] *The Poems of Emily Dickinson*, Thomas H. Johnson, ed., 3 vols. (Cambridge, MA, 1955), I, lxiii.

tion marks or exclamation points within a sentence, an acceptable practice requiring no note. The same can be said for the instances when she began a paragraph or a similar unit, like a complimentary closing, but did not include both full stop punctuation and a capital letter. The new unit itself provides sufficient clarification, for both reading and quoting.

## Letters

Letter 1 (Players)
    dateline: Letters 1 and 2 provide a curious situation. Both are originals. They are addressed to the same person on the same day and in content they are nearly identical. Letter 1 is in brown ink on buff linen stock measuring 20.5 mm x 25.5 mm, folded in the center to make four pages. "BATH" crest and name are embossed in upper left corner of pages 1 and 3. Letter 2 is in brown ink on plain white unlined paper, 20.5 mm x 25 mm, folded in the center to make four pages. From the quality of composition and the freedom from scribal error, Letter 2 seems to be a fair copy of Letter 1, which is a kind of draft.
    line 12: i.e., week. They    line 17: i.e., you. No

Letter 2 (LC--MD)
    dateline: see note for Letter 1, dateline.

Letter 3 (Players)
    line 7: i.e., presume--overwhelming
    line 8: i.e., disappointed
    line 13: i.e., acting'. Such
    lines 27-28: i.e., you. No
    line 29: i.e., Walter? He
    line 35: i.e., prayer.--If

Letter 4 (NYPL--TC)
    line 10: i.e., keeping. My

Letter 5 (Players)
    dateline: i.e., A. M. [From the first sentence it is clear that this letter was written in the early morning. See MD's comment on this matter in Letter 15, ll. 10-13.]
    lines 10-11: i.e., pleasure. If
    line 29: i.e., fail    line 30: i.e., heart--

Letter 6 (Players)
    line 3: i.e., Harrold[?] [See Letter 19, line 35.]
    line 14: i.e., "Dusseldorf Gallery"
    line 15: i.e., admire. One    line 22: i.e., *fit*.
    line 43: i.e., as soon as you can.

148   Textual Notes

           line 47: i.e., But       line 49: i.e., shall reach
           line 59: i.e., Although

Letter 7 (NYPL--TC)
      line 12: i.e., writing. Ah     line 22: i.e., me. I
      second dateline: i.e., P.M. [From the first sentence it
           is clear that this part of the letter was written
           at night. See MD's comment on this matter in
           Letter 15.]
      line 26: i.e., came. The       line 39: i.e., love". It
      line 42: i.e., you--I

Letter 8 (Players)
      line 3: i.e., 'Roborant'       line 9: i.e., long letter
      line 12: i.e., conjugated
      line 21: i.e., engagement? He
      line 23: i.e., Sothern
      line 28: i.e., you. All
      lines 30-31: written beneath ink smudges on back page
           of letter

Letter 9 (NYPL--TC)
      line 7: i.e., You       line 23: i.e., Never
      line 33: i.e., your knee
      lines 38-39: i.e., "mine the joy--mine the bliss"

Letter 10 (Players)
      line 5: i.e., This

Letter 11 (NYPL--TC)
      line 16: i.e., Most     line 18: i.e., is.
      line 33: i.e., 'baby'"--     line 38: i.e., prepared.

Letter 12 (NYPL--TC)
      line 28: i.e., My       line 29: i.e., and will
      line 42: i.e., thought

Letter 13 (NYPL--TC)
      line 8: i.e., I took
      line 10: "very" is underlined twice
      line 24: i.e., Enjoy

Letter 14 (NYPL--TC)
      line 38: i.e., Until

Letter 15 (Players)
      line 36: i.e., Queen

Letter 16 (Players)
      line 2: i.e., afternoon.     line 5: i.e., &c.
      line 6: i.e., told me Mr Clarke    line 10: i.e., Yet
      line 12: i.e., time.

Letter 17 (NYPL--TC)
    line 1: i.e., felt well      line 3: i.e., Harry
    line 23: i.e., if I were     line 23: i.e., Mr Badeau's

Letter 18 (NYPL--TC)
    line 4: i.e., Ladies      line 19: i.e., with you a
    line 23: i.e., For     line 23: i.e., Shelley says
    line 31: i.e., never told     line 35: i.e., will "tell
    line 36: i.e., Then      line 43: i.e., Adieu.
    line 44: i.e., Love

Letter 19 (NYPL--TC)
    line 3: i.e., Two     line 22: i.e., discourse'--
    line 23: i.e., difficult.      line 32: i.e., He
    line 35: i.e., Harold[?]  [See Letter 6, line 3.]
    line 51: i.e., you.  My

Letter 20 (NYPL--TC)
    line 1: i.e., after 'Richard'
    line 2: i.e., evening.--I
    line 12: i.e., proves     line 29: i.e., darling.
    lines 36-37: i.e., up last     line 55: i.e., 'B's,'
    line 61: i.e., you.

Letter 21 (NYPL--TC)
    line 13: i.e., life".      line 26: i.e., And oh
    line 35: i.e., Joe.

Letter 22 (NYPL--TC)
    line 30: i.e., This
    line 31: i.e., recalled a susceptibility
    line 33: i.e., carrying     line 34: i.e., It
    line 45: i.e., It     line 61: i.e., to study

Letter 23 (Players)
    line 4: i.e., Edwin".  That     line 9: i.e., Even
    line 32: i.e., Then      line 43: i.e., Revenge'.
    line 45: i.e., play?

Letter 24 (NYPL--TC)
    line 5: i.e., heart, and     line 34: i.e., night--be

Letter 25 (Players)
    line 1: i.e., Three      line 11: i.e., It
    line 21: i.e., yesterday.  He
    line 27: i.e., mine).  You
    line 48: i.e., You     line 49: i.e., passed.  Vary
    line 61: i.e., Then      line 65: i.e., All
    line 71: i.e., of an "ive-tipped
    line 78: i.e., makes hers so
    line 83-86: i.e., And now these vivid hours are gone,
                     Like mine own life to me thou art,
                     Where Past and Present, wound in one,
                     Do make a garland for the heart:
    line 100: i.e., acquainted.
    lines 103-104: i.e., have completed

150    Textual Notes

      line 104: i.e., I am sure
      line 108: i.e., me.  Fearful
      line 117: i.e., bad.       line 117: i.e., Adieu.

Letter 26 (Players)
      line 11: i.e., Ah       line 16: i.e., Ah
      line 22: i.e., No       line 43: i.e., But
      line 57: "<u>wishes</u>" is underlined twice
      line 57: i.e., They

Letter 27 (NYPL--TC)
      line 12: i.e., 'Lesbia'--      line 17: i.e., Heron
      line 31: i.e., Society    line 39: i.e., How
      line 42: i.e., You    line 63: i.e., Ah

Letter 28 (NYPL--TC)
      line 14: i.e., me--'when       line 18: i.e., be <u>Victor</u>
      line 32: i.e., 'as the day was long'
      line 32: i.e., "Ah",     line 33: i.e., heart'--take
      line 44: i.e., Is    line 45: i.e., Then
      line 59: i.e., When

Letter 29 (NYPL--TC)
      line 9: i.e., rewarded.        line 17: i.e., "Such
      line 22: i.e., All    line 23: i.e., Ah
      line 32: i.e., All    line 39: i.e., Many

Letter 30 (NYPL--TC)
      dateline: i.e., 11th [At the close of this letter, MD
         says she will add her "'Sunday morning' thoughts"
         presumably the next day, thereby confirming that
         this letter was written on the Saturday which fell
         on 11 February in 1860.  Letter 31 is considered
         to be entirely separate, though it likely was
         enclosed in the same envelope.]
      line 2: i.e., an hour     line 4: i.e., Now
      line 28: i.e., There!     line 40: i.e., She

Letter 31 (NYPL--TC)
      line 10: i.e., No       line 13: i.e., Ah
      line 24: i.e., 'Tis     line 25: i.e., We
      line 30: i.e., <u>They</u>     line 31: i.e., Ah
      line 35: i.e., No       lines 35-36: i.e., <u>model</u>.  Then
      line 37: i.e., If       line 39: i.e., But
      line 40: i.e, <u>We</u>       line 43: i.e., If
      line 47: i.e., <u>Why</u>      line 48: i.e., You will
      line 59: i.e., This

Letter 32 (NYPL--TC)
      lines 1-2: i.e., My teacher       line 10: i.e., Besides
      line 18: i.e., God.  These     line 26: i.e., For
      line 34: i.e., You      line 35: i.e., powers;
      line 38: i.e., No       line 46: i.e., make
      line 46: i.e., Ah       line 47: i.e., But
      lines 54-55: i.e., certainty.  This
      line 57: i.e., Selfishness     line 58: i.e., My love

Textual Notes   151

Letter 33 (NYPL--TC)
    line 2: i.e., The sun      line 27: i.e., How
    line 28: i.e., Then       line 28: i.e., A
    line 31: i.e., admirable plan
    line 36: i.e., presence. 'Tis
    line 37: i.e., Even       line 48: i.e., They
    line 55: i.e., now.       line 55: i.e., Mr Badeau
    line 57: i.e., Ah

Letter 34 (Players)
    line 2: i.e., This        line 6: i.e., poem')--then
    line 7: i.e., Perhaps     line 8: i.e., 'Mollie's'
    line 10: i.e., piano;     line 13: i.e., These
    line 13: i.e., thoughts, that encourage
    line 21: i.e., Mr Badeau      line 27: i.e., But
    line 34: i.e., Tomorrow       line 42: i.e., 'anatomist'--
    line 44: i.e., woman      line 45: i.e., She
    line 46: i.e., Booth's nature'      line 51: i.e., woman
    line 56: i.e., 'top of her compass'
    line 59: i.e., length
    line 76: i.e., 'unconsciousness'        line 79: i.e., This
    line 92:  i.e., Then
    lines 94-95: i.e.,
        They have not shed a many tears,
            Dear eyes, since first I knew them well.
    line 99: i.e., Surely       line 107: i.e., Leave
    line 108: i.e., The         line 108: i.e., A
    line 113: i.e., They        line 121: i.e., tutored me in
    line 121: i.e., Carefully

Letter 35 (Players)
    line 10: i.e., So       line 24: i.e., --And
    line 26: i.e., Now      line 30: i.e., Why
    line 30: i.e., Is       line 35: i.e., Then
    line 38: i.e., You      line 47: i.e., But
    line 50: i.e., Call

Letter 36 (Players)
    line 4: i.e., Its       line 10: i.e., She
    line 19: i.e., To       line 23: i.e., Darling
    line 30: i.e., camee    line 35: i.e., The
    line 45: i.e., thought'.  My
    line 54: i.e., "Edwin       line 65: i.e., again".  Well
    line 68: i.e., 'dismissed'.
    line 80: i.e., you.  Write

Letter 37 (NYPL--TC)
    line 1: OR leettle[?]; i.e., little
    line 12: i.e., harmonious.       line 28: i.e., Who
    line 30: i.e., Mr Badeau    line 40: i.e., 'she
    line 41: i.e., Ah       line 42: i.e., "To
    line 45: i.e., Would    line 45: i.e., No
    line 57: i.e., Give

152   Textual Notes

Letter 38 (NYPL--TC)
    line 11: i.e., They
    line 20: i.e., man OR vulgar of men
    line 28: i.e., How few    line 35: i.e., religion'.  We
    line 41: i.e., 'fitted    line 42: i.e., contemptuous
    lines 47-48: i.e., glorious to have
    line 55: i.e., And    line 59: i.e., But
    line 64: i.e., 'Tis    line 67: i.e., But
    line 76: i.e., You    line 79: i.e., Let
    line 96: i.e., seems    line 96: i.e., Every
    line 105: i.e., it;

Letter 39 (NYPL--TC)
    line 5: i.e., Year".  Were    line 8: i.e., Surely
    line 25: i.e., et you OR and you
    line 31: i.e., caresses for    line 33: i.e., give up on

Letter 40 (Players)
    line 3: i.e., Mr Cary

Letter 41 (NYPL--TC)
    line 2: i.e., and I remembered that
    line 14: i.e., But    line 40: i.e., her--

Letter 43 (Players)
    salutation: i.e., Miss Cary    line 13: i.e., When

Letter 44 (Players)
    salutation: i.e., Miss Cary    line 21: i.e., How
    line 22: i.e., disciplined--it    line 24: i.e., But
    line 42: i.e., My    line 53: i.e., Remember

Letter 45 (Players)
    line 14: i.e., Allowing    line 23: i.e., 'Haymarket'
    line 28: i.e., 'luke-warm'.  It

Letter 46 (FL--BTM)
    line 51: i.e., excellent;
    line 84: i.e., side of the water

Letter 47 (PSU)
    line 45: i.e., plants
    line 48: i.e., kindest regards to

Letter 49 (NYPL--TC)
    line 12: i.e., cap.    line 16: i.e., This
    line 21: i.e., and be patient    line 30: i.e., Isn't
    line 32: i.e., 'Cabinet

Letter 50 (FL--BTM)
    line 12: i.e., No    line 50: i.e., 'Post'
    line 74: i.e., their rambles[?]
    line 78: i.e., fears    line 84: i.e., What

Letter 51 (NYPL--TC)
    line 46: i.e., <u>guineas</u>     line 50: i.e., This
    line 52: i.e., McClellan's

Letter 52 (FL--BTM)
    line 37: i.e., "she" is underlined three times
    line 39: i.e., Now     line 42: i.e., The
    line 75: i.e., This    line 131: i.e., May

Letter 53 (Players)
    Note at head of letter is written vertically in upper
        left corner of the first page of letter.
    line 1: i.e., How     line 16: i.e., A
    line 28: i.e., have it    line 32: i.e., most <u>noble</u>
    line 34: i.e., Thackeray    line 37: i.e., Thackeray
    line 37: i.e., you darling    line 40: i.e., just suit
    line 43: i.e., needs    line 67: i.e., This
    line 86: i.e., If     line 92: i.e., told her
    line 102: i.e., might retell

Letter 54 (Players)
    line 28: i.e., after: Ah    line 29: i.e., "only
    lines 50-51: i.e., trust her again
    line 51: i.e., indignant    line 56: i.e., Aren't
    line 63: i.e., taxation'. Is
    line 73: i.e., seen, or heard
    line 93: i.e., And    line 101: i.e., 'a-comin''
    line 101: i.e., that she has
    line 108: i.e., immediately.)
    line 113: i.e., uninteresting;    line 114: i.e., Evr

Letter 55 (Players)
    line 25: i.e., sent

Letter 56 (Players)
    line 30: i.e., beauty,    line 62: i.e., Will you

Letter 57 (FL--BTM)
    line 13: i.e., to be procured    line 68: i.e., <u>You</u>
    line 76: i.e., received.
    line 82: Sheet is torn at end of word "yours"; *s*
        is presumed to have been present originally.
    line 83: i.e., In trying

Letter 58 (FL--BTM)
    Note at head of letter opposite datelines is written
        vertically in upper left corner of the first page
        of letter.
    line 7: i.e., Oh    line 35: i.e., rapidly--
    lines 47-48: i.e., "a little something" for
    line 90: i.e., for they are    line 108: i.e., as in

Letter 59 (Players)
    Note at head of letter is written vertically in upper
        left corner of the first page of letter.

154  Textual Notes

         line 27: i.e., prejudice is
         line 53: i.e, reading. I     signature: flourish

    Letter 60 (NYPL--TC)
         signature: flourish

    Letter 61 (NYPL--TC)
         line 15: i.e., Dick--he      signature: flourish

    Letter 62 (Players)
         signature: flourish

    Letter 63 (NYPL--MD)
         line 9: i.e., act of         signature: flourish

    Letter 64 (Players)
         line 18: i.e., Booth--says   signature: flourish

    Letter 65 (FL--BTM)
         line 31: i.e., content--as   line 46: i.e., well &

    Letter 66 (NYPL--TC)
         line 5: i.e., me &   line 9: i.e., 'en relaxed'

    Letter 67 (Players)
         line 13: i.e., Fields'

    Letter 68 (NYPL--MD)
         line 29: i.e., 'The Morgesons'
         line 31: i.e., Fields    line 45: i.e., It
         line 56: i.e., yourself      signature: flourish

    Letter 69 (FL--BTM)
         line 27: i.e., not dangerous
         line 85: i.e., is pulling

    Letter 70 (NYPL--MD)
         Salutation: "Elizabeth" was often spelled with an
            s by MDB and EB.
         line 24: i.e., the very
         line 60: i.e., Boston Theatre, & W. was
         lines 63-64: i.e., Is he    line 64: i.e., Tell
         signature: flourish

    Letter 71 (NYPL--MD)
         line 13: i.e., No

    Letter 73 (Players)
         signature: flourish

    Letter 74 (Players)
         line 49: i.e., tomorrow--think

    Letter 75 (Players)
         line 21: i.e., if you accomplish
         lines 22-23: i.e., that you will    line 29: i.e., No

Letter 76 (Players)
    dateline: i.e., Jan 1st [From the references to the
            newness of her Dorchester house and especially to
            EB's visit to Fortress Monroe, it is clear that
            this letter was written on either 31 December 1862
            or 1 January 1863.  From the reference to EB's
            returning "tomorrow or Saturday," it is likely
            that this letter was written on a Thursday.  1
            January 1863 fell on Thursday.  The reference to
            looking forward to her baby's first Christmas does
            not contradict this logic but probably means that
            MDB and EB celebrated Christmas a week late, after
            EB returned from Fortress Monroe.]

Letter 77 (Players)
    line 14: i.e., Morgesons      line 20: i.e., us--that

Letter 78 (Players)
    signature: flourish

Letter 79 (Players)
    line 12: i.e., i.e., Morgesons
    line 14: i.e., We will    line 20: i.e., room,
    line 33: i.e., Poor

Letter 80 (Players)
    dateline:  This letter is written on the back page of a
            letter from EB to Richard Stoddard.  MDB's letter
            bears no dateline, but EB's does and it is used
            for hers.
    line 9: i.e., Tuberoses    line 9: i.e., yesterday.  I

Letter 81 (Players)
    line 9: i.e., Tell      line 16: i.e., ensue
    line 33: i.e., 'Tuberose'       line 35: i.e., Morgesons
    line 48: i.e., would not[?] go

Letter 82 (Players)
    line 4: i.e., shuts     line 36: i.e., beings

Letter 83 (FL--BTM)
    line 21: i.e., How
    line 48: i.e., as well as she can

Letter 84 (Players)
    line 42: i.e., they have fuller

Letter 85
    line 36: i.e., Mr Booth

Letter 86 (Players)
    line 15: i.e., many familiar

Letter 87 (NYPL--TC)
    line 22: i.e., here,     line 27: i.e., 'coacher'
    line 51: i.e., "en

156   Textual Notes

                        Notebooks

Record Book (NYPL--TC), 1860
   Description:  Red tooled leather on boards 200mm x  125mm;
         blue marbled leaf edges head, foot and side; gilt
         design 97mm x 54mm centered on front and back; red
         leather spine and hinges; "RECORDS" gilt on spine;
         brown and tan mosaic design on front and back end
         papers; Players Club bookplate on front end paper.
         Leaves are not numbered.

       Notes:   lines 1-29: MDB's explanation of purpose for
                   keeping "Records" appears on recto and verso
                   of front fly leaf.

                Leaf 1 recto: *"Hurlbert" | Albion Feby 1861* in
                   MDB's hand at head center; beneath it, news-
                   paper clipping of commentary by "Hamilton"
                   regarding Charlotte Cushman's and EB's
                   Macbeths is pasted in.

                Leaf 1 verso and leaf 2 recto: Macbeth entry
                   lines 20-21: i.e., He could

                Leaves 2 verso--7 verso: blank

                Leaf 8 recto--9 recto: Hamlet entry
                   line 10: i.e., Their
                   line 17: i.e., form".  The
                   line 18: i.e., with such an
                   line 31: i.e., Other
                   line 31: i.e., dispatched,
                   line 42: i.e., in,
                addenda:  two loose leaves inserted, numbered
                   "3" and "4"
                   lines 1-2: i.e., perfectly defines the
                   line 15: i.e., "pestilent
                   line 21: i.e., contemplation,
                   line 21: i.e., personification
                   line 22: i.e., the reasoner,
                   line 23: i.e., the "players
                   line 26: i.e., intended analogy of
                   lines 28-29: i.e., depth to the superficial

                Leaves 9 verso--61 verso: blank

                Leaf 62 recto: *"Stuart"= = | Tribune.* in MDB's
                   hand at head center; beneath it, newspaper
                   clipping titled "MR. EDWIN FORREST AS
                   OTHELLO" is pasted in.

                Leaves 62 verso--82 recto: blank

Textual Notes   157

   Leaf 82 verso: *"Stuart" | Evening Post | Feby
      1861* in MDB's hand at head center; beneath
      it, newspaper clipping titled "MR. EDWIN
      BOOTH AS SHYLOCK" is pasted in.

   Leaves 83 recto--90 recto: blank

   Leaf 90 verso: *"Hurlbert" | Albion | ~~Feby~~ Novr |
      1861* in MDB's hand at head center; beneath
      it, newspaper clipping of commentary by
      "Hamilton" regarding EB's Cardinal Richelieu
      is pasted in.

   Leaves 91 recto--110 verso (final leaf): blank


Journal (Players), 1860
   Description:  Dark marbled paper on boards 250mm x 170mm;
      marbled leaf edges head, foot and side; black
      leather corners on front and back boards; black
      leather spine and hinges; green paper label
      centered on front; *DAILY | JOURNAL* gilt on
      spine.  On title page: *No. 14 | The Daily
      Journal | for 1860 | published annually | by
      Francis & Loutrel | Manufacturing Stationers | 45
      Maiden Lane | New York*.

Notes:
   4 November 1860
      dateline: At the center head of the page, the printed
         "JANUARY" is cancelled; above it is MDB's hand-
         written "Nov 4th"; "1 Sunday", printed below
         "JANUARY", is allowed to stand.  At the far right,
         opposite "JANUARY", over the printed page number
         "1" is MDB's handwritten "4".
      line 5: i.e., The      line 11: i.e., How
      line 13: i.e., How     line 23: i.e., need for a

   5 November 1860
      dateline: At the center head of the page, the printed
         "JANUARY" is cancelled; above it is MDB's hand-
         written "Nov 5th"; "2 Monday", printed below
         "JANUARY", is allowed to stand.  At the far left,
         opposite "JANUARY", over the printed page number
         "2" is MDB's handwritten "5".
      line 19: i.e., it.     line 21: i.e., 'Mary's'

   6 November 1860
      dateline: At the center head of the page, the printed
         "JANUARY" is cancelled; above it is MDB's hand-
         written "Nov."; "3 Tuesday" is printed below
         "JANUARY", but "6" is handwritten by MDB over the
         "3" while "Tuesday" is allowed to stand.  At the

158  Textual Notes

      far right, opposite "JANUARY", the printed page
      number "3" is allowed to stand.
   lines 18-19: i.e., bewail it less[?];

7 November 1860
   dateline: At the center head of the page, the printed
      "JANUARY" is cancelled; above it is MDB's hand-
      written "Nov"; "4 Wednesday" is printed below
      "JANUARY", but "7" is handwritten by MDB over the
      "4" while "Wednesday" is allowed to stand.  At the
      far left, opposite "JANUARY", over the printed
      page number "4" is MDB's handwritten "7".
   lines 3-4: i.e., cause will       line 17: i.e., Opinion
   lines 24-25: i.e., low is an excellent
   line 26: i.e., "Elective Affinities"
   line 27: i.e., what is meant

8 November 1860
   dateline: At the center head of the page, the printed
      "JANUARY" is cancelled; above it is MDB's hand-
      written "Nov"; "5 Thursday" is printed below
      "JANUARY", but "8" is handwritten by MDB over the
      "5" while "Thursday" is allowed to stand.  At the
      far right, opposite "JANUARY", over the printed
      page number "5" is MDB's handwritten "8".
   line 1: i.e., particular event
   line 11: i.e., sensational
   line 14: i.e., Shaks.  This
   line 17: i.e., Listening to
   line 22: i.e., Journals says
   line 31: i.e., author is too small, too obscure to do.
   line 31: i.e., come--

10 November 1860
   dateline: At the center head of the page, the printed
      "JANUARY" is cancelled; above it is MDB's hand-
      written "Nov--"; "7 Saturday" is printed below
      "JANUARY", but "10" is handwritten by MDB to the
      left of the cancelled "7" while "Saturday" is
      allowed to stand.  At the far right, opposite
      "JANUARY", over the printed page number "7", is
      MDB's handwritten "10th".
   line 10: i.e., is convinced that

11 November 1860
   dateline: At the center head of the page, the printed
      "JANUARY" is cancelled; above it is MDB's hand-
      written "Nov--"; "8 Sunday" is printed below
      "JANUARY", but "11" is handwritten by MDB to the
      left of the cancelled "8" while "Sunday" is
      allowed to stand.  At the far left, opposite
      "JANUARY", the printed page number "8" is allowed
      to stand.
   lines 14-15: i.e., too, is so     line 16: i.e., At 27
   line 18: i.e., dispositions--than
   line 22: i.e., know man's     line 26: i.e., The

12 November 1860
> dateline: At the center head of the page, the printed "JANUARY" is cancelled; above it is MDB's handwritten "Nov--"; "9 Monday", printed below "JANUARY", is cancelled and "12" is written by MDB to the left of the cancelled "9". At the far right, opposite "JANUARY", the printed page number "9" is allowed to stand.
> line 6: i.e., upon me[?] is
> line 11: i.e., sting' me
> line 12: "He likes" and "just" are written by Edwina Booth Grossmann over MDB's writing which is undecipherable underneath. Grossmann also wrote "youth" over her mother's "past" (line 12), but MDB's writing underneath can be deciphered.
> second dateline: At the center head of the page, the printed "JANUARY" is cancelled; above it is MDB's handwritten "Nov"; "10 Tuesday" is printed below "JANUARY", but "12" is handwritten by MDB to the left of the cancelled "10" while "Tuesday" is allowed to stand. At the far left, opposite "JANUARY", the printed page number "10" is allowed to stand.
> line 24: i.e., 'Informative'; corrected by Grossmann by writing *a* over *i*.
> line 40: i.e., 'Tis
> line 56: i.e., his 'Improvisatore'--
> third dateline: At the center head of the page, the printed "JANUARY" and "11 Wednesday" printed below it, as well as the printed page number "11", far right opposite "JANUARY", are all allowed to stand.
> line 66: i.e., Beneath

# INDEX

This index lists the principal people, places, events, titles of literary works and dramatic characters mentioned in the texts of MDB's letters and notebooks and in the General Introduction. It makes no mention of MDB or EB because their names appear on almost every page.

The index should be used in conjunction with the Textual Notes, Annotations and the Calendar of Letters and Notebooks. The Calendar lists the recipients of MDB's letters and the location of the various repositories in which the letters are stored. Those people and repositories, along with those mentioned in the section of the General Introduction entitled The Search for MDB Documents, have not been included in this index.

Agassiz, Louis, xxvi, 82
Agassiz, Elizabeth Cary, xxvi, 80
Aldrich, Thomas Bailey, xxviii, 99
Aldrich, Mrs. T. B. *See* Woodman, Lillian
Alice, 28, 42
Andersen, Hans Christian, 116
Anderson, Captain, 69
Andrews, Mrs., 68
Ann, 68, 69
"Anne Hathaway," 50
Arch Street Theatre, 13
Artists' Reception, 98, 100

Badeau, Adam, xii, xiv, xv, xxiii, xxiv, xxv, xxvi, 15, 18, 22, 23, 25, 27, 32, 35, 40, 46, 47, 48, 68
Baker, Benjamin A., 5
Ballow, Mrs., 105
Baltimore, xi, 107
Baltimore Museum, xx, xxi

Barrett, Lawrence, xxii
Barstow, Wilson, xxviii, 96, 100
Bartlett, Frances Amelia, 22
Beacon Street, xxvii, 87, 88
Beale, Dr. & Mrs., xii
Bell, Mrs., 103
Bertha, 17
Bethel, 51, 52
Boker, George Henry, 100
Booth, Asia, xxii, 37; *The Elder and the Younger Booth*, xxii; *The Unlocked Book*, xxii
Booth, Edwina, xv, xvi, xviii, xxvi, xxviii, 61, 62, 63, 65, 66, 67, 68, 69, 71, 72, 73, 74, 75, 77, 78, 79, 81, 82, 83, 84, 85, 89, 93, 95, 96, 97, 99, 102, 104, 106; *Edwin Booth: Recollections by his daughter,* xv

162  Index

Booth, John Wilkes, xxii, xxiii, 22, 27, 45, 69, 101, 105
Booth, Joseph Adrian, xxii, xxiii, 8, 9, 11, 12, 18, 19, 20, 22, 23, 24, 26, 27, 29, 30, 38, 41, 45, 46
Booth, Junius Brutus, xxii, 82
Booth, Mary Anne Holmes, xxii, 9, 11, 12, 22, 23, 26, 27, 50, 104
Booth, Rosalie (Rose), xxii, 9, 11, 12, 23, 27, 104
Booth's Theatre, xxii
Boston, xi, xii, xxiii, xxv, xxvi, xxvii, xxviii, xxix, 3, 13, 18, 20, 33, 41, 51, 52, 53, 56, 57, 59, 62, 66, 75, 81, 82, 83, 84, 85, 86, 88, 89, 90, 91, 96, 101, 103
Boston Museum, xxiii
Boston Theatre, 3, 4, 91
Boswell, James, xxiv, 18
Boucicault, Dion, xiv, 71
Boughton, George Henry, 70, 71
Brackett, Louise, 5, 12, 22, 33, 41
Brackett, Walter, xi, xii, xiii, xxi, 5, 12, 22
Brampton, 58
Brennan, John C., "John Wilkes Booth's Enigmatic Brother Joseph," xxii
British Museum, 71
Broadway, 22
Brooke, Gustavus Vaughan, 70
Brooklyn, 89, 91
Buffalo, 4, 16, 20, 21
Bull, John, 75
Bulwer-Lytton, Edward, 64

Cambridge, 55, 57, 64, 73, 74, 78, 80, 93, 96
Camp Andrew, 51, 52
Cary, Elizabeth. See Agassiz, Elizabeth
Cary, Emma F., xxvi, 72, 81, 84, 85
Cary Family, xxvi, 53
Cary, Georgie, xxvi, 53, 55, 74, 81, 82, 83, 85
Cary, Helen, xxvi, 53, 55, 74, 79, 80, 81, 82, 83
Cary, Mary. See Felton, Mary

Cary, Richard, xxvi, 50, 52, 53, 57, 59, 64, 72, 73, 79, 80, 81, 82
Cedar Mountain (Virginia), xxvi
Charleston, 45
Chicago, xi
Choate, Rufus, 93, 103
Civil War (including Union, Confederate, North, South), xv, xxiii, xxvi, xxviii, 51, 53, 54, 55, 57, 60, 62, 64, 70, 73, 82, 83
Clarke, Asia Booth. See Booth, Asia
Clarke, John Sleeper, xxii, xxiii, 17, 33
Cooke's Royal Amphitheatre, 44
Corbyn, Miss, 69, 70
Corbyn, Mrs., 70
Cousin, Victor, 48
Cremorne, 70
Crow, Wayman, xx
Cushman, Charlotte, xi, xiv, xv, xx, xxvi, xxvii, 57, 64, 66, 77, 85, 101
Cushman, Edwin Charles Merriman, xx, xxvii, 57, 63, 67, 76, 85, 90
Cushman, Emma Crow, xx, xxvii, 65, 69

Daley, Mr., 106
Davenport, Adolphus Hoyt, 5
Davenport, Edward Loomis, xiv, 20
Davenport, Fanny Elizabeth, 3, 4, 67
De Bar, Benedict, 5
Devlin, Catherine Celestine. See Magonigle, Catherine Devlin
Devlin, Charles, xxi, xxii, 11, 16, 17
Devlin Family, xxi, xxii, 11, 17
Devlin, Nancy Ann, xxi, xxii, 11, 16, 17
Devlin, William H., xxi, xxii, 17
Dickens, Charles, 64, 75
Dora Spenlow, 77, 79
Dorchester, xxviii, xxix, xxx, 87, 89, 90, 92, 93, 96, 97, 98, 100, 101, 102, 103

Drew, John, xiv
Duflex, Mrs., 68
Dusseldorf Gallery, 7
Dwight, Wilder, 82

Eame's Hotel, 52
Eddy, Edward, 5, 106
Edinburgh, 57, 59, 63
*Elective Affinities, (Die Wahlverwandtschaften)*, 112
Emancipation Proclamation, 82
England, xv, xxvi, xxvii, 4, 46, 52, 53, 54, 56, 63, 67, 73, 74, 78, 79, 85, 91
Exhibition (Royal Institute of British Architects), 59, 66, 75

Fauntleroy, Anne M., "The Romance of Mary Devlin Booth," xi
Fechter, Charles Albert, 74
Felix, 91
Felton, Cornelius, xxvi, 64, 72, 73, 74, 78
Felton, Mary Cary, xxvi, 53, 55, 57, 59, 73, 74, 78
Fenno, A. W., xxii
Field, Mary Katherine (Kate), 66, 89
Fields, James Thomas, 86, 87, 92, 94
Fifth Avenue Hotel (New York), 50
Florence, Malvina Pray, 71
Florence, William Jermyn, 71
Ford, John Thompson, xxi, 19
Forrest, Edwin, xiv, xxiii, xxiv
Fortress Monroe (Virginia), xxviii, 92, 94, 95, 96, 97
*Four Georges, The,* 67
France, 62
Fuller, Margaret, xxvi

Garrick, David, xxiv
Germany, xv, xx
Goethe, Johann Wolfgang von, 108, 112
Gordon, George H., 81, 82, 83
Gould, Thomas Ridgeway, 106
Graham Family, 57, 62, 67, 71

Graham, James Lorimer, xxvii, xxviii, 58, 62, 67, 71
Graham, Josephine, xxvii, 57, 62, 67, 71
Graham, Miss, 58, 59
Grant, Ulysses S., xxiii
*Great Eastern,* 57
Grisi, Giulietta, xxiv
Grossmann, Edwina Booth. *See* Booth, Edwina

Harlow Brothers, 44
Harold, Prof., 7, 20, 25, 31, 32, 34, 37
Harvard College, xxvi
Hawthorne, Nathaniel, 46, 64
Haymarket Theatre, 54
Hazlitt, William, xxiv
Heron, Matilda Agnes, xiv, xxiv, 31, 35
Hoboken (New Jersey), xxii, xxv
Hodson, George, 71
Hollister, Gordon Hiram, xxiv, 28
Holmes, Oliver Wendell, 13
Horch, Mr., 32
Horticultural Gardens, 67
Howe, Florence, xxvii, 51, 100, 101
Howe, Julia, xxvii, 51, 91, 100, 101
Howe, Julia Ward, xxvi, xxvii, 56, 86, 87, 88, 91, 93, 94, 96, 100, 101
Howe, Laura, xxvii
Howe, Maud, xxvii
Howe, Samuel G., xxvi, 27
Hughes, Archbishop, 22
Hugo, Victor, 32, 114

Italy, xv, xx, 116
Ives, Mr., 93

Jackson, A. W., 105
Jarrett, Henry, xxi
Jefferson, Joseph, xi, xiv, xx, xxi, 4, 17, 19, 23, 33, 44, 45, 47
Jefferson, Mrs. Joseph, xxi, 4, 19, 44
Jones, Avonia, 70
Jordan, George, 31, 47

Kean, Charles John, 71
Kean, Edmund, xxiv

Kean, Ellen Tree, 71
Keats, John, 24
Kellogg, Clara Louise, 75
Kemble, Frances Anne (Fanny), 64
*King's Bell, The,* xxviii, 91, 94, 97
Kuntzie, Edward J., 70

Leitch, Capt., 3
Lemaître, Frédéric, 77
Lennox, William Pitt, 70
Lincoln, Abraham, 72, 82
Liverpool, 52, 75
London, xx, xxiii, 52, 54, 55, 56, 57, 58, 59, 60, 61, 62, 63, 64, 66, 72, 73, 74, 75, 76, 77, 78, 79
Ludlow, Fitz Hugh, xxviii, 102
Lyon, Nathaniel, 53

McClellan, George B., 64
McEntee, Jervis, xiv, xxviii
Macnair, Andrew, 69, 70, 71
Macready, William Charles, xxiv
Manchester, 62
Magonigle, Catherine Devlin, xxi, xxii, 39
Magonigle, John Henry (Harry), xxi, xxii, 16, 18, 27, 29, 30, 40, 45, 49
Magonigle, Sarah, xxii, 41
Marie, 104
Marion, General Francis, xxvi
*Married Life of Albrecht Dürer, The,* 104
Marshall Theatre, xxi
Mathews, Charles, xxiv
Mathews, Charles James, 68, 69
Mathews, Mrs. Charles James, 68, 69, 70
Matlack, James, *The Literary Career of E. B. Stoddard,* xiv, xxviii, xix
Mayhew, Horace, 68, 70
*Le Mémorial François,* 25, 32, 37
Memphis, 38, 39, 41, 44
Miller, Dr. Erasmus, xxvii, xxviii, xxix, xxx, 87, 88, 89, 90, 92, 95, 96, 97, 98, 100, 101, 105

"Miller's Daughter, The," 23, 27, 28, 41
Mobile, 33
*Monitor,* 75
Monroe County (Pennsylvania), xii
Montgomery, 27
*Morgesons, The,* xxviii, 87, 96, 97, 99
Mowett, Mr., 67
Murdock, James E., xiv

Nash, Julia, 39, 40, 41
National Theatre, xxi
New Orleans, 29, 38
New York, xii, xx, xxi, xxii, xxiii, xxiv, xxvi, xxvii, xxviii, xxix, 4, 5, 11, 17, 19, 23, 57, 62, 63, 80, 82, 83, 84, 87, 88, 90, 96, 100, 101, 102, 103
Newport (Rhode Island), 51

*Newspapers and Journals:*
  *Atlantic Monthly,* xxiv, 87
  Boston *Post,* 62
  London *Telegraph,* 71
  London *Times,* 54, 62
  New York *Post,* xxviii, 70
  *Spectator, The,* 28
  *Sunday Times* (Noah's), xxiii
  Troy *Times,* xxi

Niagara Falls, 4, 14
Niblo's Garden (New York), xii, 5, 44

O'Flaherty, Edmund. *See* Stuart, William
Oggel, L. Terry, "Guide to the Edwin Booth Literary Materials at NYPL," xv

Paradise Valley (Pennsylvania), xii, 4
Paris, xx, 73, 75, 76, 77, 79, 83, 96
Parker, Theodore, xxvi
Parsons, Dr. Thomas William, 94, 98
Paton, Mary Ann, 70
Père La Chaise, 77
Philadelphia, xx, xxii, xxiii, xxv, 4, 11, 12, 14, 80

Pike, Mrs., 90
Players, The, xxii
*Players, The*, xi, xxi

Plays and Dramatic
Characters:
  *Camille*, 39
  *Camille*, 31
  *Cardinal Richelieu*, 35
  *Don Caesar*, 77, 85
  *Edward Mortimer*, 85, 91
  *Eily O'Connor*, 69
  *Faust*, 29, 35
  *Fool's Revenge, The*, 25, 113
  *Hamlet*, 83, 105, 108
  *Hamlet*, xiv, xx, 41, 48, 108, 109, 115
  *Henry II*, xxiv
  *Hippolytus*, xxvi
  *Jester*, 113
  *Julius Caesar*, 103
  *Lesbia*, 31
  *Lesbia*, 31
  *Lily of Killarney*, 68
  *Lord Dundreary*, 78
  *Macbeth*, 108
  *Medea*, 31
  *Painter of Athens, The*, 71
  *Polonius*, 109
  *Richard III*, 21
  *Richard*, 7
  *Le Roi s'amuse*, 32, 114
  *Rosencrantz*, 110
  *Ruy Blas*, 104
  *Shylock*, 54, 55, 56

Pocono Mountains (Virginia), xxi
Potomac, Army of the, 63
Pratt, Mrs., 103
Pray, Isaac Clark, 3, 4
Princess's Theatre, 71
Pry, Lucy J., xxvii, 58, 61, 62, 67, 75, 78, 84, 89, 101, 102, 103, 104, 105

Rachel, Elisa Félix, xxiv
*Remains of the Late Mrs. Richard Trench, The*, 91
Richmond, xi, xxi, xxiii
Ristori, Adelaide, 77
Robertson, Agnes, xiv
Rome, 57
Royal Circus. *See* Cooke's Royal Amphitheatre
Russell, John, 70

Sallie, Miss, 53
*San Jacinto*, U.S.S., 60
Sand Lake (New York), xxi
Sandford, Mrs., 66, 89, 101
Shakespeare, William, xxiii, 20, 50, 79, 108, 110, 113, 114
Shattuck, Charles, *The Hamlet of Edwin Booth*, xiv, xv, xxiv
Shaw, Mrs., 80
Shelley, Percy Bysshe, 19
Siddons, Sarah, xxiv
Silsbee, Joshua, 59
Simpson, Dr., 57, 58
Sims, Dr., 90
Skinner, Otis, *The Last Tragedian*, xv, xvi
Slidell, John, 60
Smith, Miss, 58
*Songs of Summer*, 97
Sothern, Edward Askew, 9, 10, 78
Spofford, Richard Smith, xi, xii, 5, 10
St. Louis, xx, 89
Stamford Villas, 61, 62, 64, 68, 74, 77, 79
Stedman, Edmund Clarence, xxvii, xxviii
Stoddard, Edwin, xxviii
Stoddard, Elizabeth Barstow, xiv, xxv, xxvii, xxviii, xxix, 97, 98, 104, 106
Stoddard, Richard Henry, xxv, xxvii, xxviii, 82, 86, 87, 88, 91, 94, 96, 99, 100, 102, 103, 104, 105
Stuart, William, 91, 102

Tarrytown (New York), xxiii
Taylor, Bayard, xxviii
Taylor, Tom, 22, 113
Tennyson, Alfred, 91
Thackeray, William Makepeace, 68
Thierry, Jules, 31
Thompson, Launt, xxviii, 106
Titian (Tiziano Vecellio), 36
Tompkins, Orlando, xxx, 90, 94, 105
Tremont House, 105
Trench, Melesina (Mrs. Richard), 91
Trent Affair, 62, 63

Troy (New York), xx, xxi, 105
"Tuberoses," xxviii, 98, 99
Tudor Hall, xxii, xxiv
*Two Men,* 95, 98

"Vagabond, The," xxiii
Le Vert, Octavia Walton, 39

Walden, Miss, 105
Wallack, James William, xiv, xxiv, 31
Washington, D.C., xxi
Washington, George, xxvi
Westminster Abbey, 53
Whipple, Edwin Percy, 87, 91

Whipple, Mrs., 87, 91
Williams, Roger, xxvi
Wilson, Harry, xxv, xxvi
Winchester, Battle of, 83
Winter Garden, xxviii, xxix, 31, 106
Winthrop House, The, 105
Wood, Mary Ann. *See* Paton, Mary Ann
Woodman Family, 106
Woodman, Lillian, xxvii, xxix, 99, 106; *Crowding Memories,* xxvii
Woodman, Matilda, 106

Zoyara, Ella, 44

**About the Editor**

L. TERRY OGGEL is Associate Professor of English at Northern Illinois University. His earlier works include four volumes of the *Index to Reviews of Bibliographical Publications*, the revised edition of *American Literary Manuscripts*, and numerous articles in such journals as *Theatre Survey*, *Bulletin of Research in The Humanities*, and *Western Humanities Review*.

Recent Titles in
Contributions in Drama and Theatre Studies
Series Editor: Joseph Donohue

A Whirlwind in Dublin: *The Plough and the Stars* Riots
Robert G. Lowery, editor

German Actors of the Eighteenth and Nineteenth Centuries:
Idealism, Romanticism, and Realism
Simon Williams

William Archer on Ibsen: The Major Essays, 1889-1919
Thomas Postlewait, editor

Theatre for Working-Class Audiences in the United States, 1830-1980
Bruce A. McConachie and Daniel Friedman, editors

Hamlet on Stage: The Great Tradition
John A. Mills

America's Musical Stage: Two Hundred Years of Musical Theatre
Julian Mates

From Farce to Metadrama: A Stage History of *The Taming of the Shrew*, 1594-1983
Tori Haring-Smith

Prophet of the New Drama: William Archer and the Ibsen Campaign
Thomas Postlewait

The Theatre of Meyerhold and Brecht
Katherine Bliss Eaton

Ten Seasons: New York Theatre in the Seventies
Samuel L. Leiter

Sam Shepard's Metaphorical Stages
Lynda Hart

JU